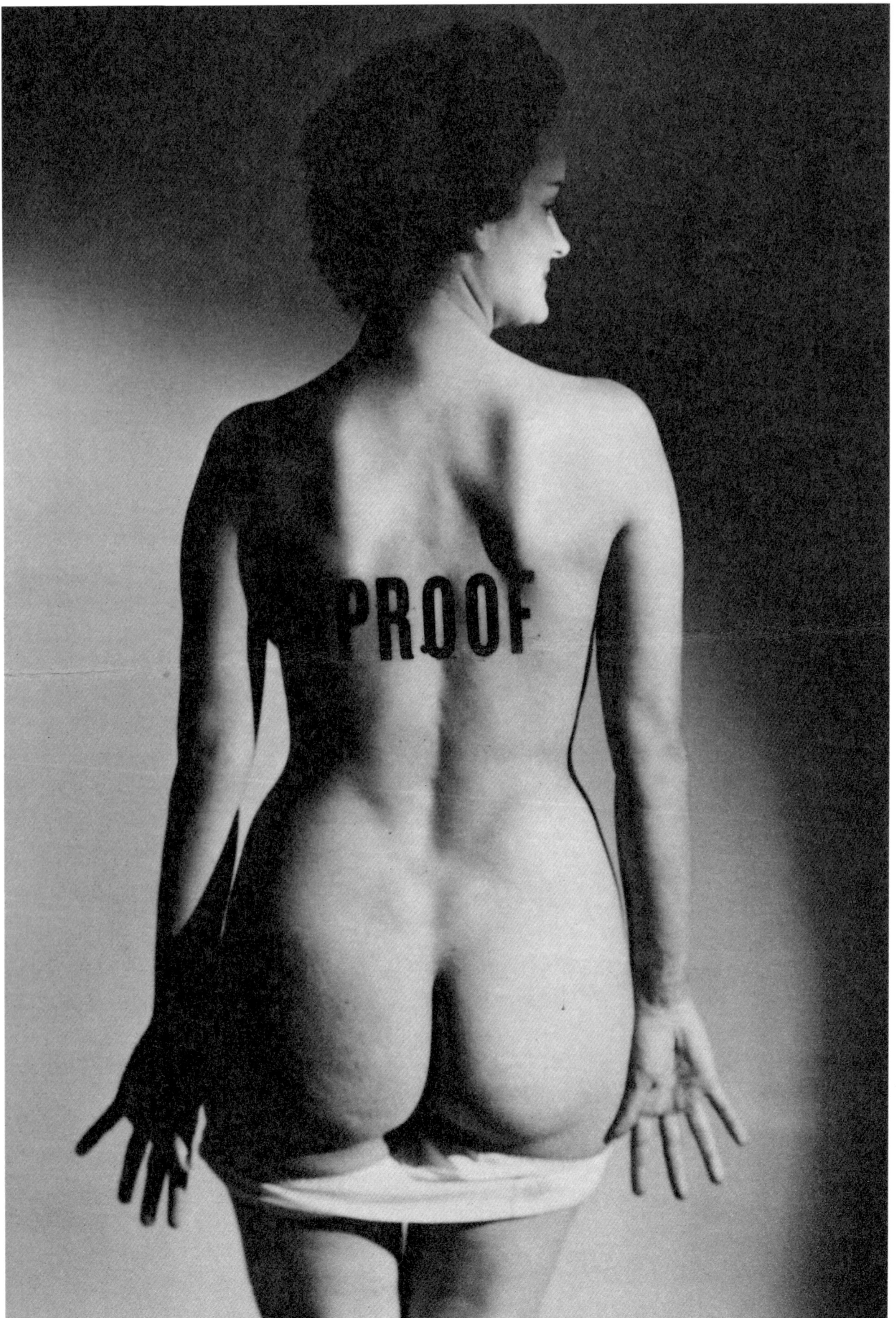
PROOF

Peek

PHOTOGRAPHS FROM THE
KINSEY INSTITUTE

Arena Editions

PREFACE

Over the years, we have been fortunate to collaborate with the staff of the Kinsey Institute on several projects. This work has allowed us to explore the vast holdings of art, photography, and ephemera at the institute, arguably the largest collection of erotica in the world. Of particular importance is the photography collection, which is by far the biggest component, containing over 75,000 images. These pictures are not only scientifically important because they are a visual record of sexual practices from the late nineteenth century to the present, but many of the images in the collection are of incredible beauty and should be shared with a wider audience.

The pictures in the Kinsey Institute collection were made for many reasons and for a variety of consumers. There are a number of erotic images produced by professional photographers for commercial purposes. The collection contains cinematic stills from American and European movies made throughout the twentieth century. There are documentary photographs made for scientific use, and promotional photographs for models and performers. In addition, there are important photographs produced by fine art photographers, including Wilhelm von Gloeden, George Platt Lynes, and Judy Dater, among others.

One thing that sets the Kinsey apart is the significant number of amateur photographs represented in the collection. As the process of photography became more accessible in the early to mid-twentieth century, people began to learn how to take black and white pictures, process their film, and print their own photographs. This allowed them to make images without fear of arrest or censorship. The Kinsey collection contains a large number of amateur "homemade" photographs, and these pictures, a kind of folk art, reflect tremendous diversity in sexual behavior. Some of the images are crudely fashioned while others are remarkable for their beauty, spontaneity, and energy. Some were arranged in groups or albums, indicating that the owners or makers organized and categorized these photographs for their own purposes. Many pictures show signs of wear, such as folding or creasing, indicating that they were used and sometimes passed on from one person to another. Some images have cutouts or blacked-out heads, erasing the subjects' identities, while other photographs show signs of drawing, collage, or other handwork.

The collection encompasses a wide range of pictures that reflect numerous aspects of the history of photography from the late 1880s to the present day. The earliest photographs are albumen prints, some hand colored to enhance their realism. Many of the early French photographs and postcards, which were produced as commercial erotica, utilized beautiful historic printing processes such as gold-toned gelatin and collodion printing out paper. The Kinsey contains examples of both mainstream and unusual photographic processes. For example, there are quite a few erotic stereo cards, which were mass-produced between 1900 and 1925. The collection also contains a number of erotic Stanhopes, which are microscopic photographs designed to be seen through a special viewer. Several early black and white Polaroid prints exist in the collection. The invention of the Polaroid instant print process in the late 1940s opened up the field of amateur photographic erotica to people who needed no knowledge of the fundamentals of photography. Color pictures are rare until the 1960s, when color photographic print processes became widely available.

The selection process for this book was a daunting one, because of the number of photographs. Since we worked as a team with Jennifer Yamashiro, curator of the Kinsey Institute, we were able to go through the entire collection together reasonably quickly, picking out the most compelling photographs. We selected over one thousand images after the initial pass, and then culled our choices to end up with a group of pictures that met our criteria. We wanted each example in the book to be unique and visually arresting in its own way. Some pictures were selected because of the quality of composition, the beauty of the lighting, the intended humor, or the unique representation of sexuality. Others are products of unusual photographic accidents or techniques, which give the pictures immediacy and confirm that many are one of a kind. Still others were chosen because they seem to be at odds with and even defy many of today's standards for beauty. Many of the most interesting and unusual photographs are the most imaginative, and reveal the importance of fantasy in the tableaux that are pictured.

Our selections have attempted to demonstrate the broad visual range that exists within this significant collection. Many pictures depict important cultural trends, reflected in the clothing, sets, and objects seen in the photographs. In some images props illustrate the creativity of the photographers and their subjects. The people in these pictures are in many cases participants and performers, either directing or collaborating with the photographers, who occasionally appear themselves as models in the images.

The erotic photography collection at the Kinsey Institute is one of the most unique and important in the world, and this volume includes a very small number of images from the overall archive. The Kinsey collection is largely made up of commercial and amateur erotica produced during the time when still photography dominated such endeavors. The efforts of many contemporary artists/photographers notwithstanding, it is likely that video and the Internet have supplanted silver-based still photography for most contemporary depictions of human sexuality. The examples of commercial and amateur erotica depicted in this book indicate the continued importance of the still photograph as visual documentation of the science and art of sexuality.

Betsy Stirratt, Director, School of Fine Arts Gallery, Indiana University
Jeffrey A. Wolin, Ruth N. Halls Professor of Photography, Indiana University

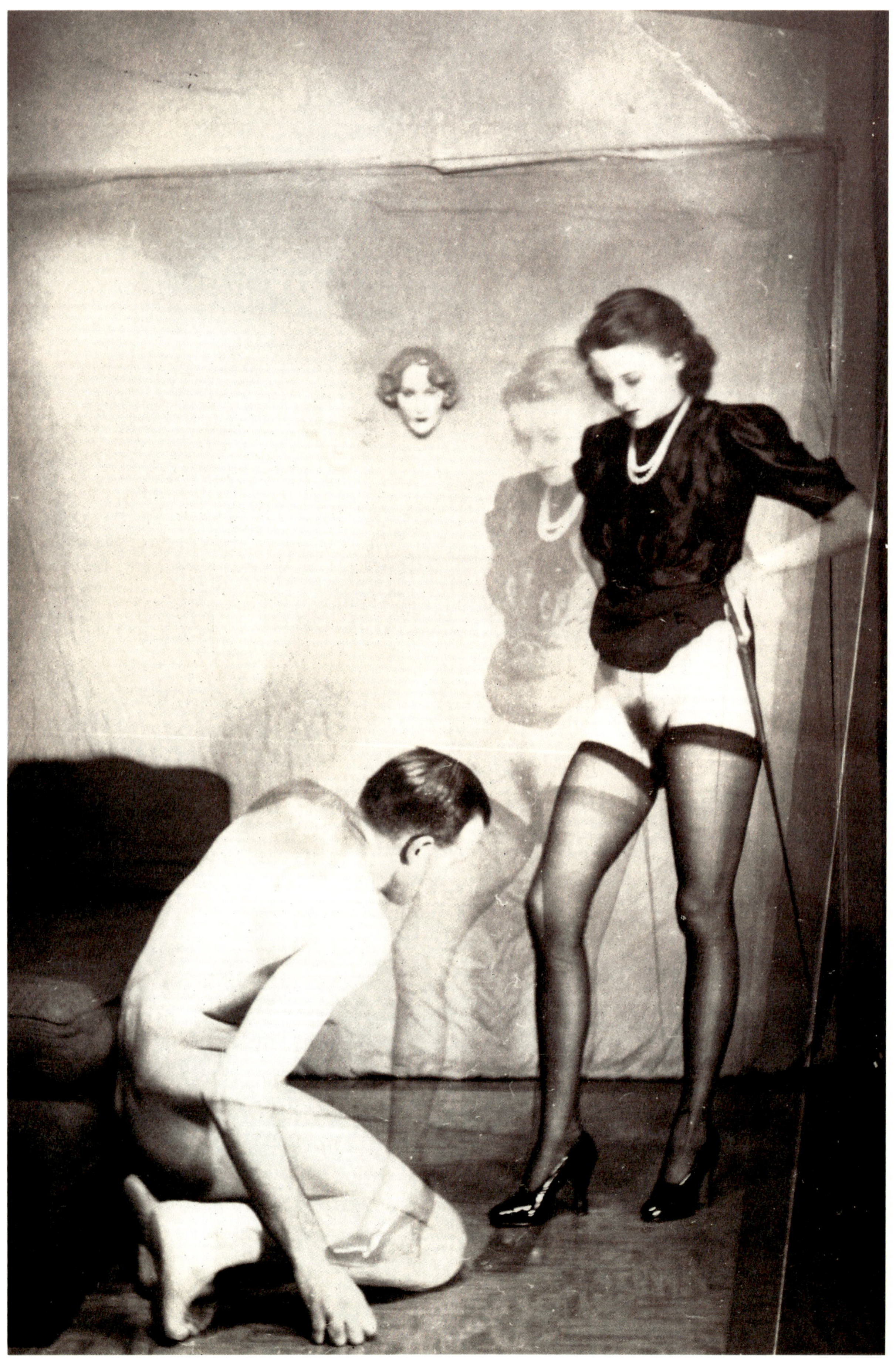

AN INTRODUCTION TO A BOOK OF SEXUAL PHOTOGRAPHS

What is pornography and what makes it different from erotica or art? Right-wing moralists and anti-porn activists answer that by lumping almost any imagery of the naked human body into the category of pornography.[1] Art historians take pains to differentiate between the contemplative aims of art and the arousing aims of pornography.[2] For some feminist critics, drawing distinctions between the various genres makes very little difference, since the very act of looking at a representation of an unclothed female body, regardless of its categorization, occurs within a patriarchal sexual economy.[3] There is no consensus on the question, which remains a social, cultural, and political battleground.

Indeed, the majority of people might not want to think about the issue at all, mostly because of the disrepute that still surrounds images of the nude and/or sexual body. Such images seem to exist mainly to arouse, to confront us with our sexual selves. That task seems indecent and improper, even worse than the ubiquitous use of erotic imagery in advertising and movies, where it is deployed to sell us products and entertainments. Being aroused to go out and purchase a lipstick or a car is definitely more acceptable than simply being sexually aroused.

Of course, the two forms of stimulation are different. One is motivated by the holy injunction to spend; the other is motivated by the unholy desire to experience bodily pleasure, which conflicts with nineteenth-century ideas that have been in revival since the 1980s. In the wake of the Civil War, sensual expression was seen as being in conflict with the middle-class values spelled out by purity crusaders and moral reformers like the fearsome Anthony Comstock, a Connecticut dry goods salesman who became one of the most powerful censorious voices in American history. In 1872 Comstock began a successful campaign against abortion, contraception, and any public expression of sexuality in literature or art, and the legacy of his oppositions is with us still.[4] Since then the United States has grown into an extraordinarily hedonistic culture that revolves around the joys of consumption, but bodily gratification of the sexual type, along with images of it, still provokes protest, shame, and fear.

The images in this volume were taken from a collection that was begun and nurtured in the midst of such an atmosphere and was closed off from general public scrutiny. They are from the archive of photography at the Kinsey Institute for Research in Sex, Gender, and Reproduction, and this is the first volume that is drawn from the entire scope of the institute's collection. For it the editors have culled over one hundred and twenty images (along with pages of multiple images taken from amateur albums), dating from the 1880s to 1998. The majority of images show the naked or partially clothed human body both in repose and engaged in sexual acts or postures and are, by turns, unexpected, playful, strange, puzzling, and witty. Their ability to arouse, like their beauty, lies in the eye—and the psyche—of the beholder.

That the collection exists at all is extraordinary. It was started in the late 1930s and routinely faced difficulties, chief among them federal obscenity laws and public codes of morality. One of its early contributors was Paul Gebhard, an anthropologist who worked with Kinsey and functioned as photographer to the collection for a few years in the 1940s, taking pictures of erotic objects, drawings, and photos that collectors allowed them to copy, but didn't want to donate to the institute. The sensitive nature of the material meant that the collection was kept secret from the public, even after the groundbreaking, publicity-inciting 1948 publication of Kinsey's *Sexual Behavior in the Human Male.* "Since we looked upon this as an extremely touchy thing," said Gebhard, "the existence of our collections and the fact that we did photography was a deep state secret."[5]

The Kinsey state secret broke wide open in 1950, when a new Customs official, unaccustomed to okaying the importation of sexual images into the state of Indiana, confiscated a package from Denmark destined for the institute. Kinsey decided to take the Customs Bureau to court to resolve the issue of whether he could legally import sexual images for scientific use. One Customs official responded by taking some of the seized items to the press, which reported on them in a predictably outraged, hostile, and condescending manner: "'Science' Says Kinsey: 'Dirty Stuff' Says U.S." screamed a headline on the *Indianapolis Star.*[6]

Anyone who grew up in the American Midwest of the 1950s would recognize the sentiments and wording of the headline: "dirty" was a favored pejorative term. "Dirty" and "sex" were often uttered together, and throughout the 1950s the very name "Alfred Kinsey" meant sex. Not that someone who was a child at the time (as I was) would know that Kinsey wrote two groundbreaking studies, one on male sexuality in 1948 followed by one on female sexuality in 1953. One's knowledge of Dr. Kinsey was more general than that. His name floated in the air in those years loosely trailed by an aura of the forbidden.

That kind of overt association of a public figure with sex is commonplace now, but then it was very mysterious and unusual. Because Dr. Kinsey was a buttoned-down academic at a midwestern university, his chosen profession as a sex professor seemed somehow minimally acceptable. The adults talked about him like he was a bit of crackpot, but they seemed to grudgingly accept his endeavors.

Their tolerance proceeded from Kinsey's status as a scientist. His professional credential meant that he was a serious individual doing the arcane stuff called "science," which was almost as mysterious as "sex." He was presumably closeted in some laboratory where he scientifically gathered information about sex and then thought about his sex information very hard before writing about it.

This fuzzy impression of the eccentric college professor was challenged in 1950 when the news of his collection of erotica, especially the photographs, hit the papers. Kinsey assembling scientific "facts" was one thing; buying and looking at steamy pictures was quite another. The science of sex must surely consist of highly technical concepts and theorems about sex written in dull language, the average person may well have thought (although both Kinsey Reports were best-sellers). Pictures of sex, on the other hand, were produced for an entirely different audience with completely different aims and could, seemingly, never have intellectual value. As the *Anniston Star* (Alabama) put it: "Pictures of moral degenerates in degenerate poses hardly can reveal much of real scientific worth." Such pictures were made to arouse, and the culture-wide perception of them, as papers around the country proclaimed, was that they were just plain "dirty."

Of course, the adults in my remembered fantasy of the 1950s knew more than I did of the world and would have realized the voyeuristic possibilities inherent in even Kinsey's most intellectual pursuits. I wonder how conscious they were of the erotica and pornography that was around; what is freely available on the Internet today was in those years hidden and proscribed. Given the amount of it that seems to have been made, it must not have been terribly difficult to obtain, especially in larger cities. Obviously, some of them were cognizant of this stuff, because someone was buying it and even making it themselves.

Indeed, a sizable portion of Kinsey's collection consists of amateur pornography, which are some of the most intriguing pictures in this book. Like other types of amateur photography they are often lacking in the technical know-how and pictorial sophistication that make professional photography so seamlessly appealing. In amateur photographs you can see the seams—the single light source, the awkward pose, the less-than-perfect bodies. The interest of amateur pornography lies precisely in the inability to smooth over the rough spots, to either normalize or glamorize the homespun sexual pursuits.

A lot of the amateur images, in fact, are downright odd. Take the image on page 24, of a nude woman doing a back-bend in a homey-looking bedroom, circa 1940. She was probably used to performing her nimble calisthenics in public, albeit in appropriate garb. The gymnastic pose produces a crotch-toward-the-camera position that insures the display of her genitals in a particularly thorough and open way. Genital display is one of the main—if not *the* main—goals of much pornographic imagery. Rather than simply presenting a woman sitting spread-eagle on the floor, adventurous amateur photographers conjured up more creative postures, even if the images ended up being a tad awkward in terms of their overall erotic charge. Like many other amateur shots, this was probably a private picture, meant only for the eyes of the photographer and model. We can only speculate on how long the photographer may have fantasized about making this photo, sitting through one hometown football game after another, or multiple gymnastics exhibitions, before he won the confidence of his athletic muse.

Fantasy, of course, is at the heart of sexual imagery, although the content and boundaries of the fantasy are often unavailable to the uninitiated. In one image, which is dated "before 1959," a nude male figure lounges head first down a flight of stairs while propping his genitals up with one hand. The sheer weirdness of the pose inspires an obvious question: What in the heck is he doing? Once again, genital display seems to be the issue, although the pose looks so clumsily uncomfortable that the eroticism is difficult to locate. But there is obviously erotic potential for the people involved, which is one reason Kinsey may have been interested in the photo. He was looking for the largest sample of sexual behavior he could get, and in so doing had discovered the tremendous variety of human sexual experience. "Above all," Paul Robinson writes of Kinsey's ideas, "there was the extraordinary extent of individual variation, including many different techniques of intercourse and an even wider variety of psychological attitudes associated with sexual acts."[8] The activity in this image probably doesn't qualify as a "sexual act," but it raises questions about where the sexual allure resides in this down-the-stairs posture—and how many people might share in it.

As the result of his research, Kinsey plotted human sexual practice along a continuous arc, rejecting the binarism of "normal" versus "abnormal" sexuality.[9] Sexual pictures might be charted, too, proceeding along a curve that moved from the most private and arcane fantasies, like the previous image, to those that have readily identifiable sources, such as advertising and editorial photography. On pages 146–147, a woman perches on the running board of a car clutching a dog and smiling for the camera as she pulls up her dress and spreads her legs, exposing her genitals. It's an amateur's mischievous vision, circa 1923, of a visual trope that was useful to the automobile industry for much of the twentieth century: Woman as an essential prop in advertising and selling automobiles.

Women and cars were a particularly potent combination in the 1920s because the invention of the car helped foster a sexual revolution. The automobile was a symbol of the dangerous liberty that was becoming more available to women. An enclosed, mobile space, it could carry women away from the surveillance of parents and chaperones and into the clutches of sexually venturesome young men.[10] The wily amateur who took this picture neatly sums up the problem and the pleasures of the new car culture in a blatant way that would probably horrify auto industry executives of the day. The industry's own equation of sex, cars, and women was expressed in its ads with an elegance and subtlety that tried to sublimate the obvious sexual pitch.[11]

The irony of amateur pornography is that amateurs often use those near to them—especially wives and girlfriends—as the subjects/objects of the pornographic image. At the root of the arguments against pornography is a notion that unacceptably sexual images must be controlled or even censored to keep them away from designated groups of vulnerable or incompetent people who would be harmed by exposure to them—including women, children, and the uneducated; some of the very people who are supposed to be protected by legal strictures from such material are the models within it, a circumstance that moral crusaders never come to terms with.[12]

In addition to the work of enterprising amateurs, there are other types of sexual photography in this volume, including pinups, physical culture and nudist imagery, art, ethnography, and commercially produced pornography. There are several photos of male nudes by George Platt Lynes, drawn from the institute's large collection of nearly 600 prints by him. His nude photos point to the difficulty of precisely defining the motivations, purposes, and definitions of sexual images, and return us to the question that opened this essay: What is pornography and how is it different from erotica and art?

Lynes was a successful portrait, fashion, and advertising photographer in the 1930s and early 1940s. As a young man he had ambitions to be a serious writer, but abandoned them and took up photography in 1927. Soon after he learned the medium, he began making photos of male nudes, which became increasingly more sexually explicit.[13] In the 1930s he was included in several important shows at the Museum of Modern Art and had exhibitions at significant galleries, but also did commercial and editorial work in order to make a living. Throughout both his busy, successful years and his years of declining popularity and ultimate bankruptcy in the later 1940s and 1950s, Lynes continued to make homoerotic male nudes, even after he had lost interest in doing any other kind of photography.

Lynes was at a low point in his fortunes when he met Alfred Kinsey in 1949. The following year Kinsey began acquiring photos by Lynes, eventually amassing nearly 600 prints that included the entire range of Lynes's subjects. Lynes rebelled against Kinsey's penchant for labeling his images in terms of their sexual content, and was especially put off by Kinsey's use of the term "pornographic" in relation to his photos. Kinsey may have suggested that Lynes create images of homosexual intercourse, which Lynes was hesitant to do. Lynes hoped to exhibit his less sexualized nudes to a general audience, although the mores of the day made that virtually impossible. There was open opposition to gay artists and themes within the art community in the 1930s, and increasing discrimination in general against gays in the 1940s and 1950s. The best Lynes could do was to publish his nudes under the name Roberto Rolf in *Der Kreis*, a gay magazine in Switzerland.[14]

How are we to categorize Lynes's sexual pictures? He shot them using the same stylistic strategies of posing, composition, and lighting that he employed in his more respectable commercial and portrait work. He made them with a dedication and single-mindedness usually associated with the making of art. But he never exhibited them—that we know of—in any of the upscale galleries and museums that showed his other work. Nor was he able to publish them except in a foreign country under an assumed name. In the five years before his death in 1955, he sold them to Kinsey for the purpose of science, but worried about them being confiscated by postal officials, who would have called them pornography.

Lynes lived his life as a secret sexual photographer during a time of social and cultural change that didn't come fast enough to do him any good. World War II had whet the appetites of American men for new sexual images, which they brought back with them from Europe and Asia; the war also mandated sex-segregated activity and living quarters that fostered same-sex intimacy and a postwar gay subculture.[15] Kinsey's reports on male and female sexuality opened a window onto human sexuality in its many permutations that was unprecedented, and made sex a topic of everyday conversation. One of his most shocking findings concerned the prevalence of homosexuality in the United States: over one-third of his respondents admitting to having had a postadolescent homosexual experience that resulted in orgasm.[16] *Playboy* magazine debuted on newsstands in 1953, and an enormous underground manufactory of erotica and pornography blossomed in the United States.[17] Starting in 1957, the Supreme Court handed down rulings on obscenity cases—including the Kinsey Institute's test case, *U.S. v. 31 Photographs*—that progressively condoned the use of sexual speech and sexual imagery in public expression.[18]

Yet, as I write, sexual expression of all kinds, from strip clubs to artists' photographs, are under continuing attack; the lines separating the artistic from the pornographic or the pornographic from the obscene are faintly drawn and subject to ongoing argument and reinterpretation. Although many of Lynes's nudes and sexual photographs have migrated from the twilight domain in which they were made into the province of art, the judgments that elevated them would be vehemently condemned by some outside the field of art and photography. Indeed, the more explicit photographs might well be "pornographic," although I'm not too certain of what that means.

What I do know is that one sexual image by Lynes is particularly powerful for me. The untitled photo, dated 1955, is straightforward in its rendition of male genitalia but ambiguous as to how it could be classified as an image.[19] In it a man is seen from mid-forehead to mid-thigh, naked from the waist down, with his genitals, stomach, and thighs brightly lit. His head, chest, and hands, which are buttoning a shirt over his nakedness, are in shadow. He leans against a nondescript piece of furniture, a pack of cigarettes and a cut-glass ashtray visible next to him.

Although there is no sexual activity taking place, this image could not be reproduced in many magazines and books even today because of a prohibition against showing the human penis. Displaying the photo in a museum might well create controversy and protest. Yet the penis is not the only element of the photograph. If we say that the "point" of the image is merely to display his sex, what are we to make of the image's other elements? What does it mean that I hesitate over his shadowed face and wonder at its purpose? If his face is in shadow merely to shield his identity, that could have been accomplished by simply cropping his head out. Instead, Lynes seems to set up an opposition between sexuality and identity, as if to say by owning his sexuality the sitter must give up his identity. That dilemma, which is familiar to gay men and lesbians, gives the image an unnerving sadness.

An argument could be made that I have perused and considered this image in a way that is "contemplative"—which is an aim of art—rather than "arousing"—which is the aim of pornography. Whether the image is pornographic or not is a wholly subjective decision; another viewer might dismiss my analysis completely and see nothing but base purposes at work. Just as Lynes's intentions were not clear-cut when he was making his sexual images, there is nothing clear-cut about their reception now.

Sexuality and its depictions remain contested, which is not all bad. Despite the evident threat from moral crusaders, sexual pictures shouldn't be normalized as "art" just so that they'll be considered fit to view, nor should they be sorted into predetermined categories. The difference between "pornography" and "erotica" may, in fact, simply be one of style. Ideally, the entire realm of sexual imagery will remain ambiguous and fugitive, hard to pin down; in its fleeting refusals and taunting provocations, it will maintain substantial disruptive power.

Notes

[1] The group Morality in Media, for instance, which was founded in 1962, states in its listing of programs for 1999 that it devotes itself completely to working "through constitutional means to combat obscenity (hardcore pornography)." Its definition of obscenity is, however, extremely elastic. On January 7, 2000, the organization issued a press release announcing that it had successfully "asked" the Kroger supermarket chain to display *Cosmopolitan* magazine in blinder racks, which block the entire magazine cover except for the logo. The reason: the magazine carries "headlines with lurid sexual content."

[2] Lynda Nead, *The Female Nude: Art, Obscenity and Sexuality* (London and New York: Routledge, 1992). See 27, especially, for a summation of the issue by Kenneth Clark.

[3] Abigail Solomon-Godeau, "Reconsidering Erotic Photography: Notes for a Project of Historical Salvage," *Photography at the Dock: Essays on Photographic History, Institutions, and Practices* (Minneapolis, MN: University of Minnesota Press, 1991), 220–37.

[4] John D'Emilio and Estelle B. Freedman, *Intimate Matters: A History of Sexuality in America* (New York: Harper & Row, 1988), 159–64.

[5] James H. Jones, *Alfred C. Kinsey: A Public/Private Life* (New York: W. W. Norton & Company, 1997), 605.

[6] Ibid., 670. The newspaper is dated November 15, 1950.

[7] Ibid., 671.

[8] Paul A. Robinson, *The Modernization of Sex: Havelock Ellis, Alfred Kinsey, William Masters, and Virginia Johnson* (New York: Harper & Row, 1976), 50.

[9] Ibid., 54–55.

[10] D'Emilio and Freedman, 239–41; 257.

[11] Automobiles accessorized by women became a familiar sight not only in auto advertising but in fashion and other types of editorial images as well. For a recent example of the pairing, this time in editorial fashion photos, see *Harper's Bazaar*, February 2000, 222–31.

[12] Nead, 91–96.

[13] James Crump, "Iconography of Desire: George Platt Lynes and Gay Male Visual Culture in Postwar New York," *George Platt Lynes: Photographs from the Kinsey Institute* (Boston: Bulfinch Press, 1993), 151. Most of the biographical information about Lynes in my introduction comes from Crump's two essays in this book.

[14] Ibid., 150–53.

[15] D'Emilio and Freedman, 280; 288–89.

[16] Jones, 528.

[17] D'Emilio and Freedman, 279–80.

[18] For a thorough account of this case, see Jennifer Pearson Yamashiro, "In the Realm of the Sciences: The Kinsey Institute's 31 Photographs," *Porn 101: Eroticism, Pornography, and the First Amendment* (New York: Prometheus, 1999), ed. James E. Elias et al., 32–52. The argument on pornography versus obscenity is outside the scope of this paper. For discussions on it see Marjorie Heins, *Sex, Sin, and Blasphemy: A Guide to America's Censorship Wars* (New York: New Press, 1993) and Nadine Strossen, *Defending Pornography: Free Speech, Sex, and the Fight for Women's Rights* (New York: Scribner Books, 1995).

[19] The image was first reproduced as plate 57 in Jack Woody, *George Platt Lynes: Photographs, 1931–1955* (Los Angeles: Twelvetrees Press, 1980).

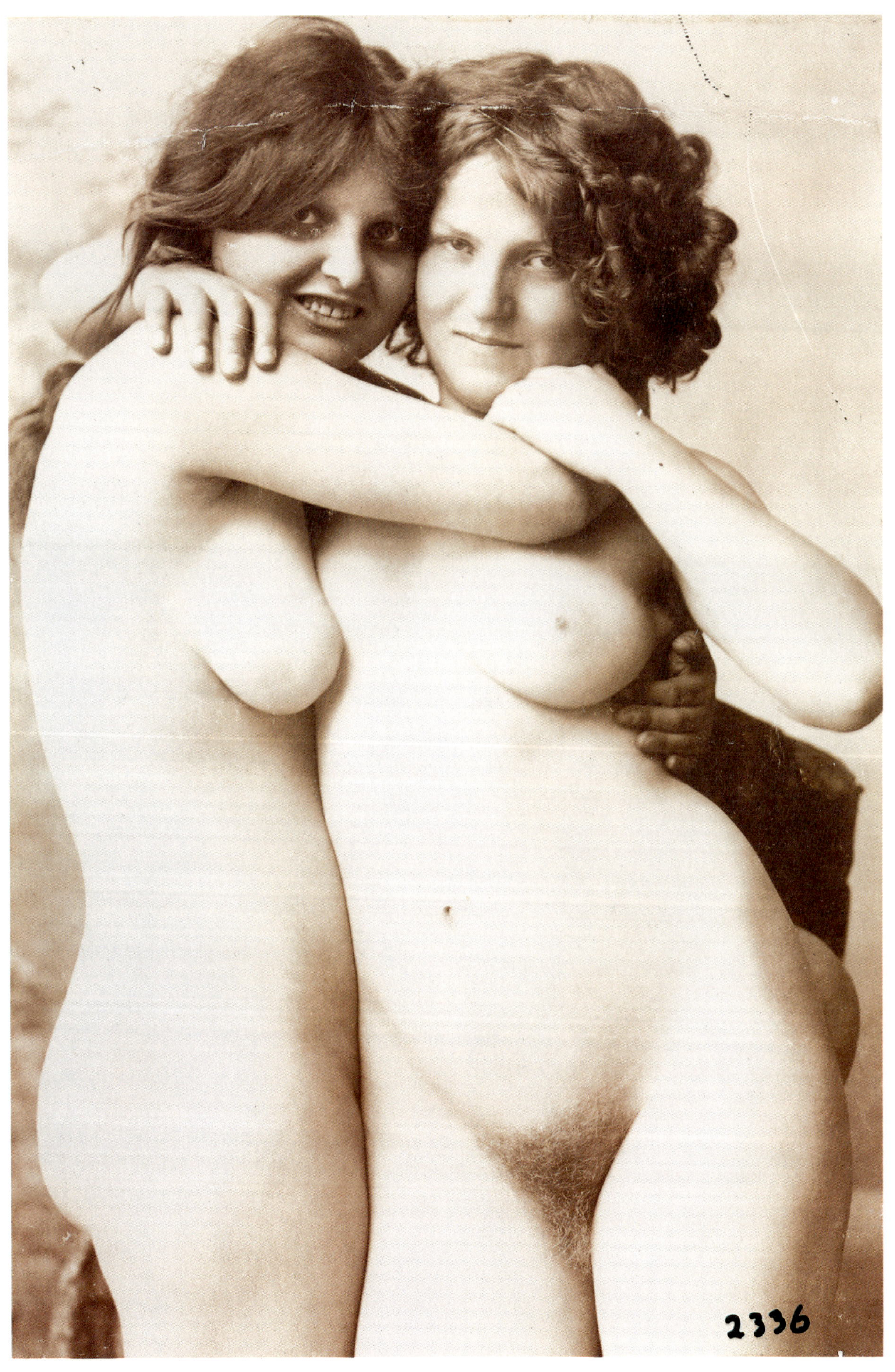
2336

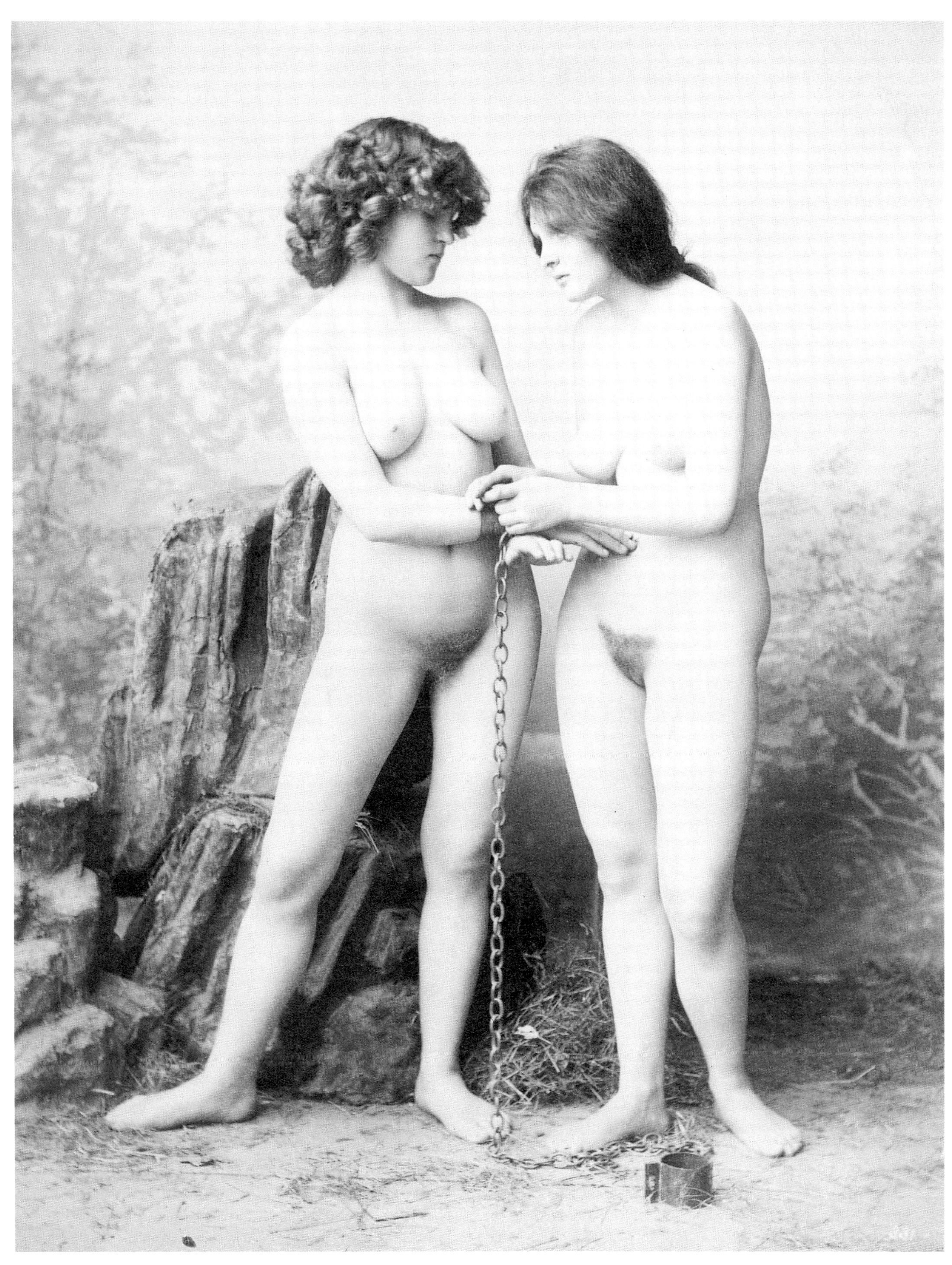

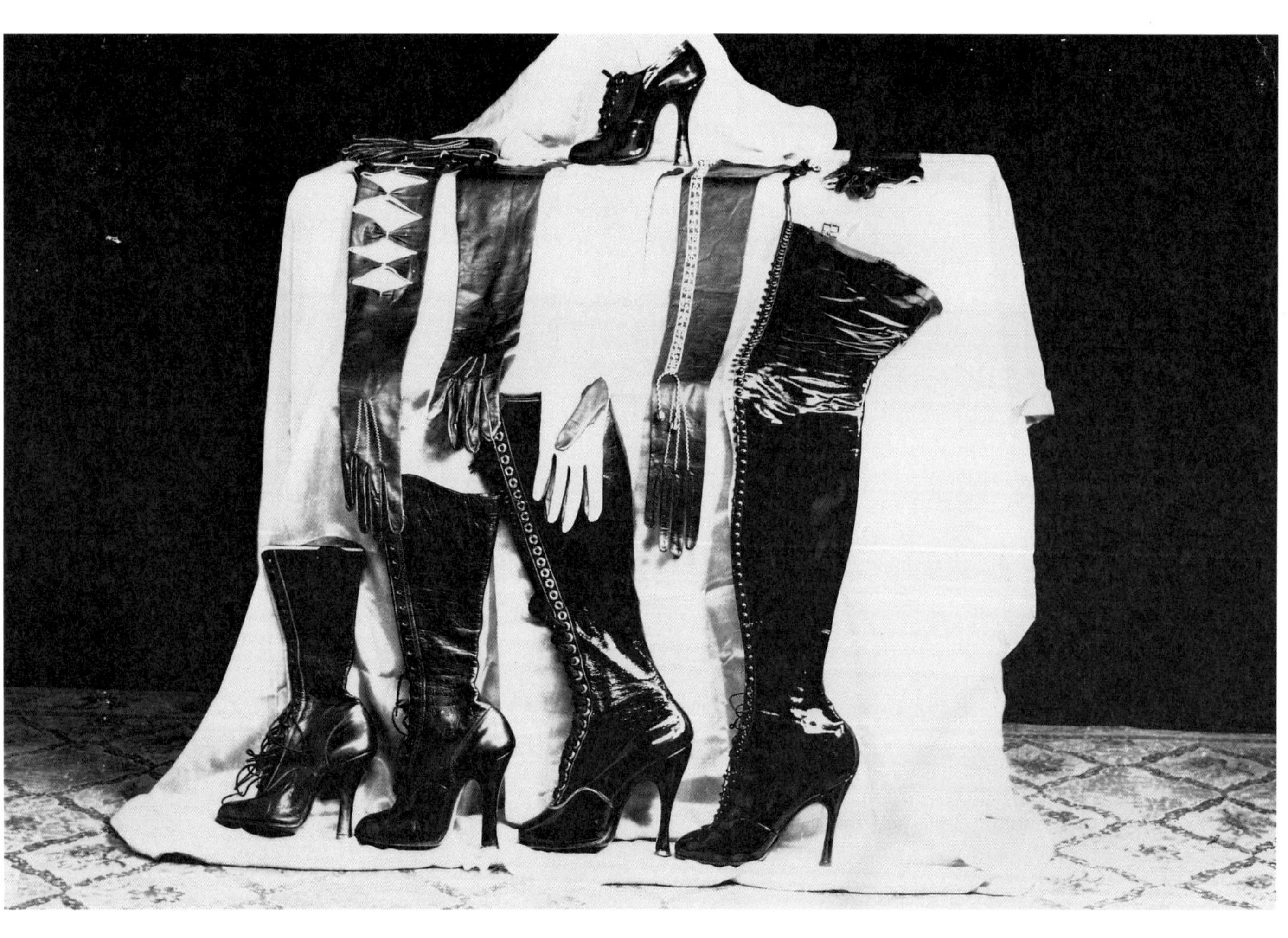

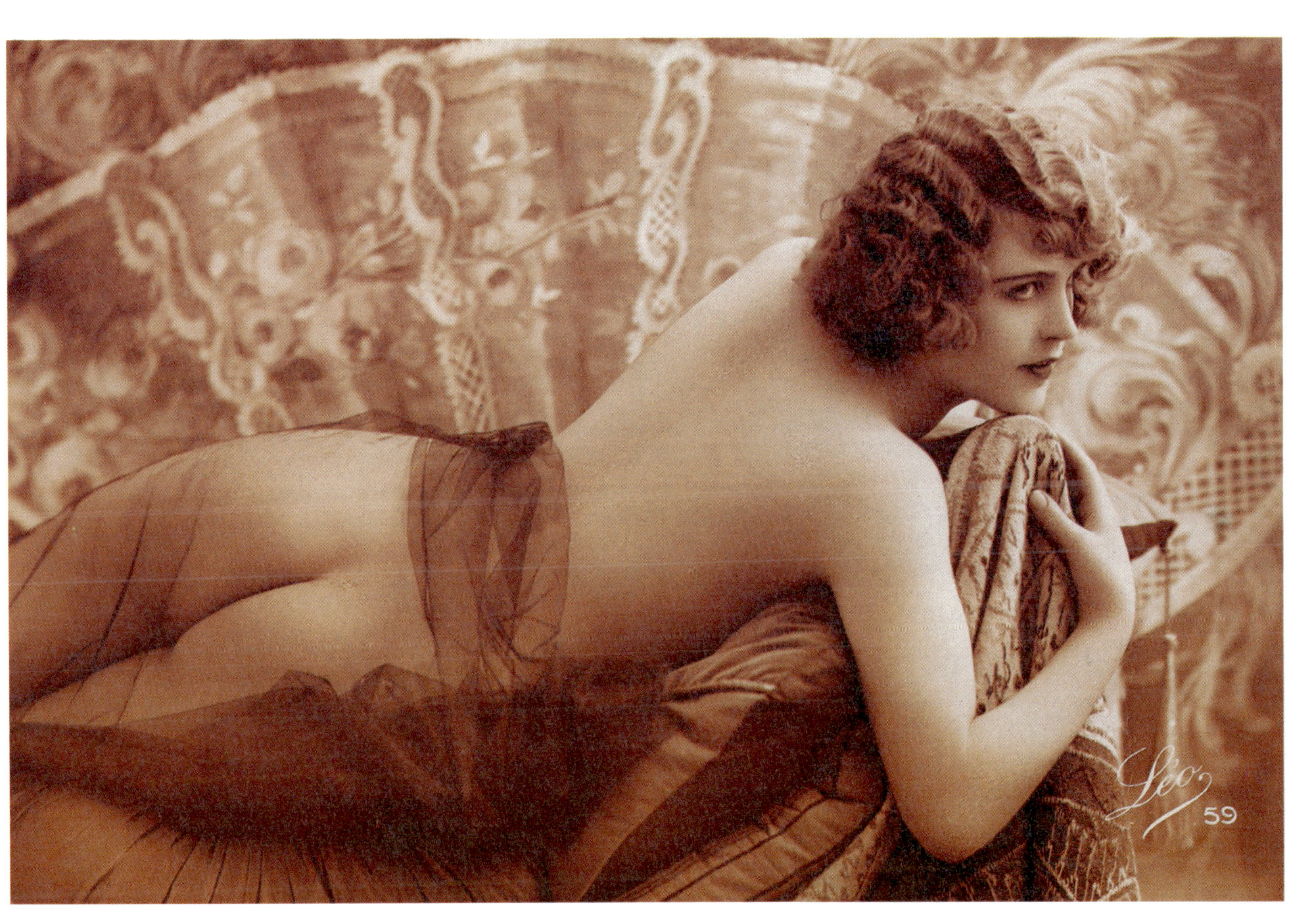
Léo
59

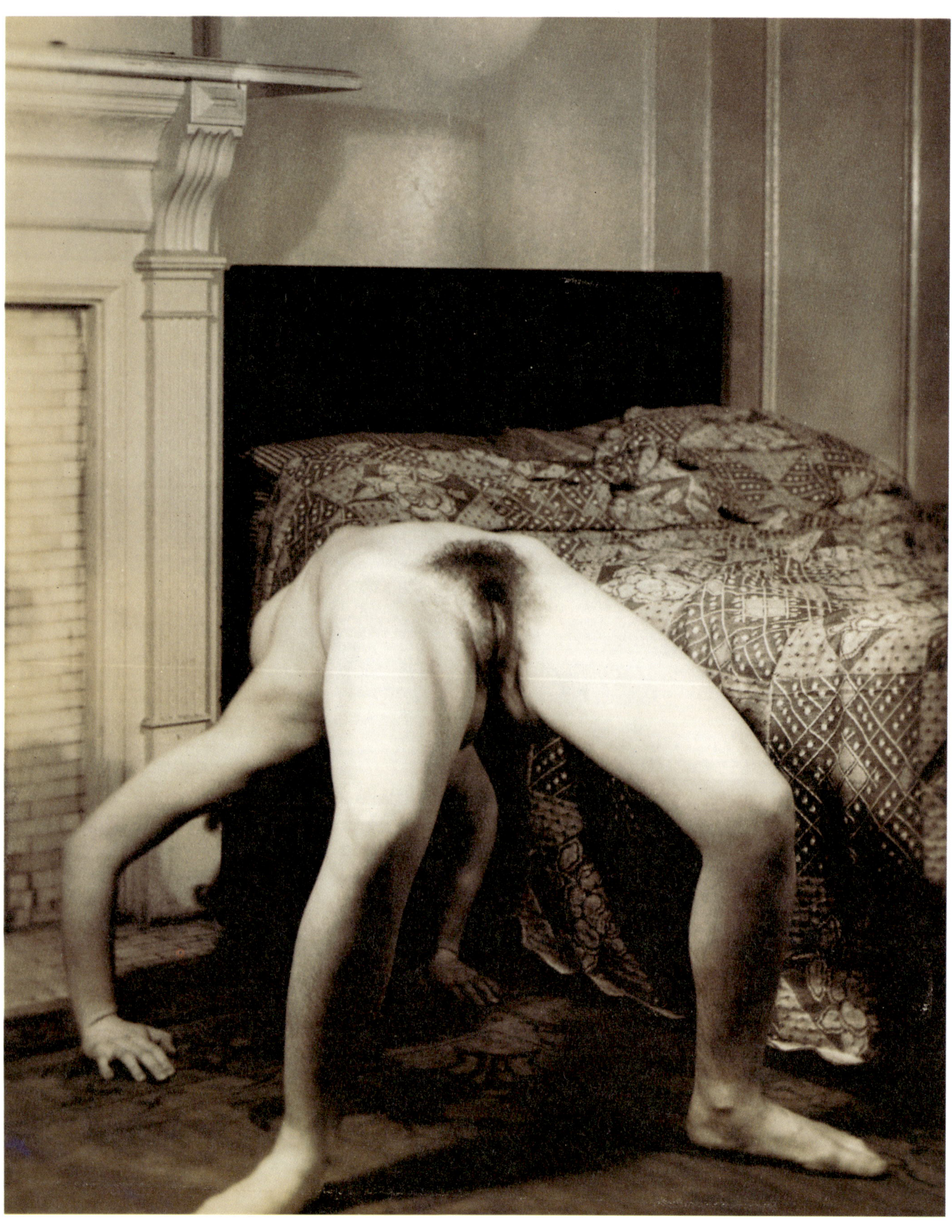

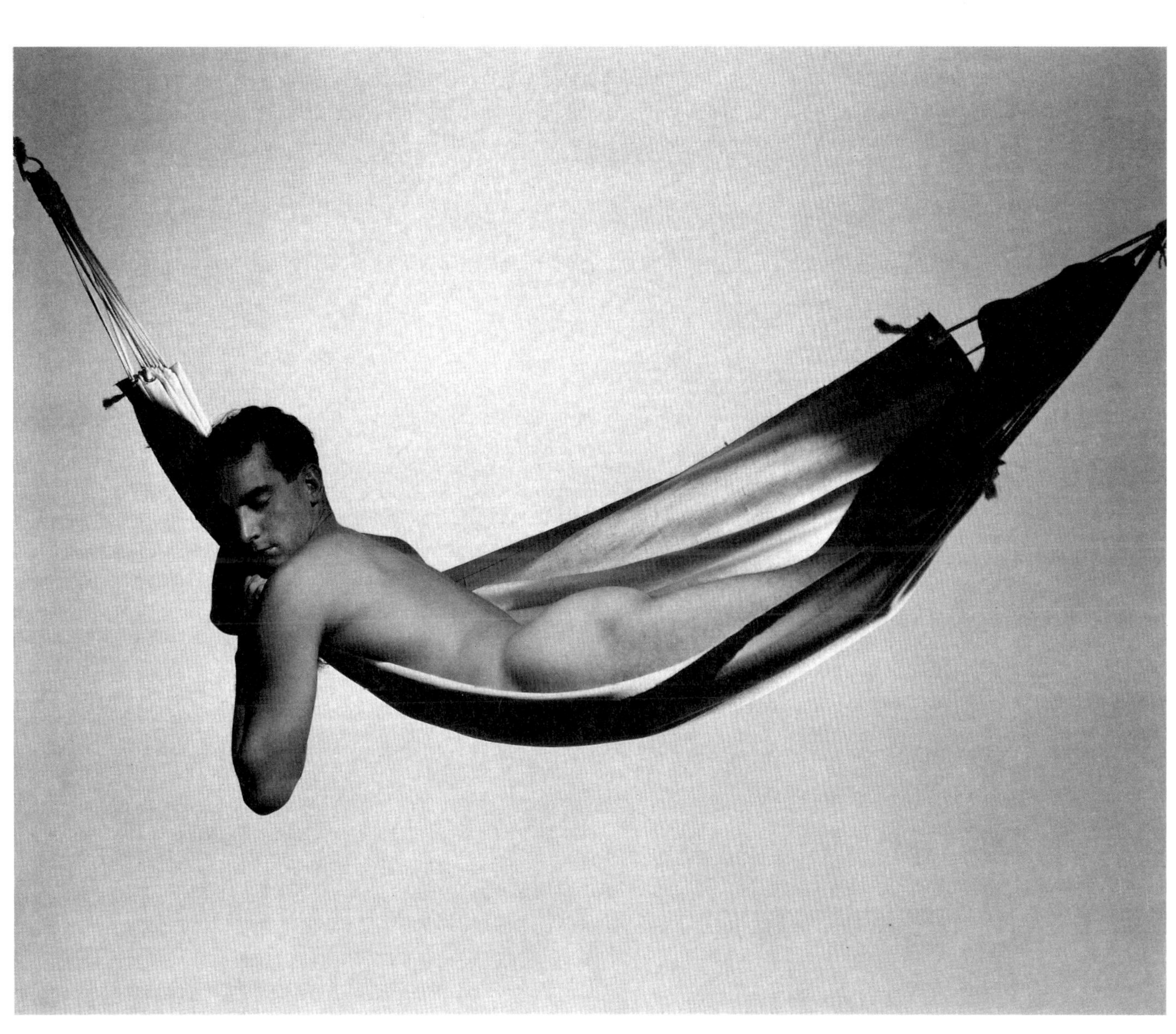

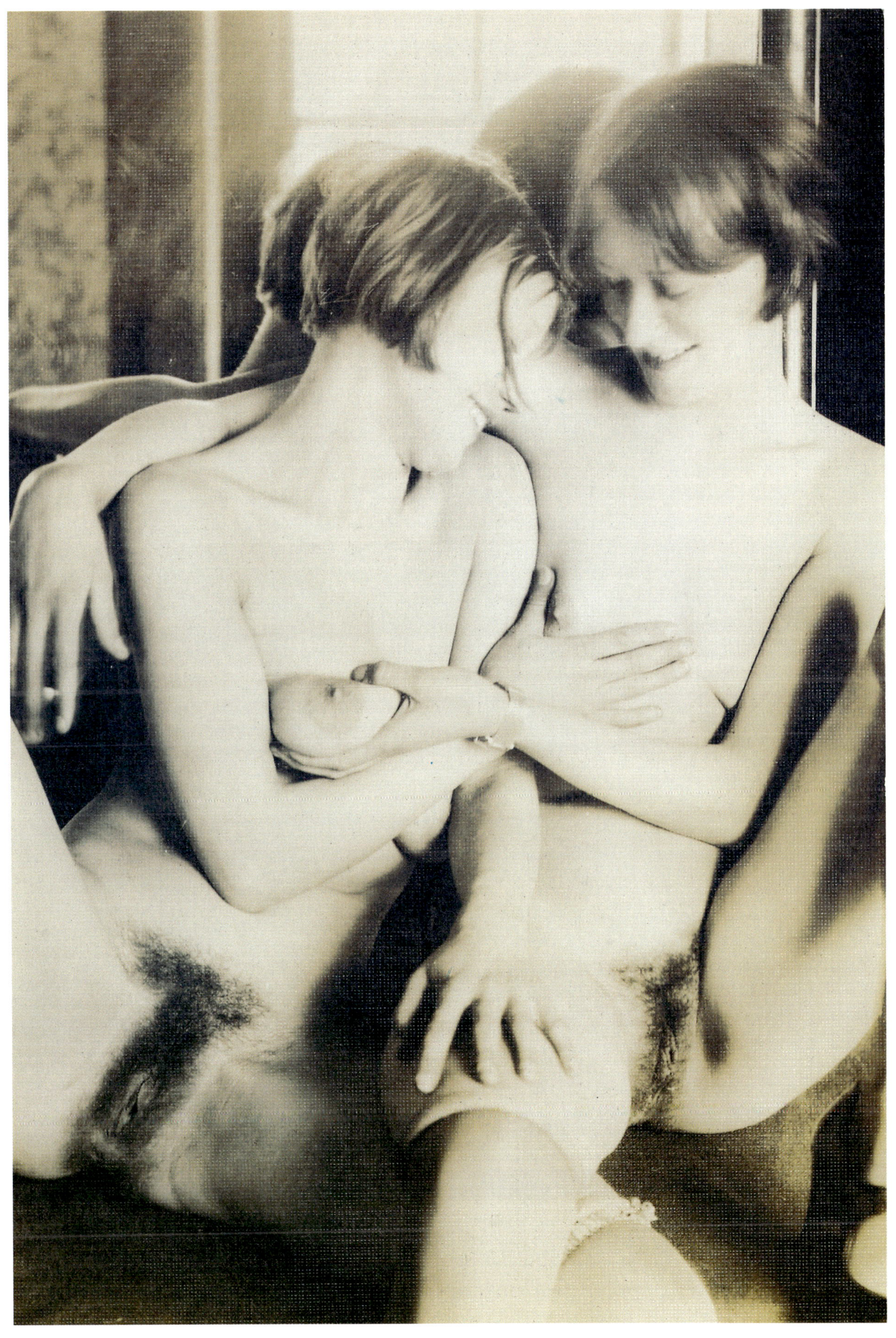

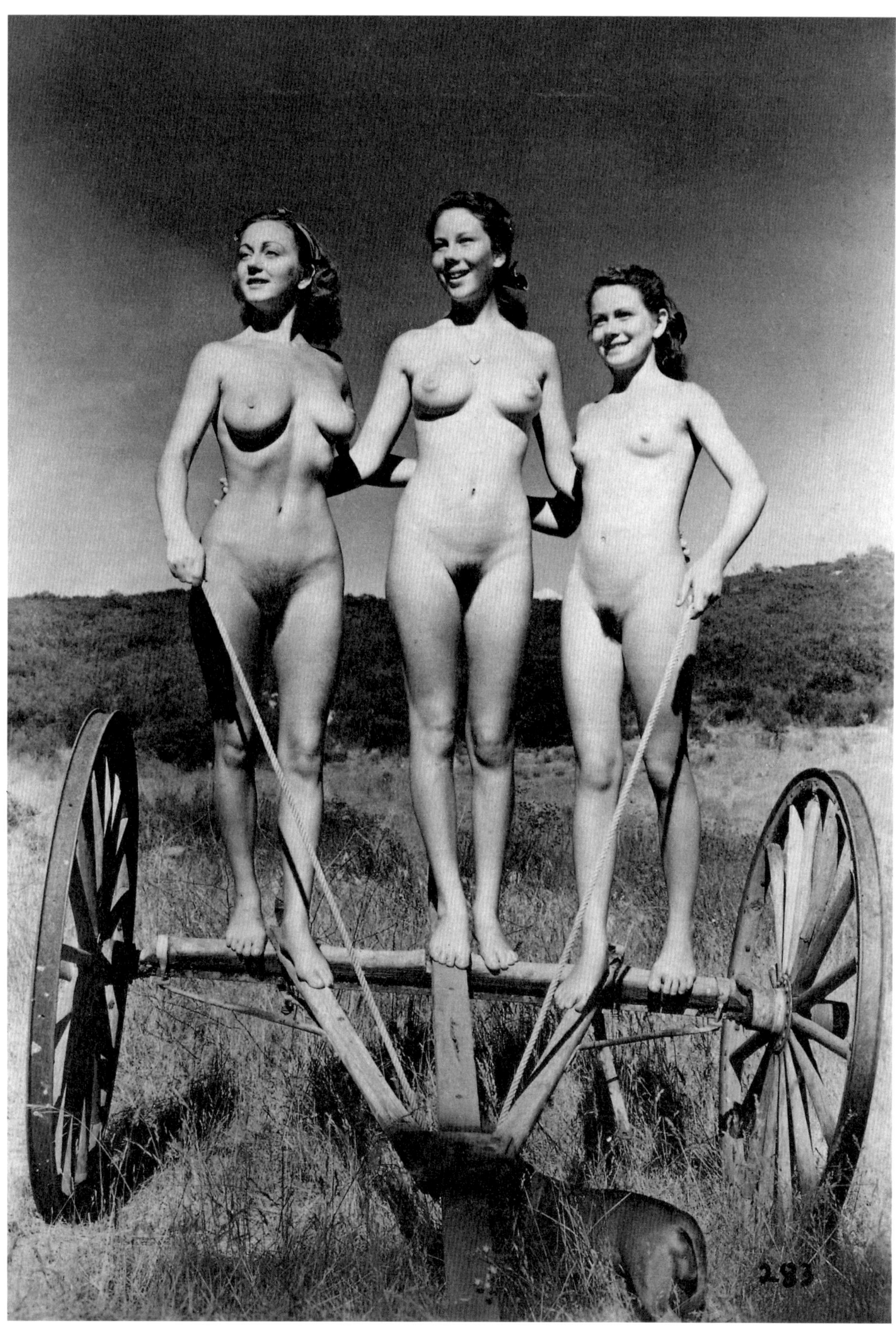

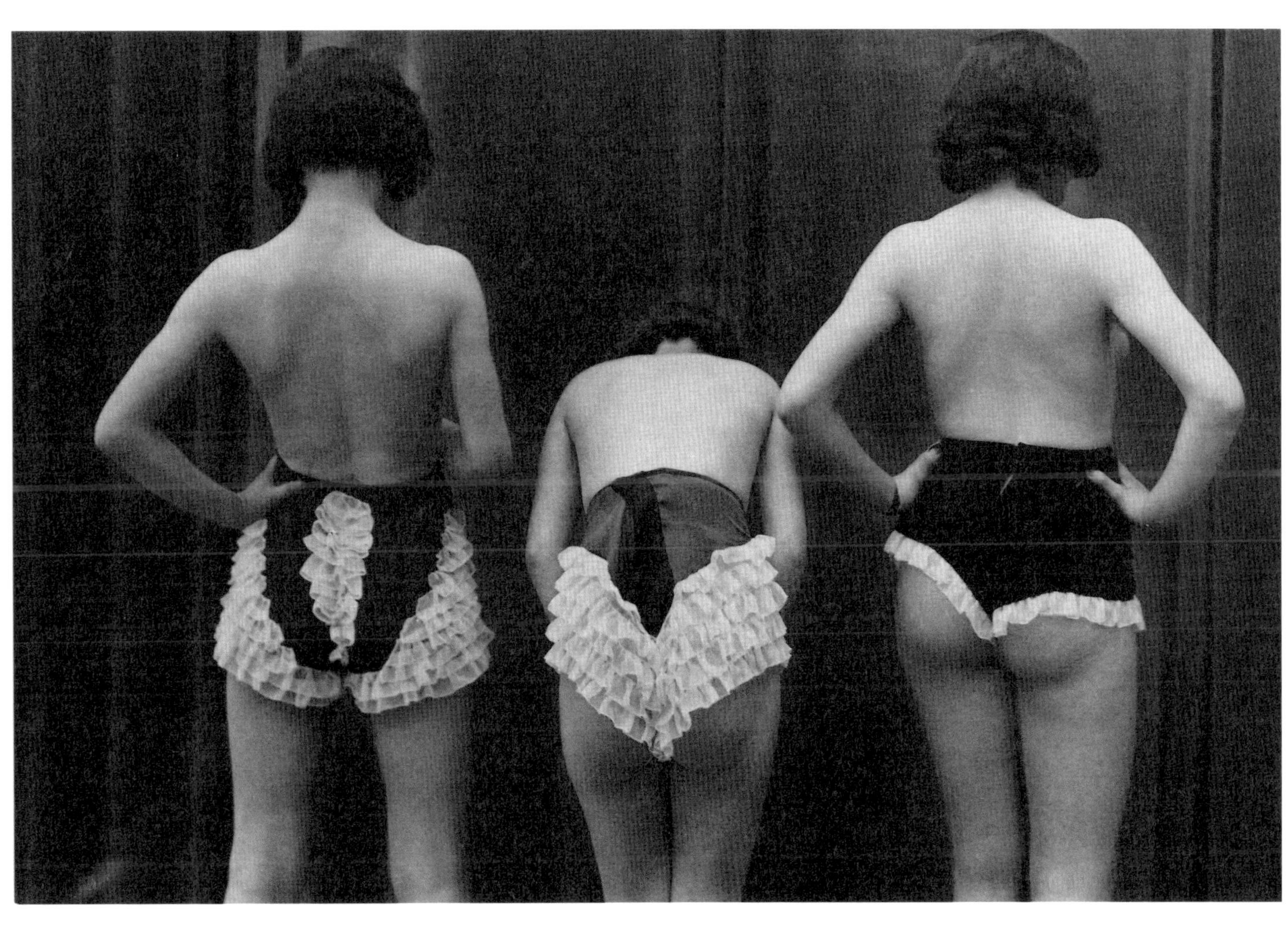

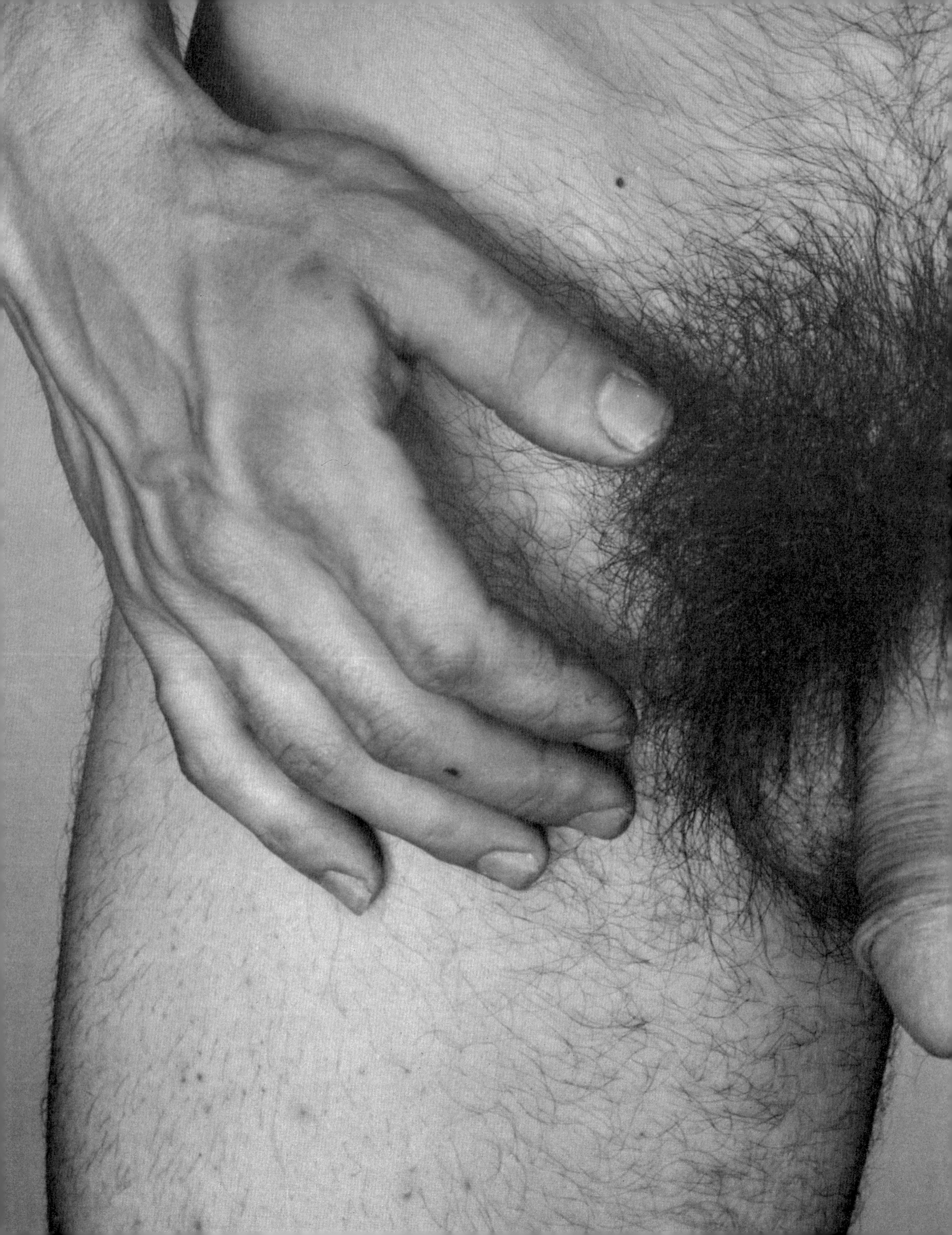

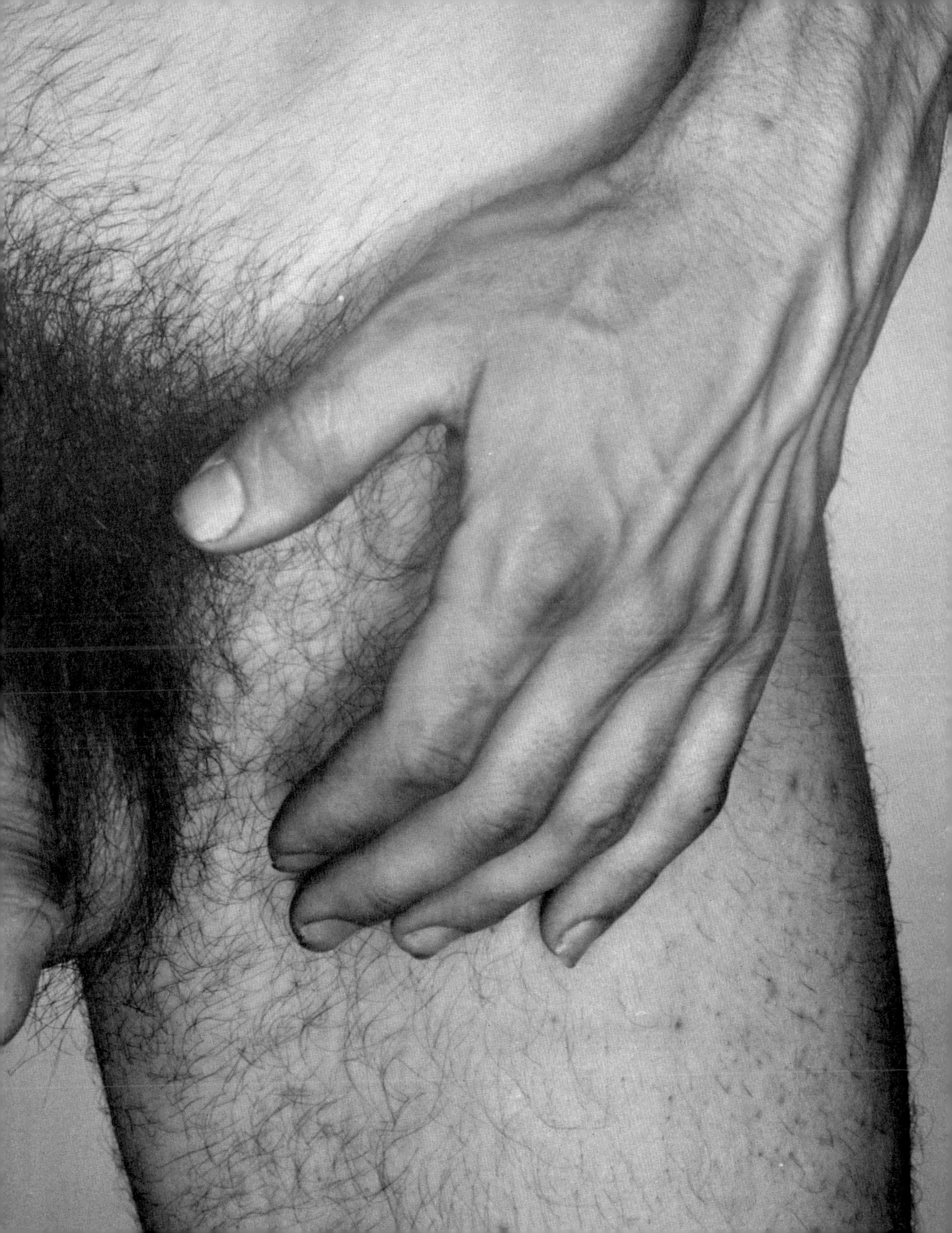

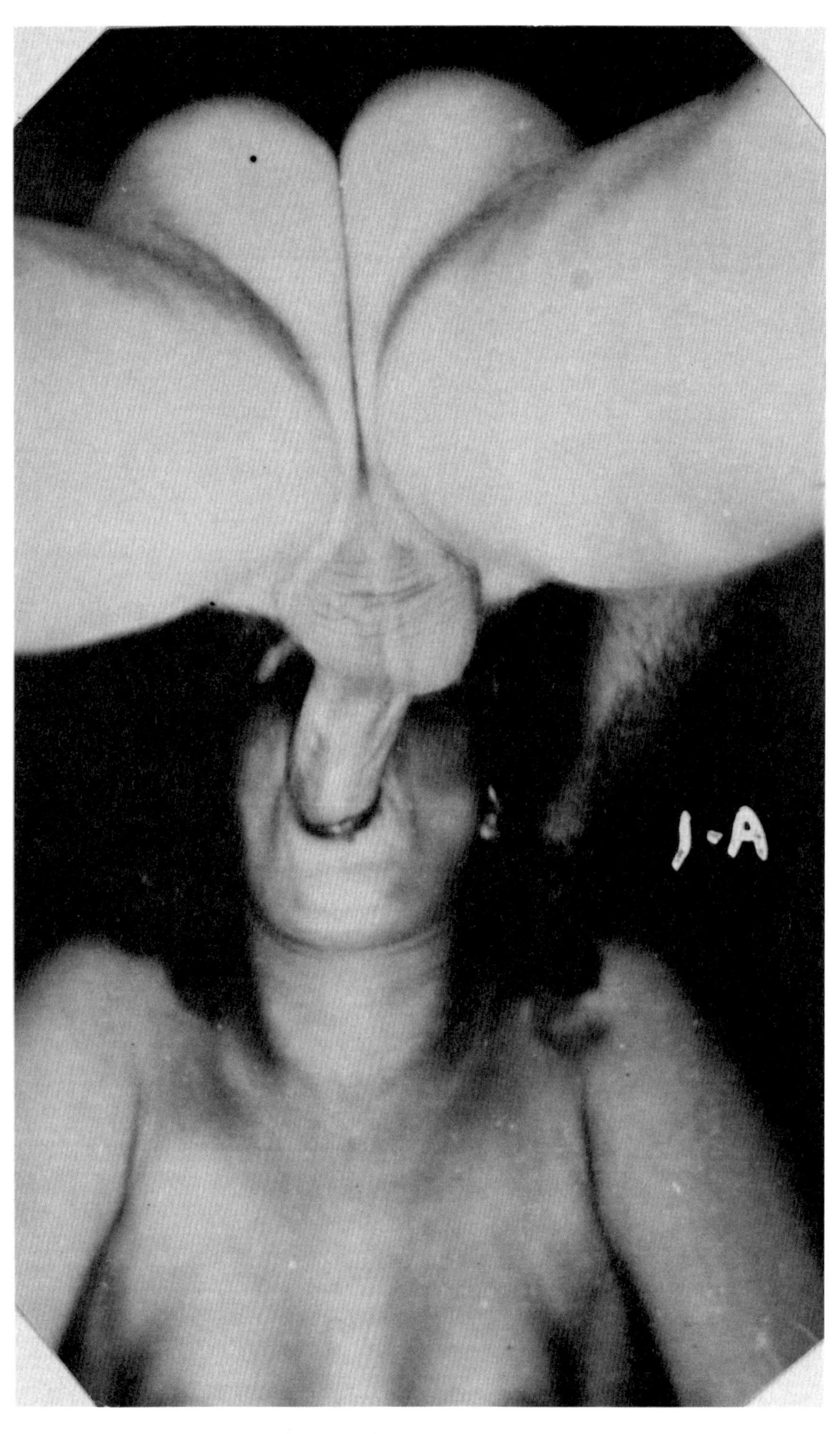J-A

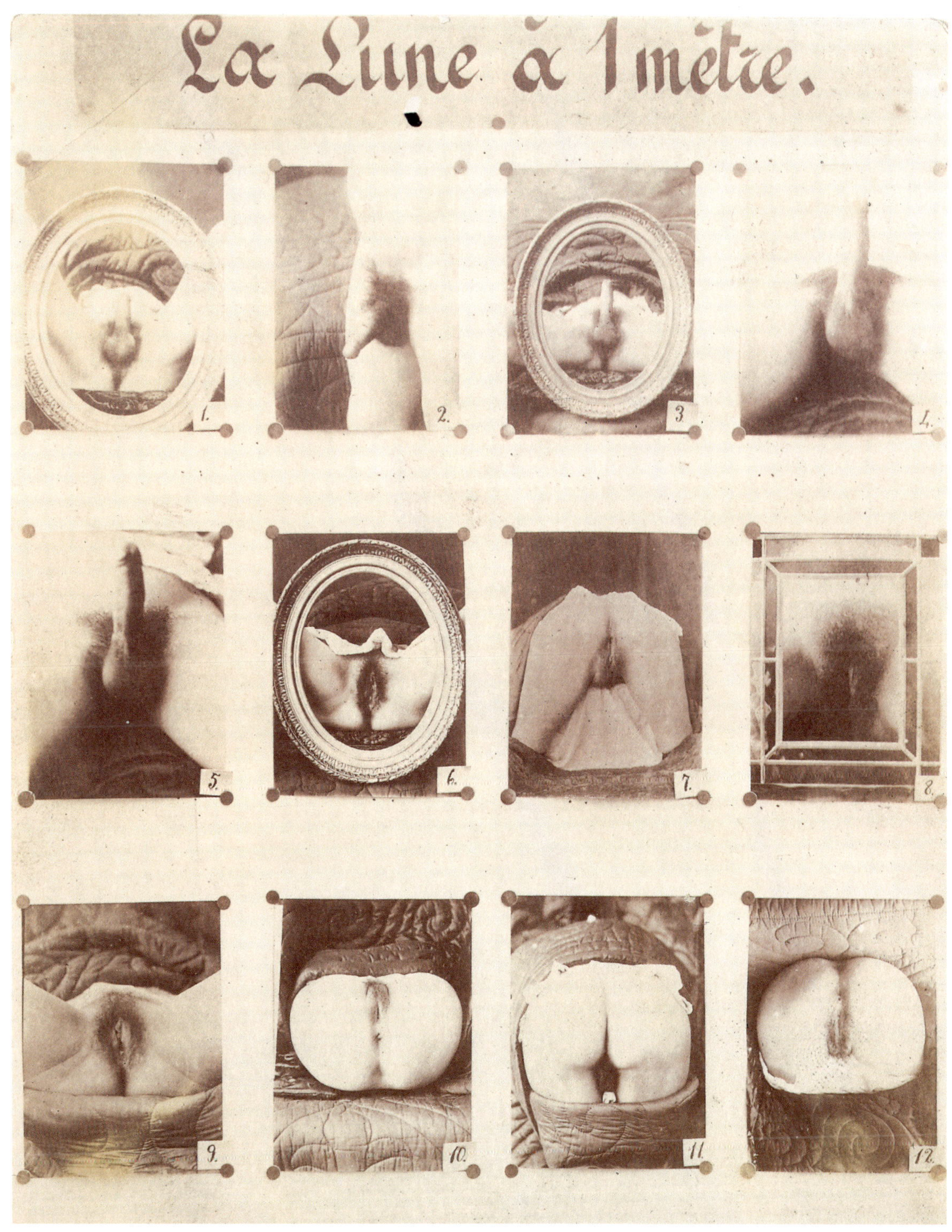
La Lune à 1 mètre.

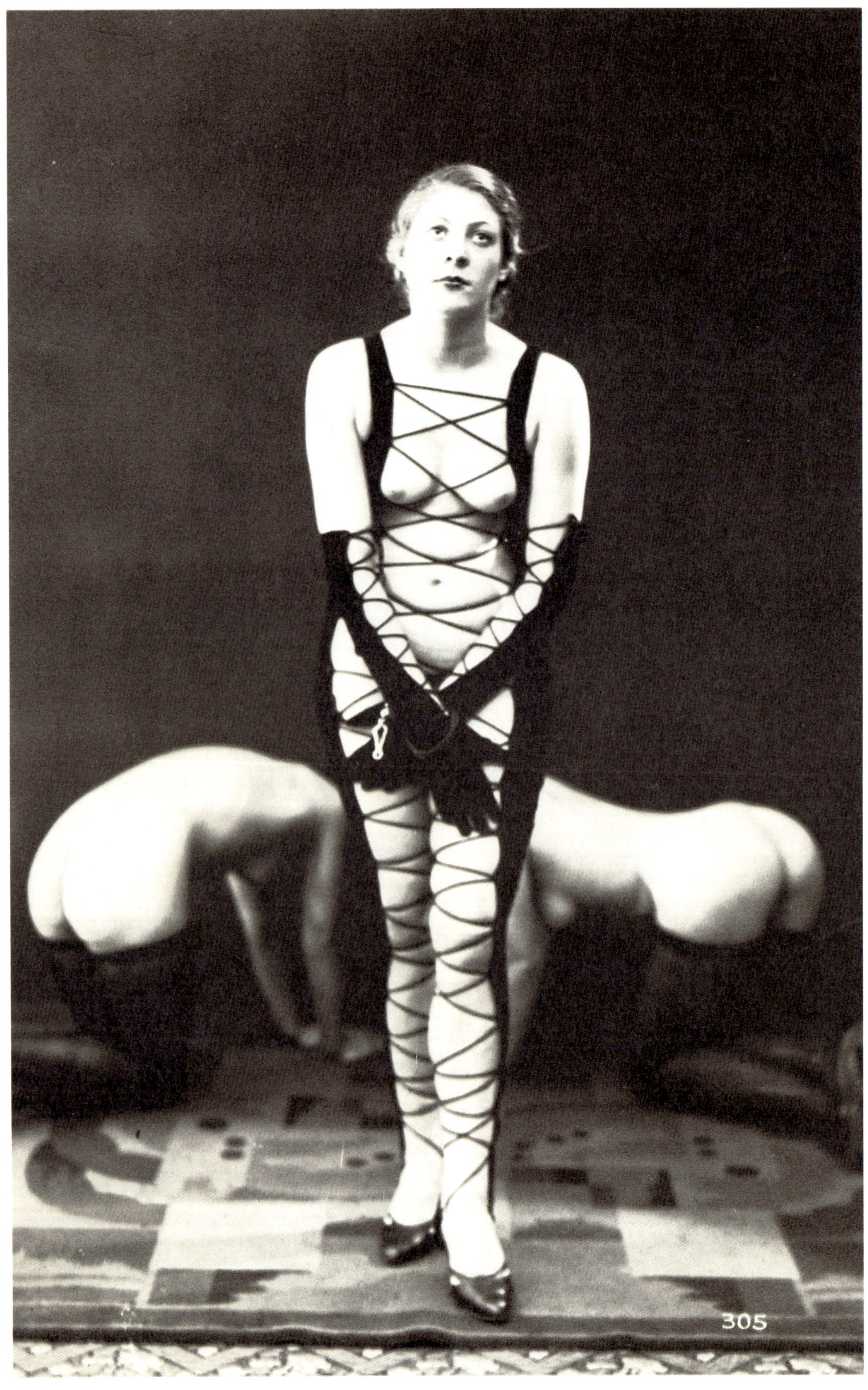

305

34

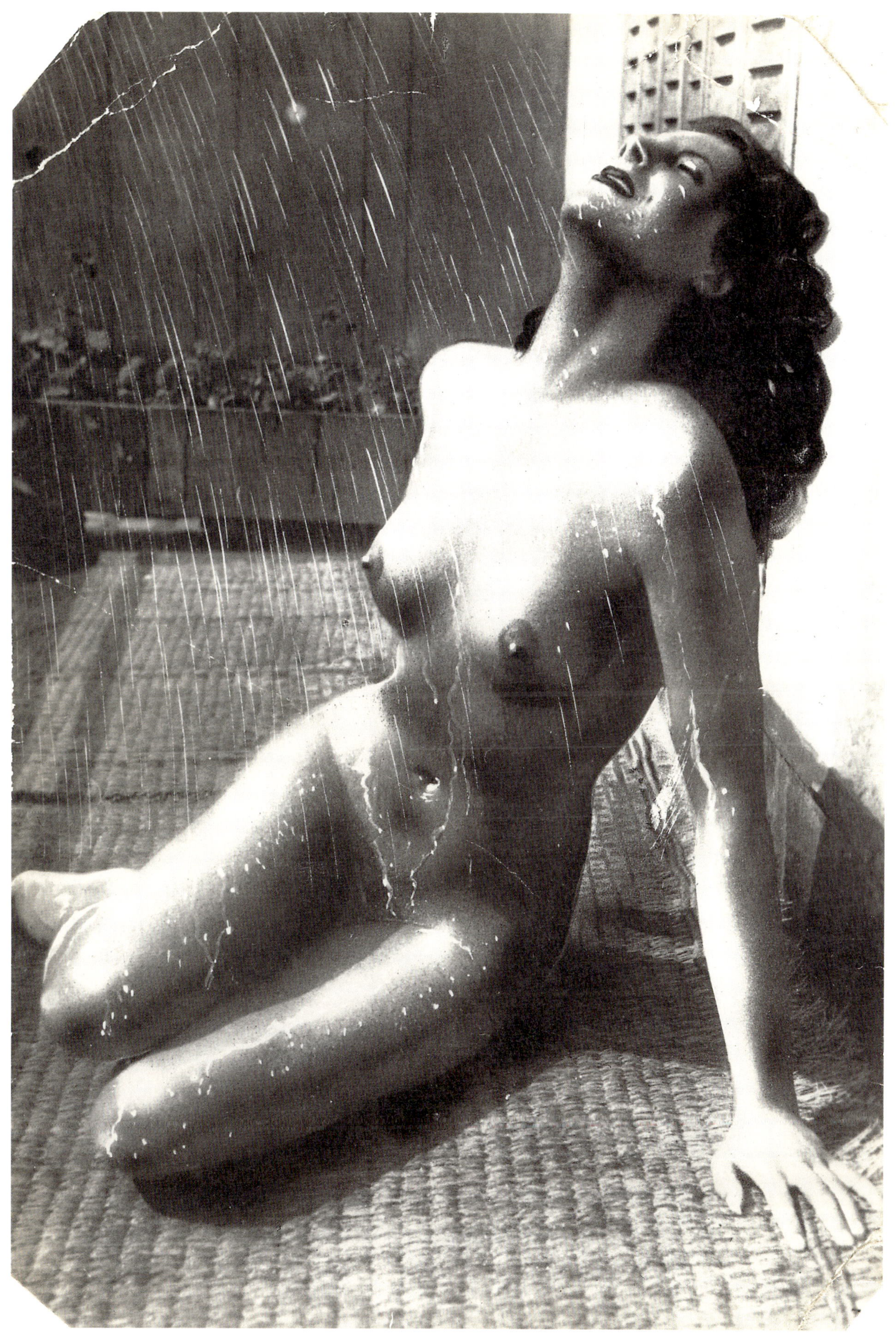

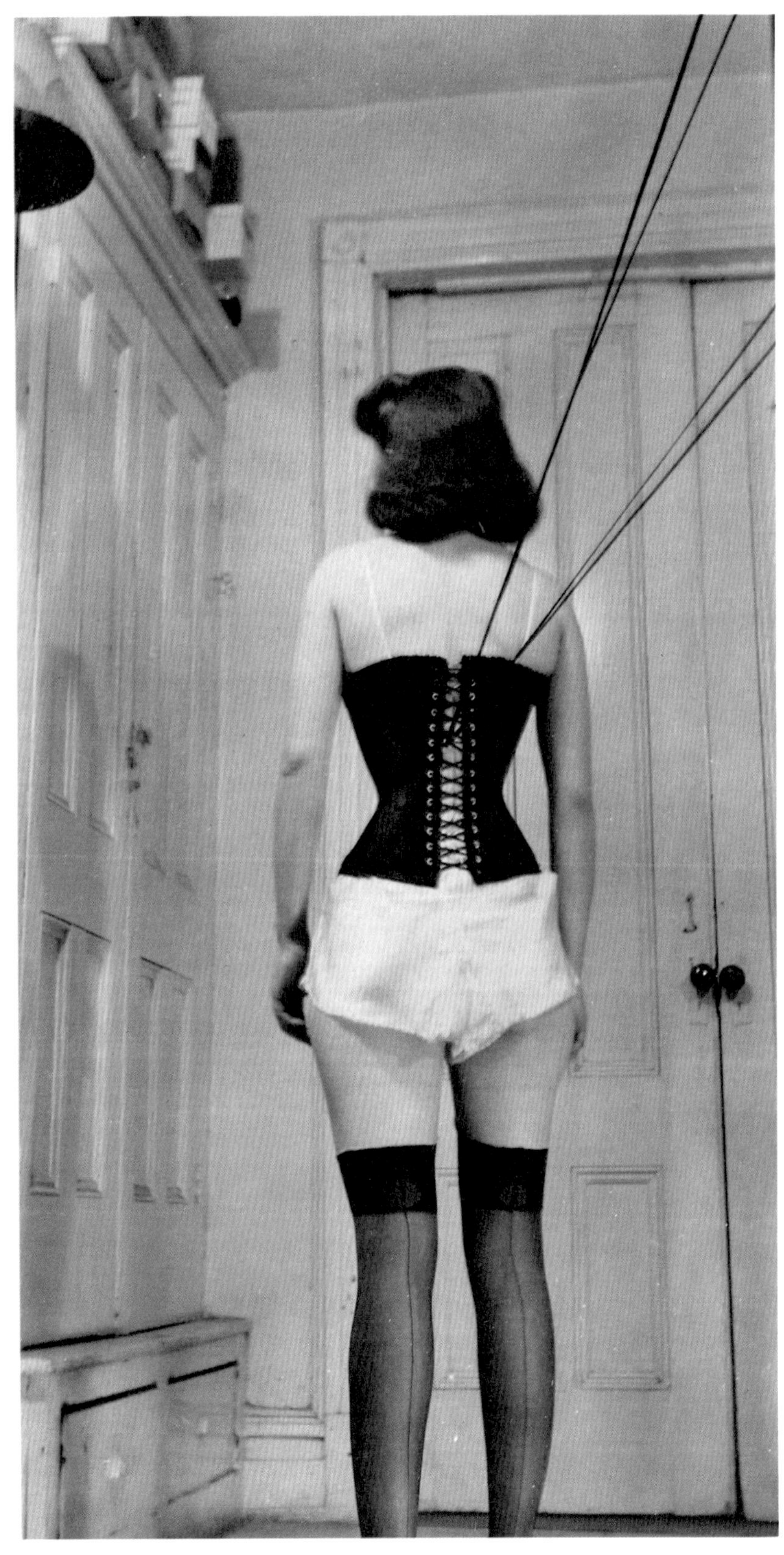

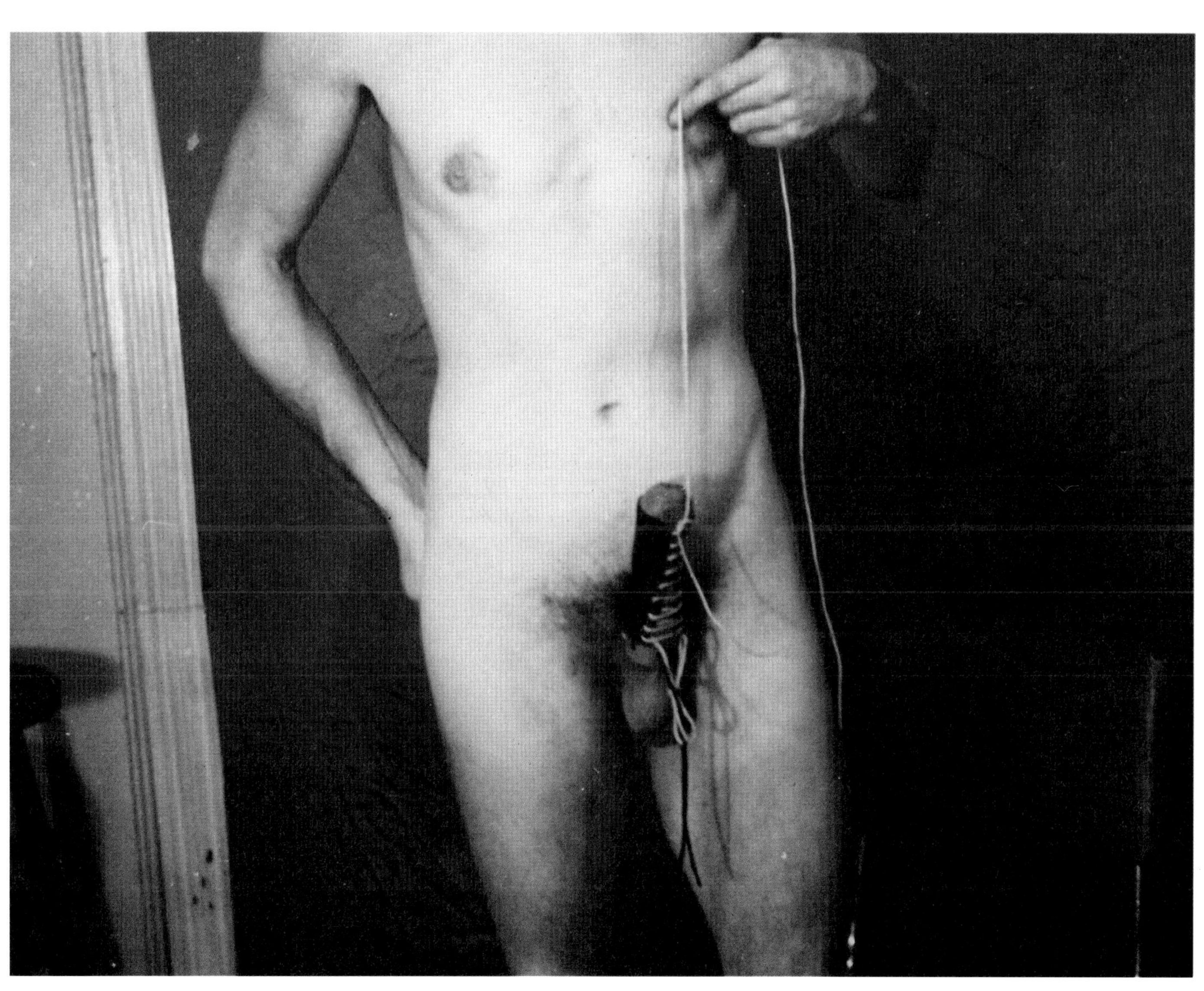

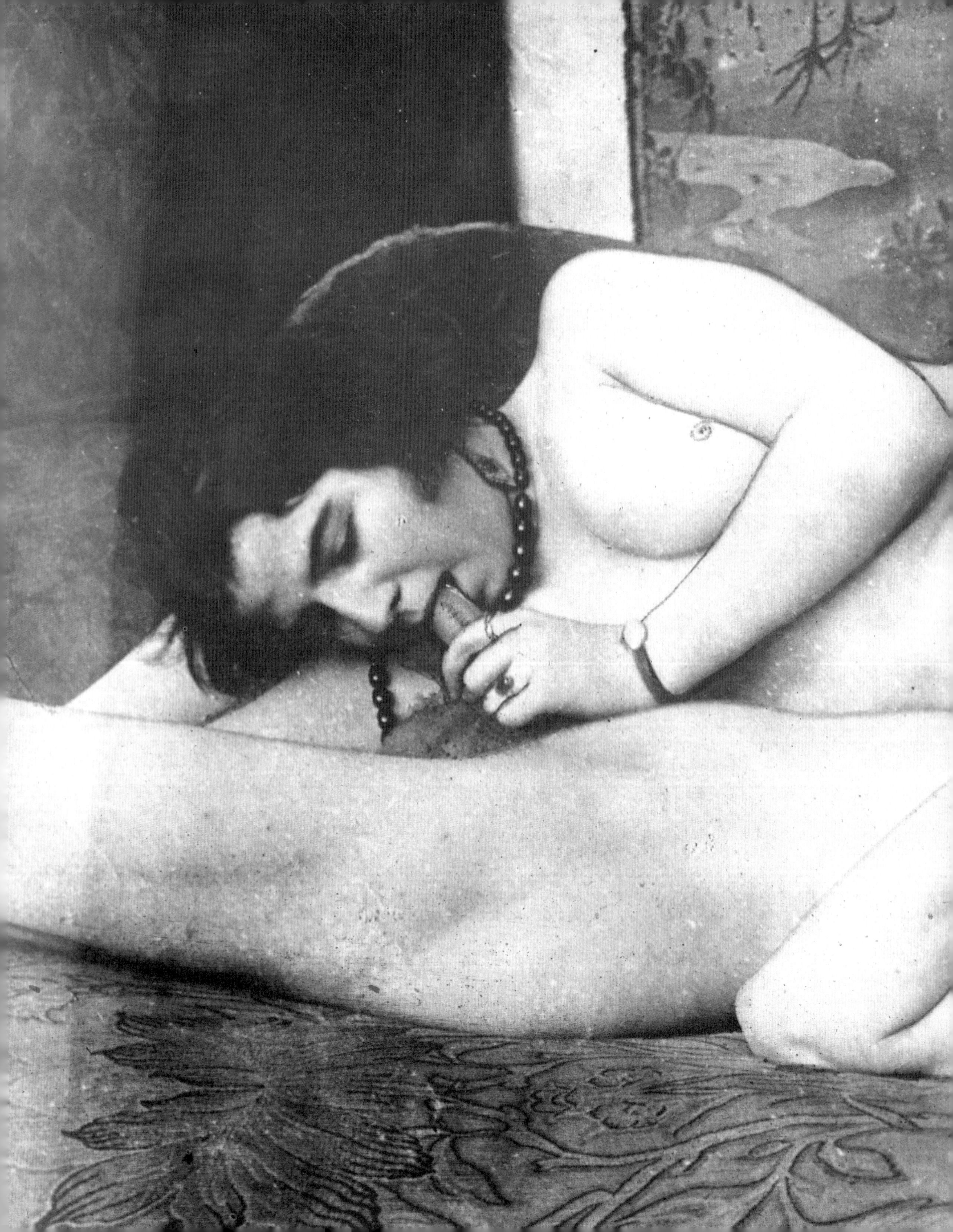

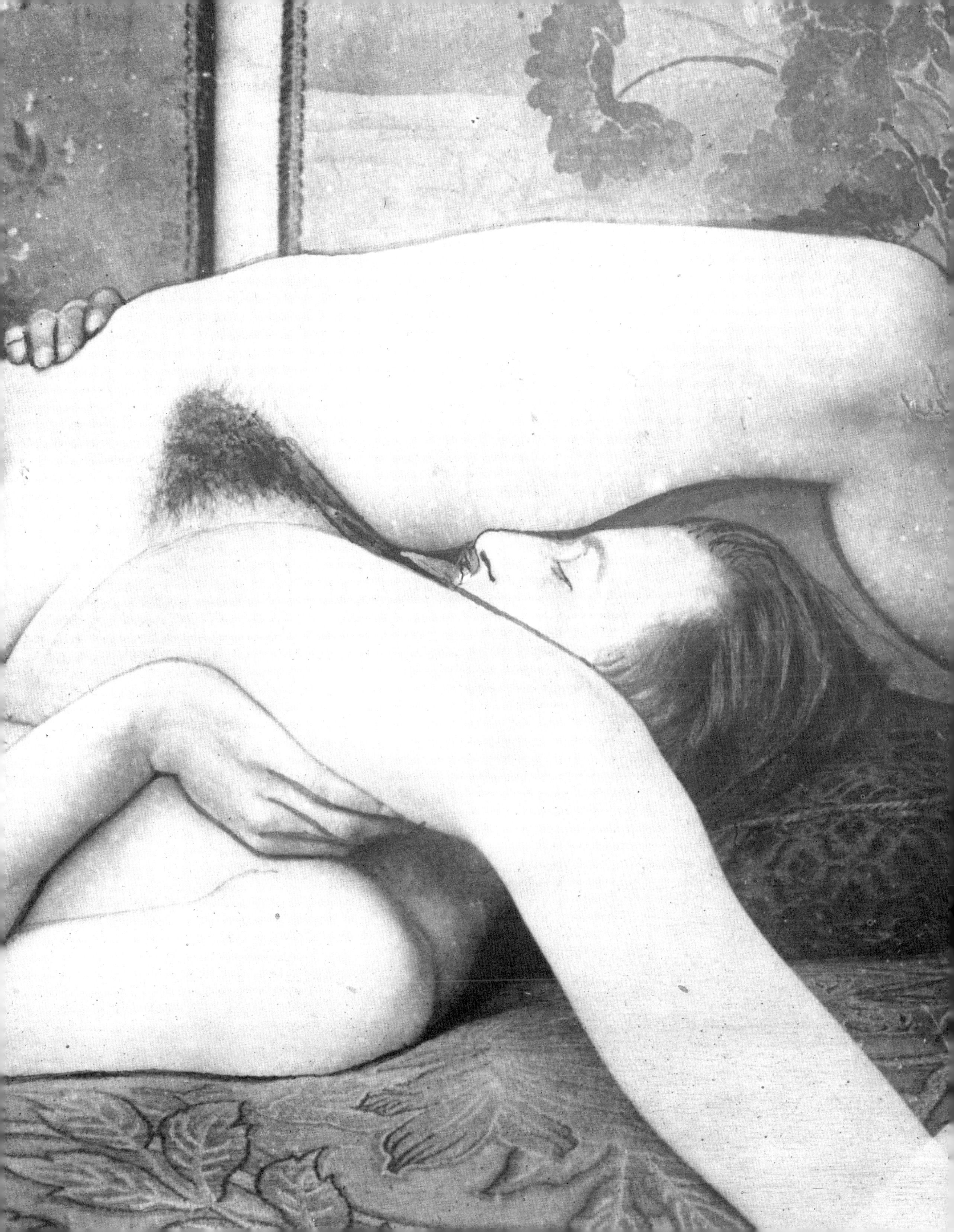

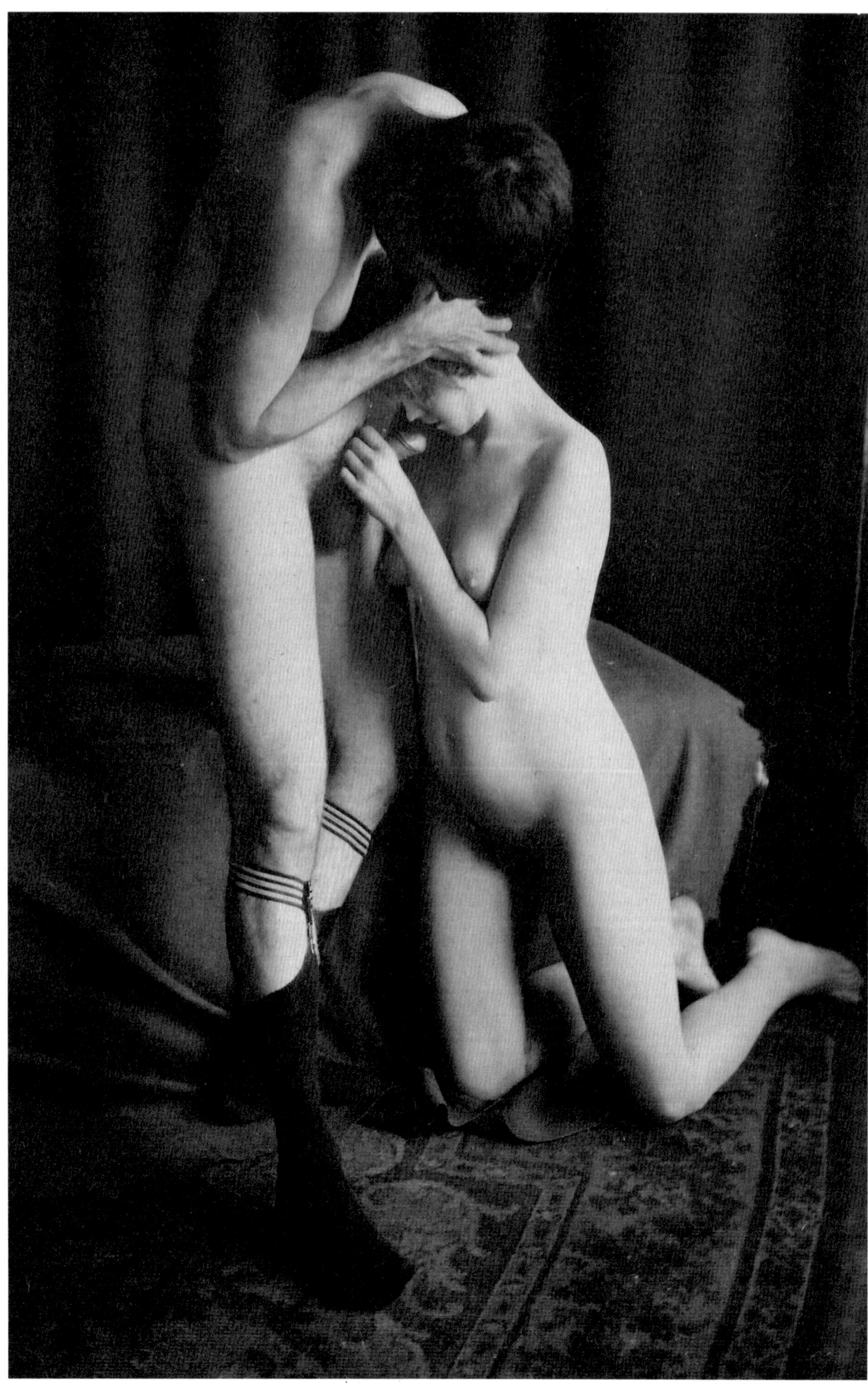

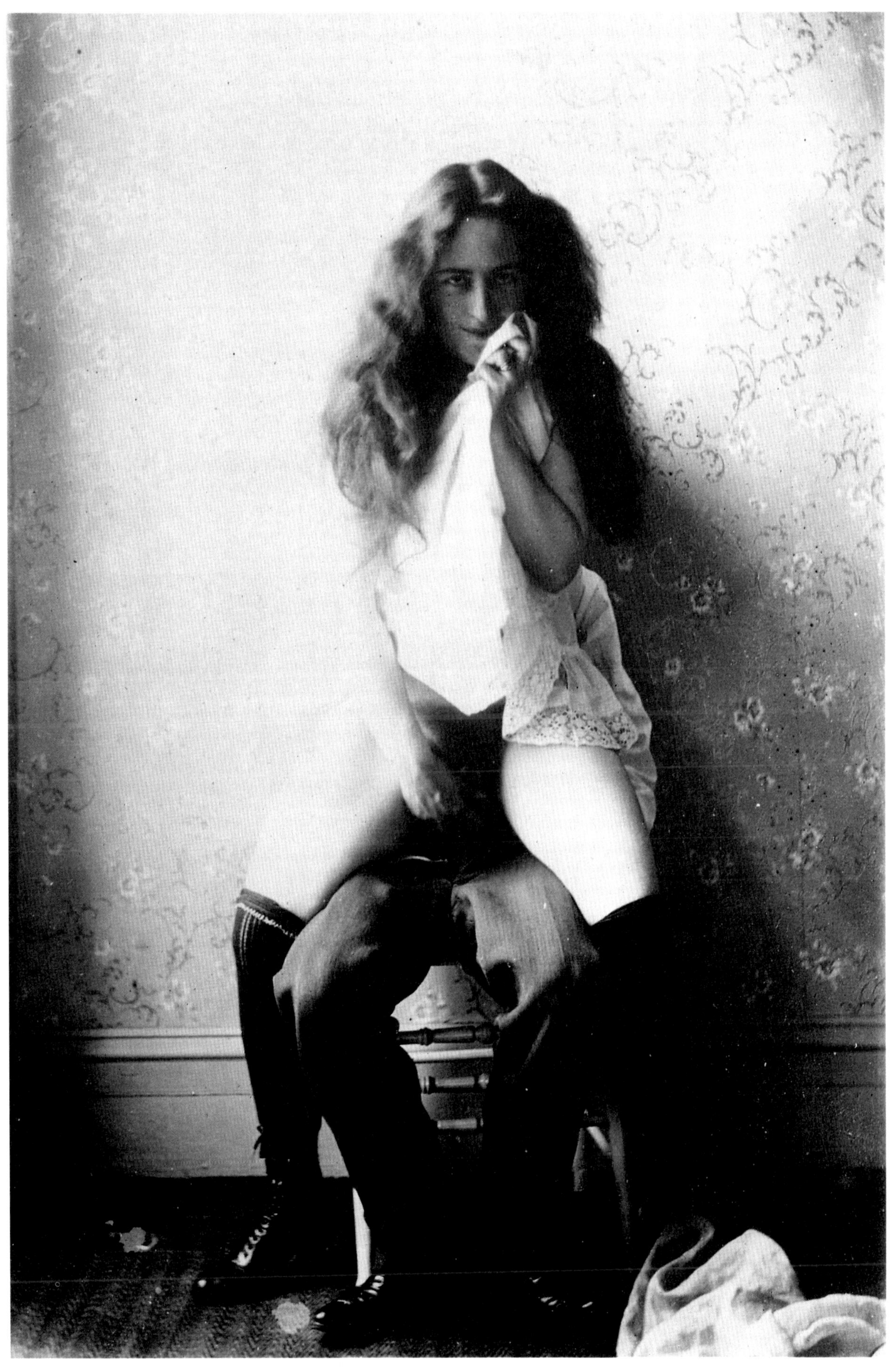

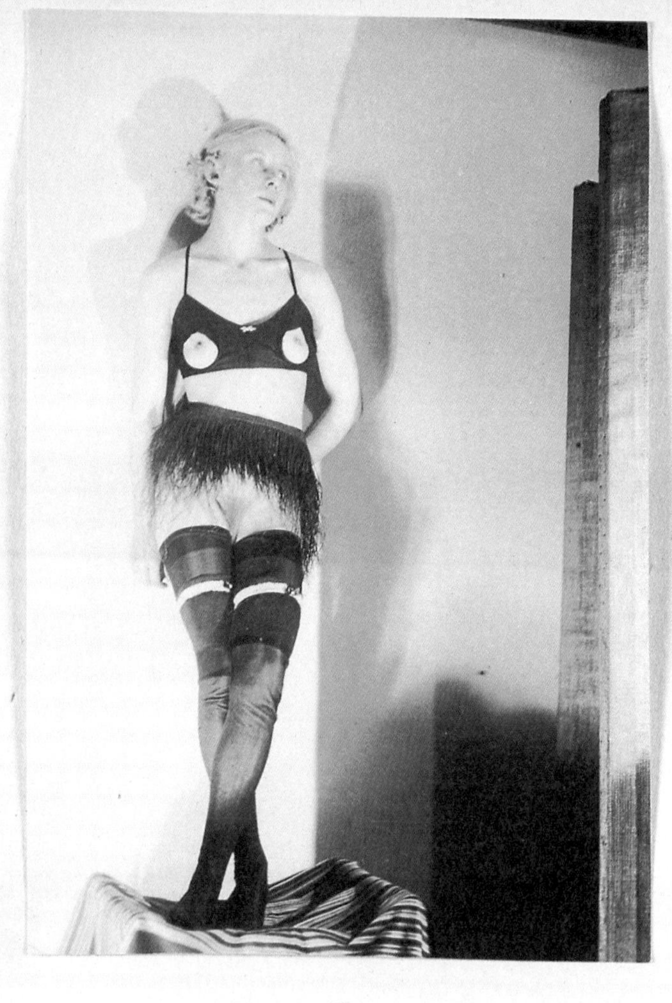

5

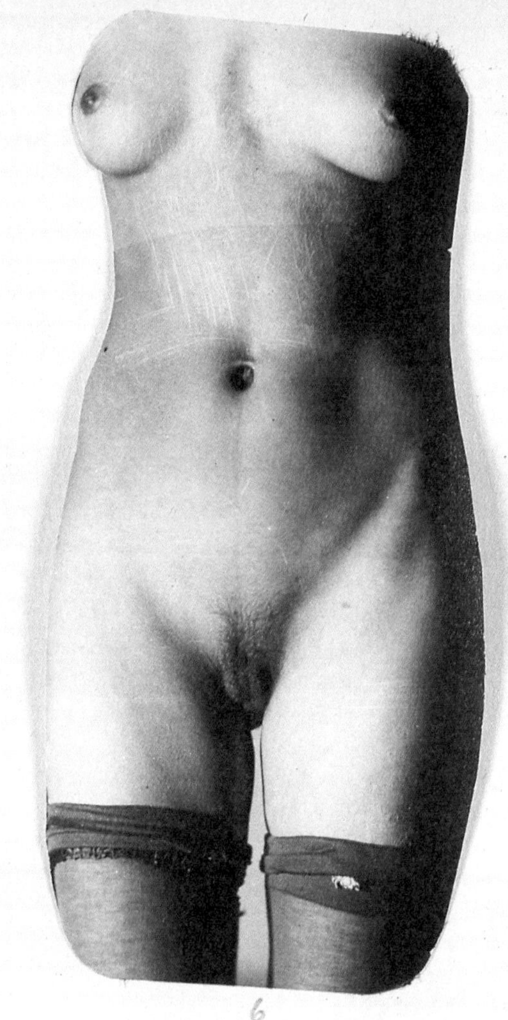

6

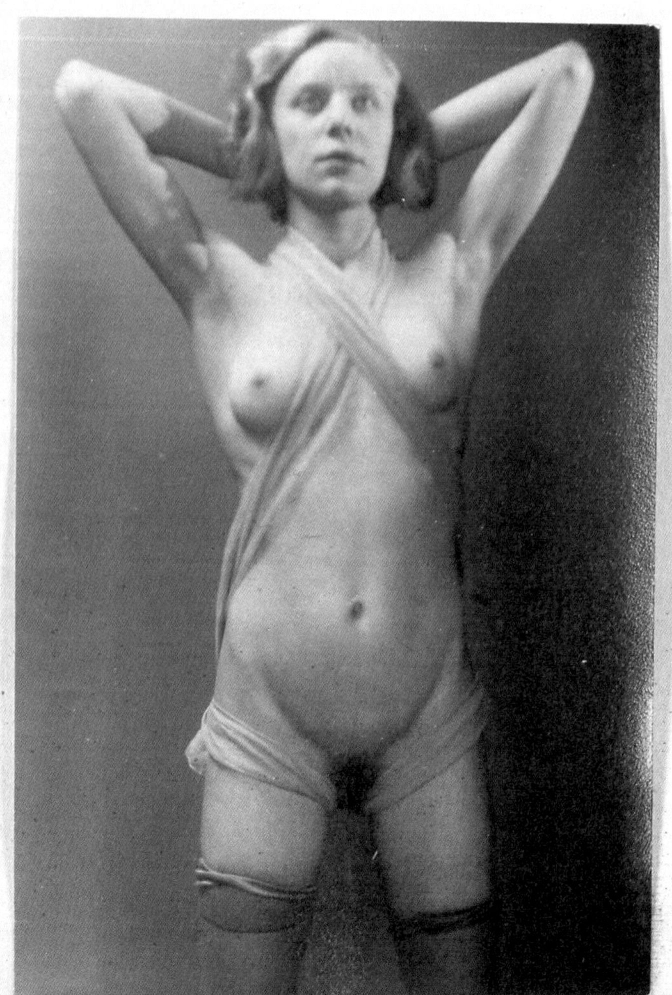

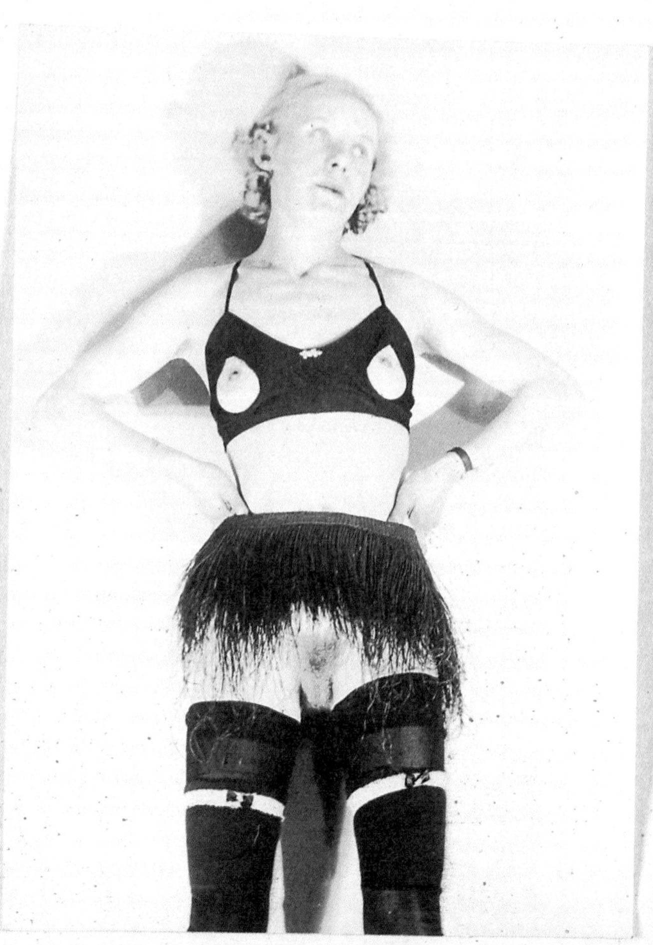

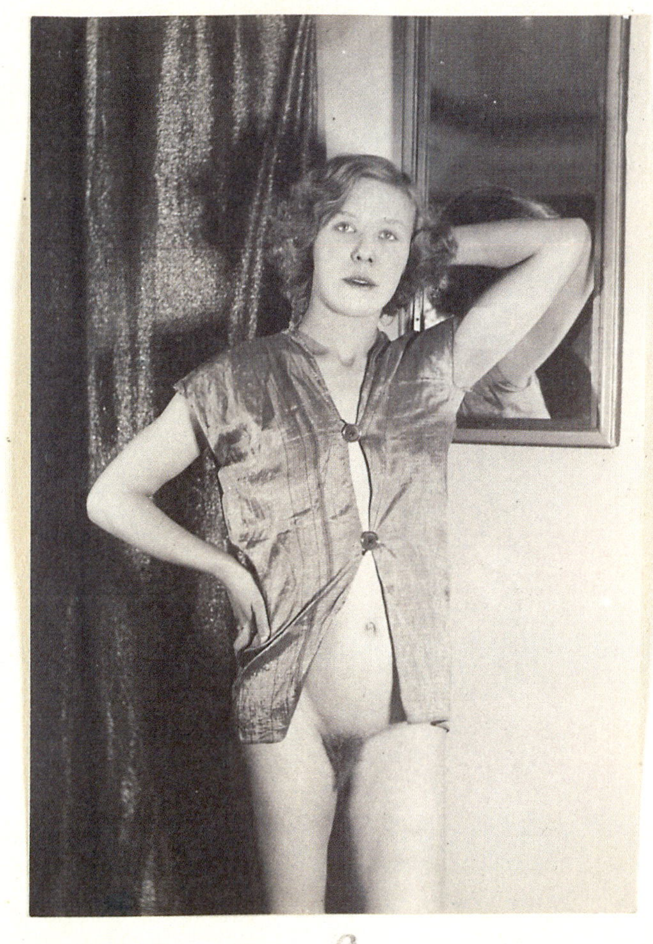

9

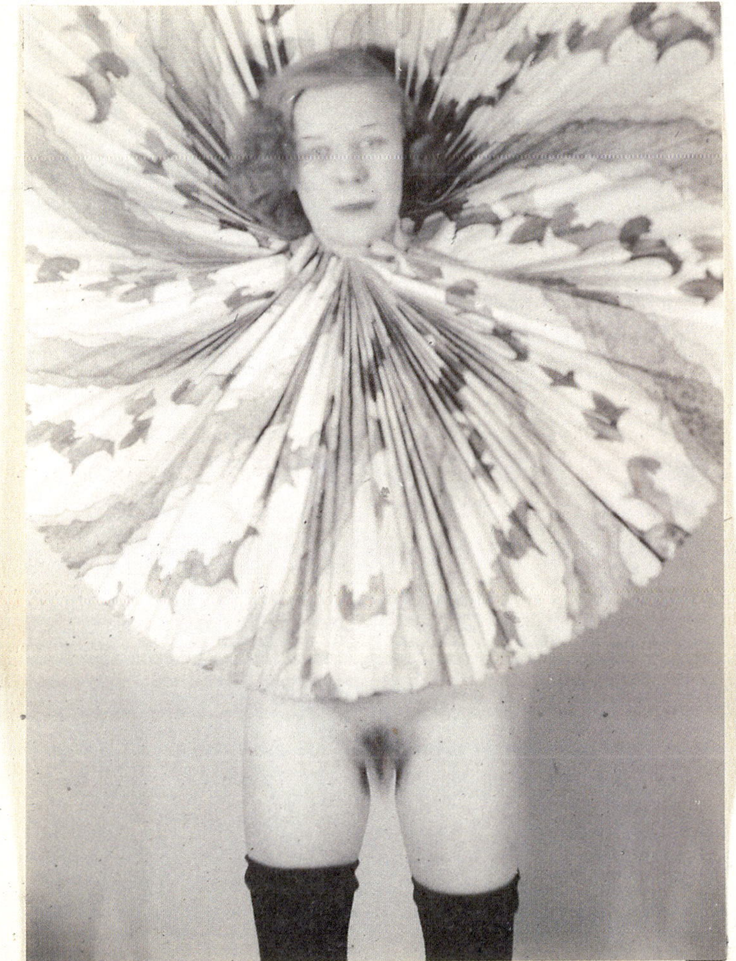

10

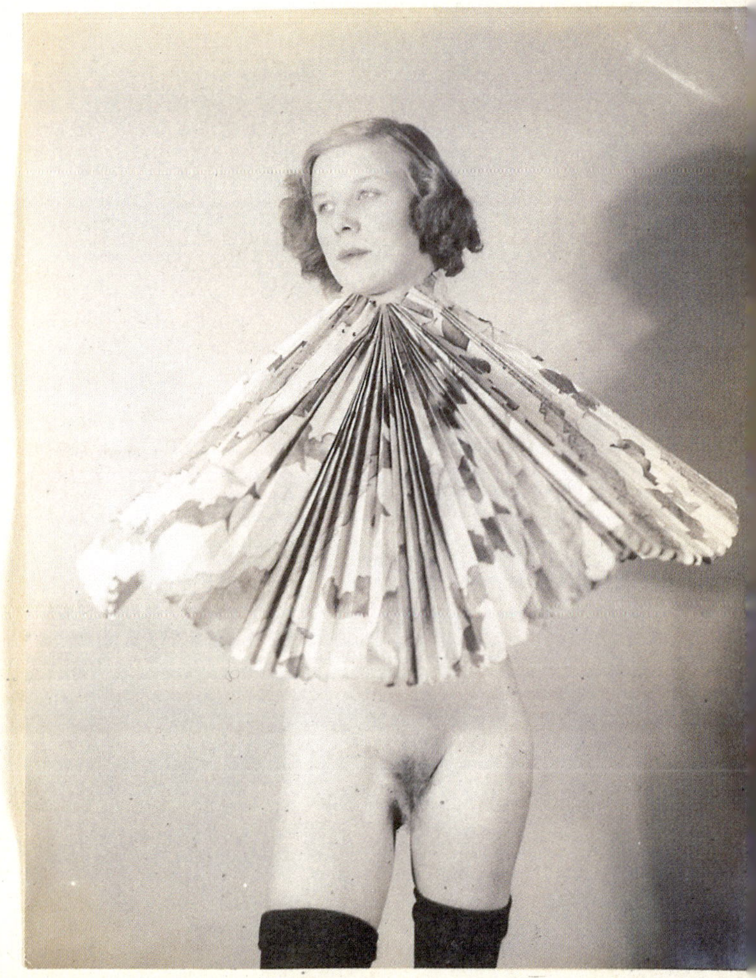

11

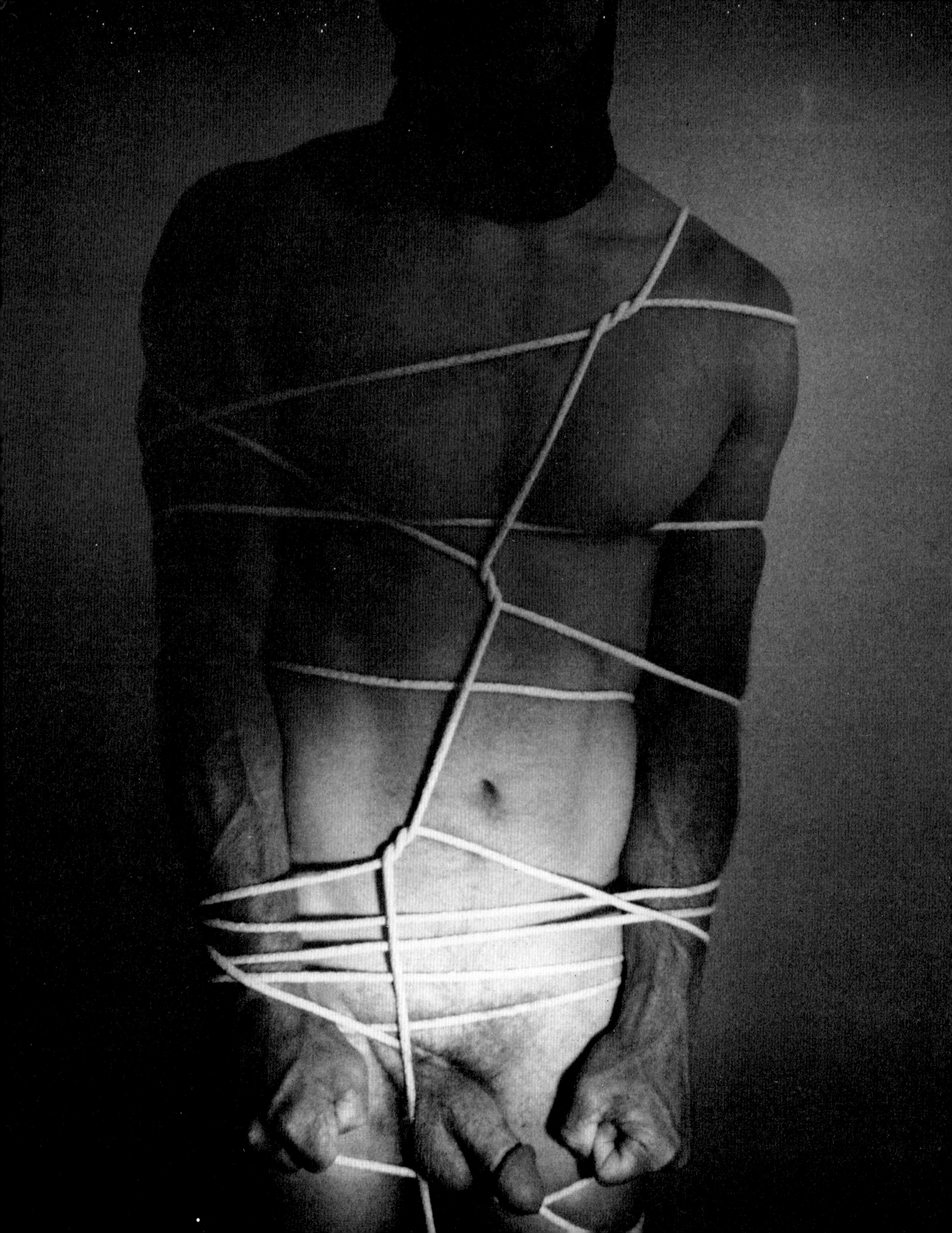

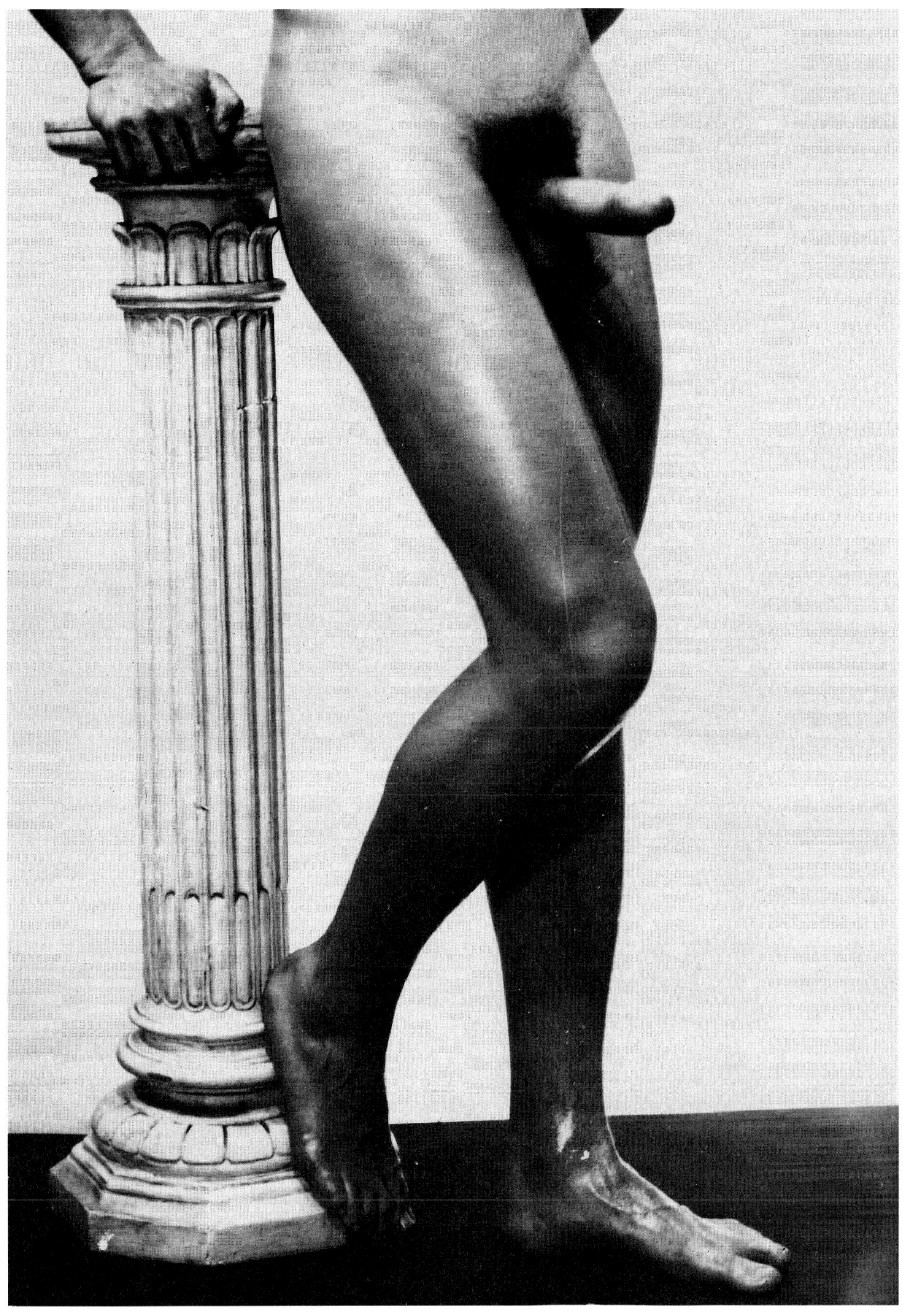

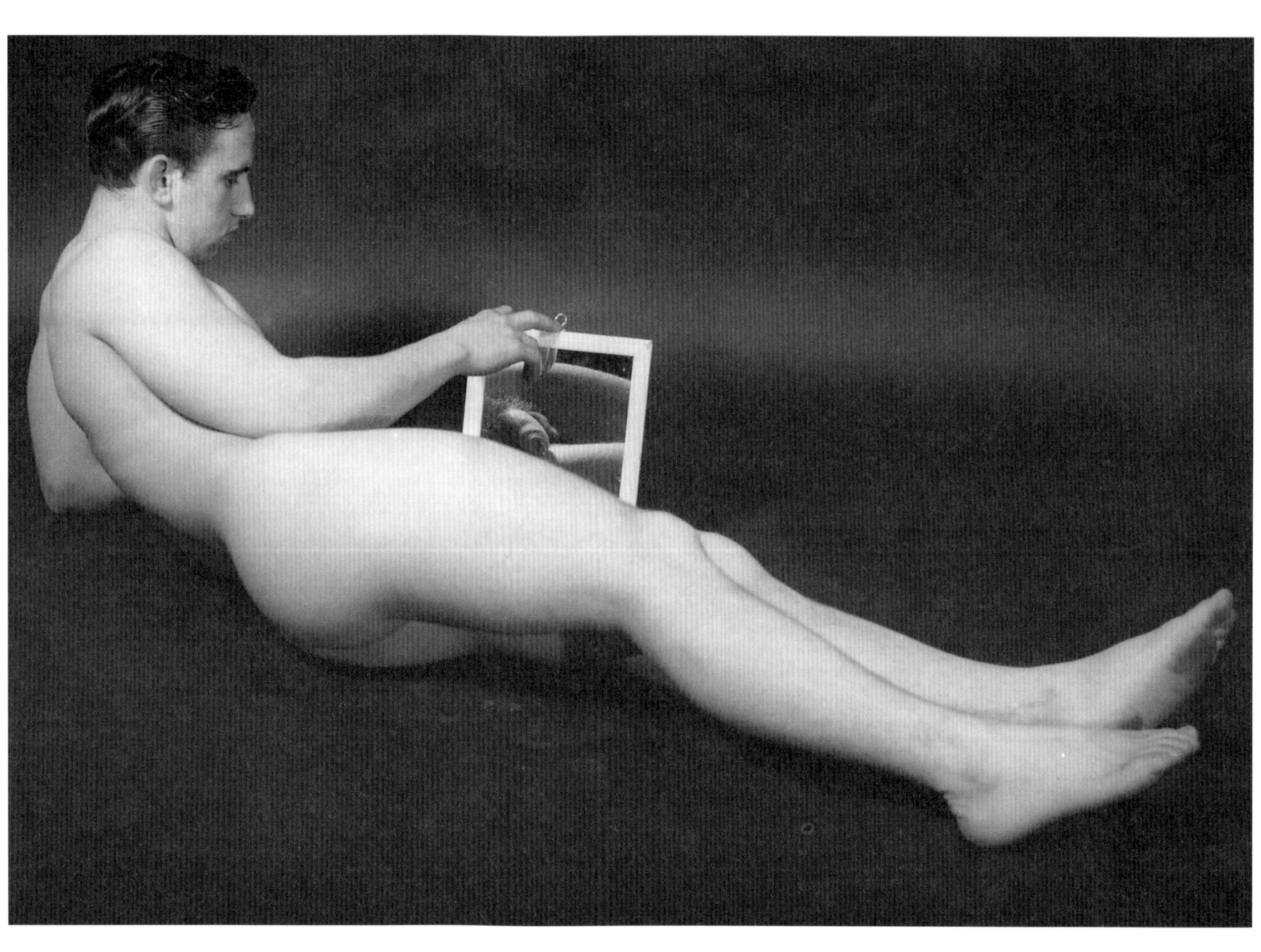

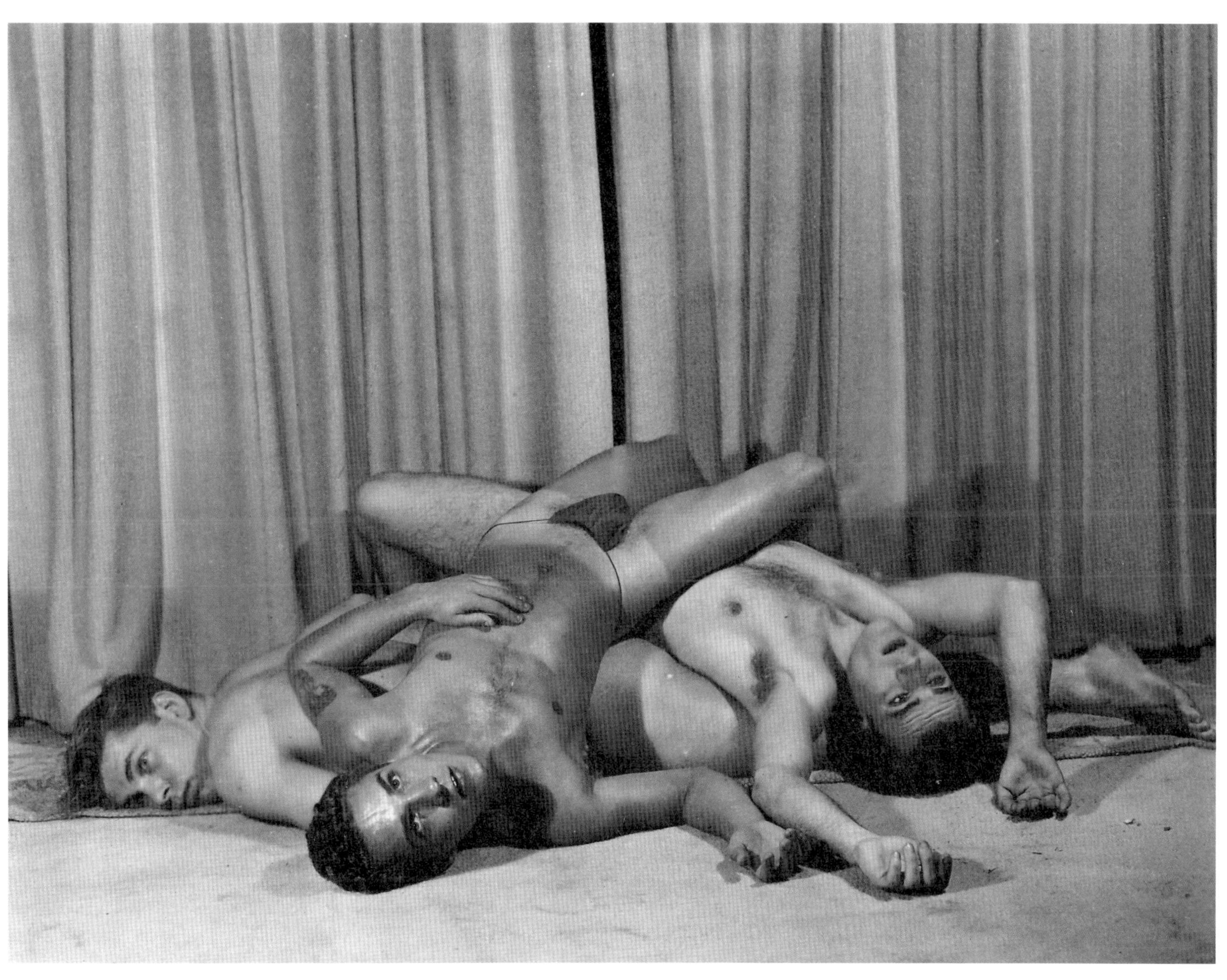

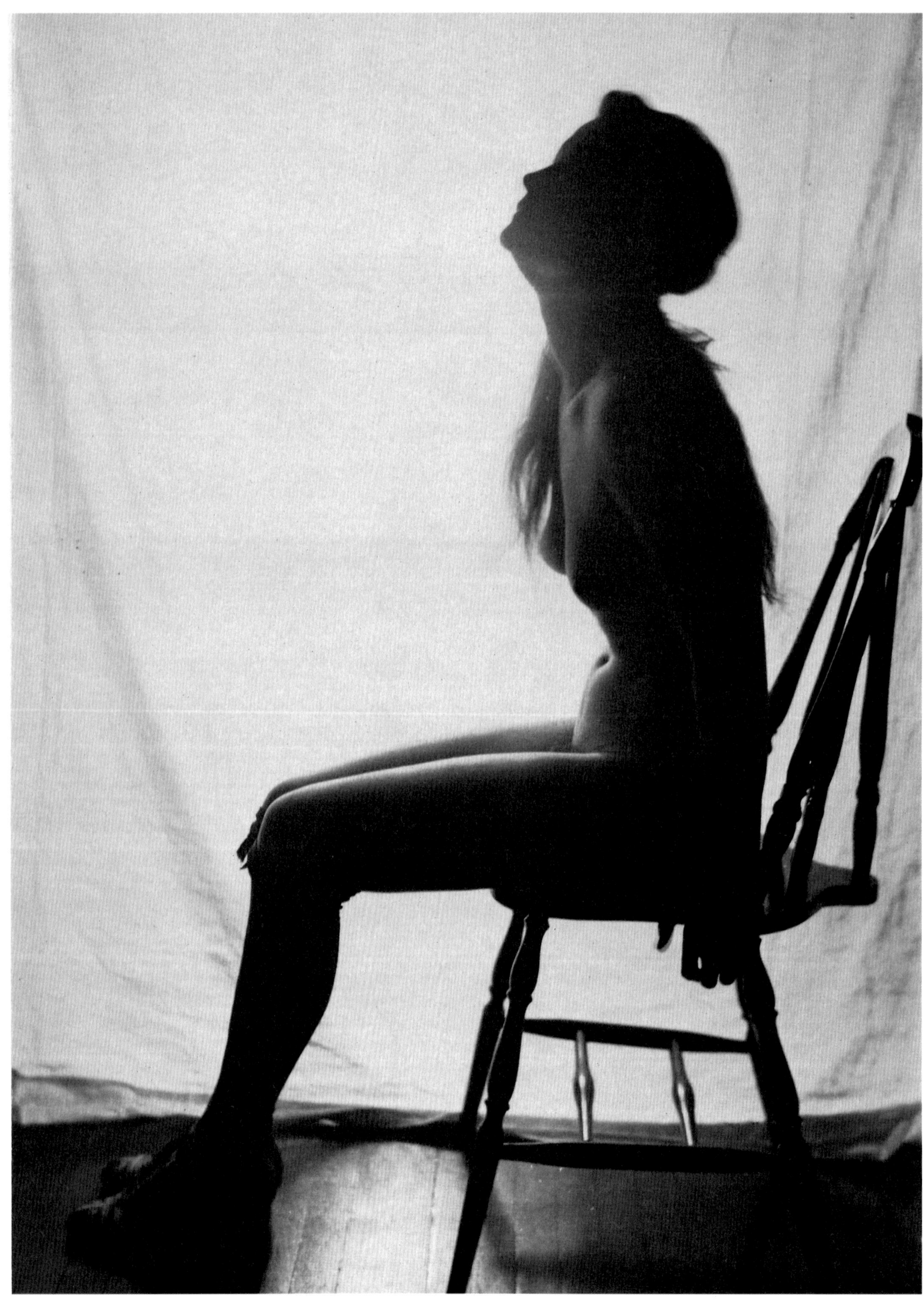

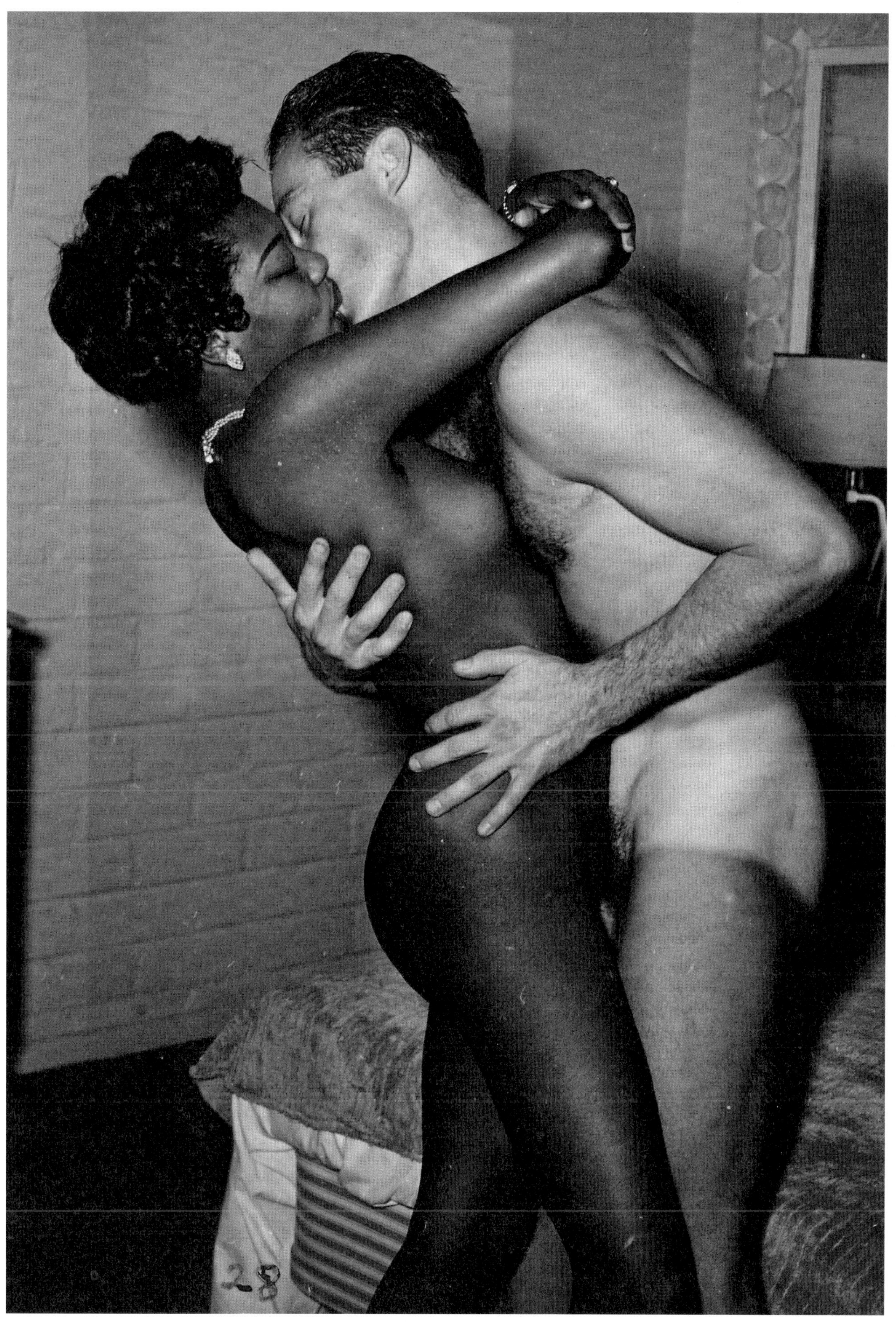

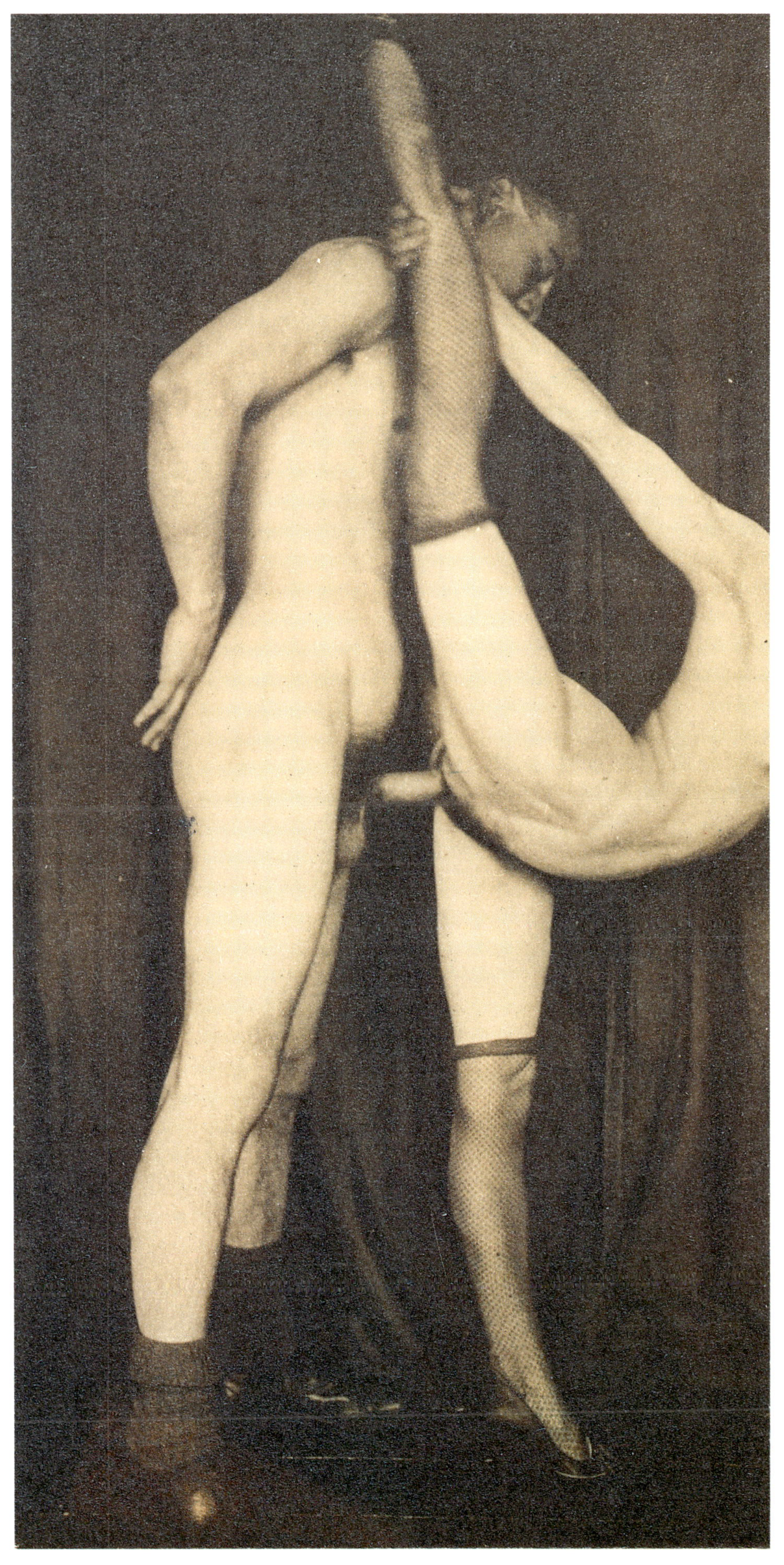

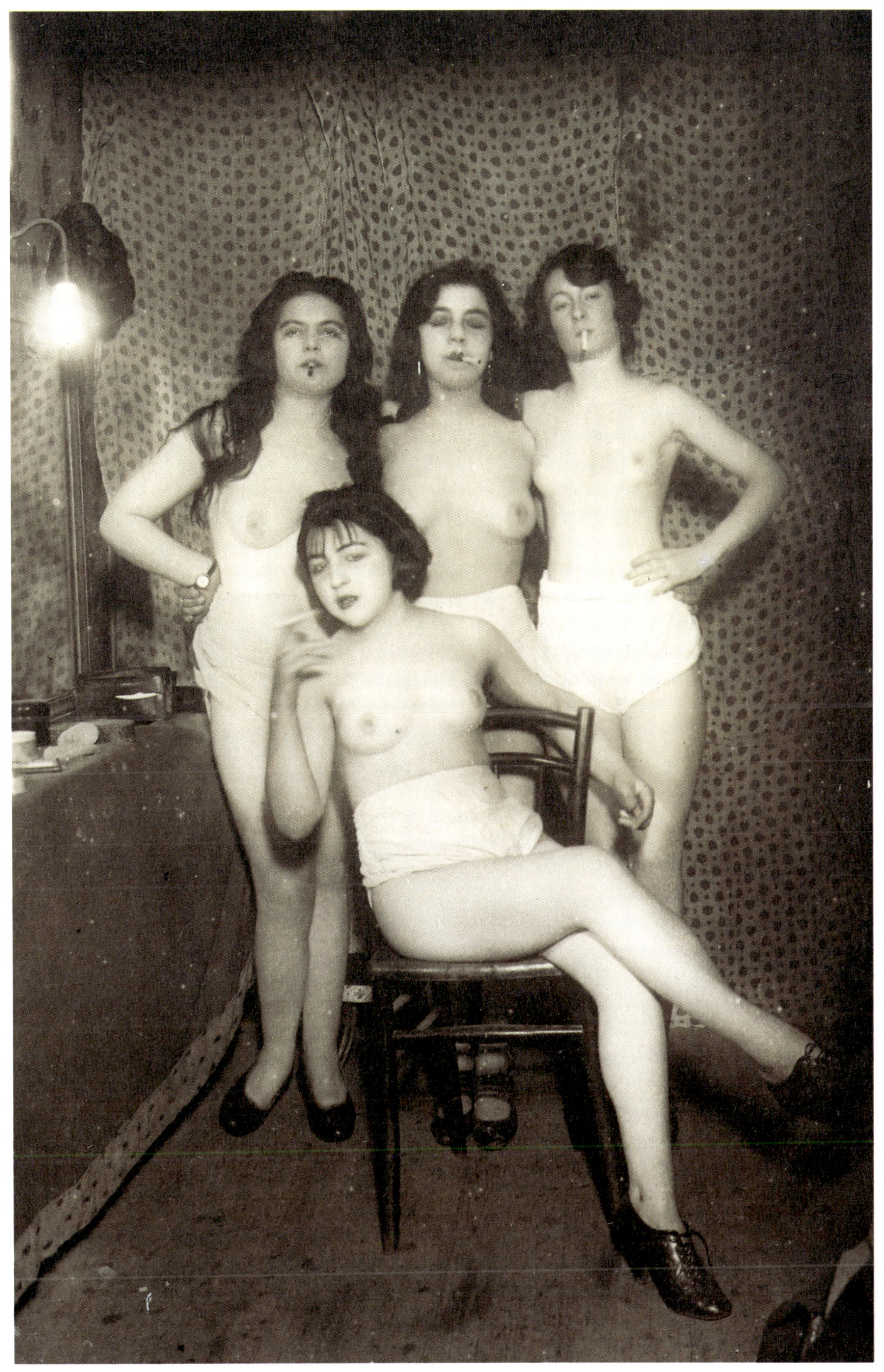

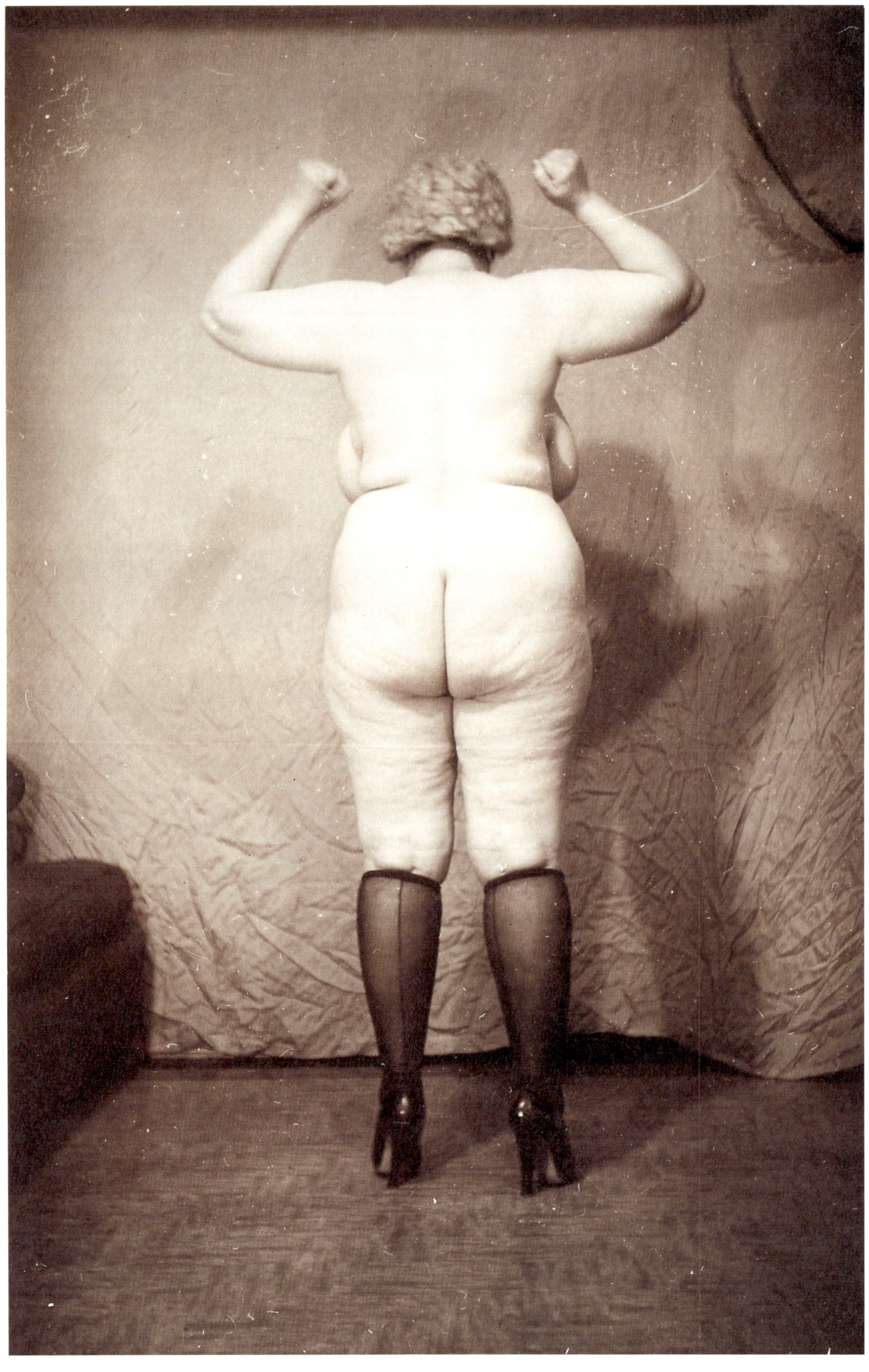

54

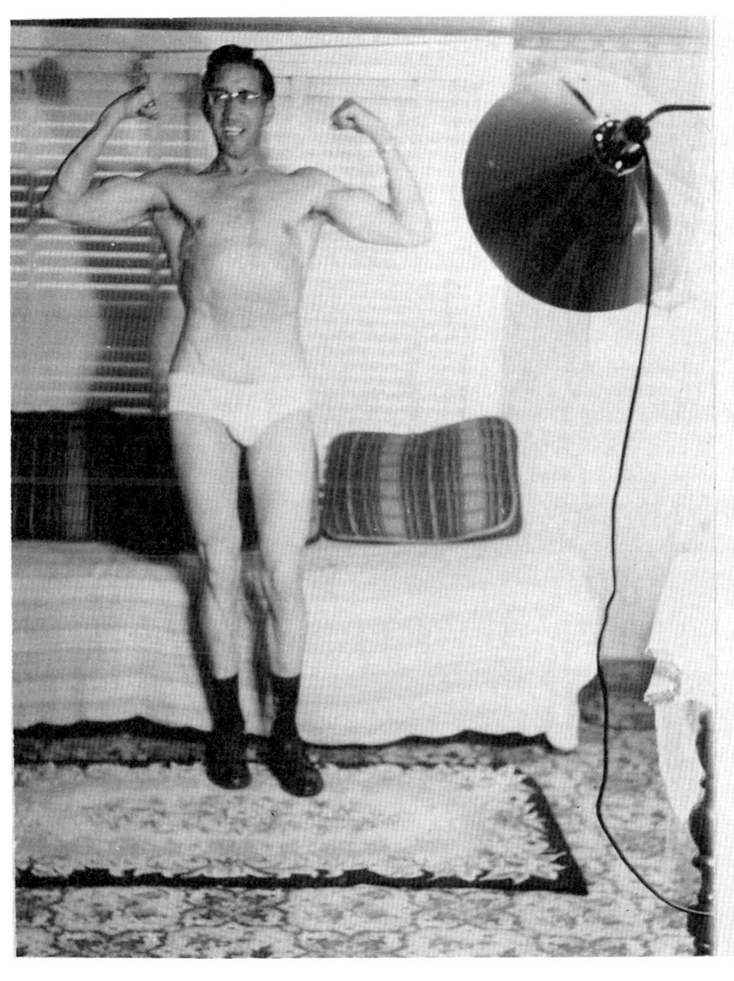
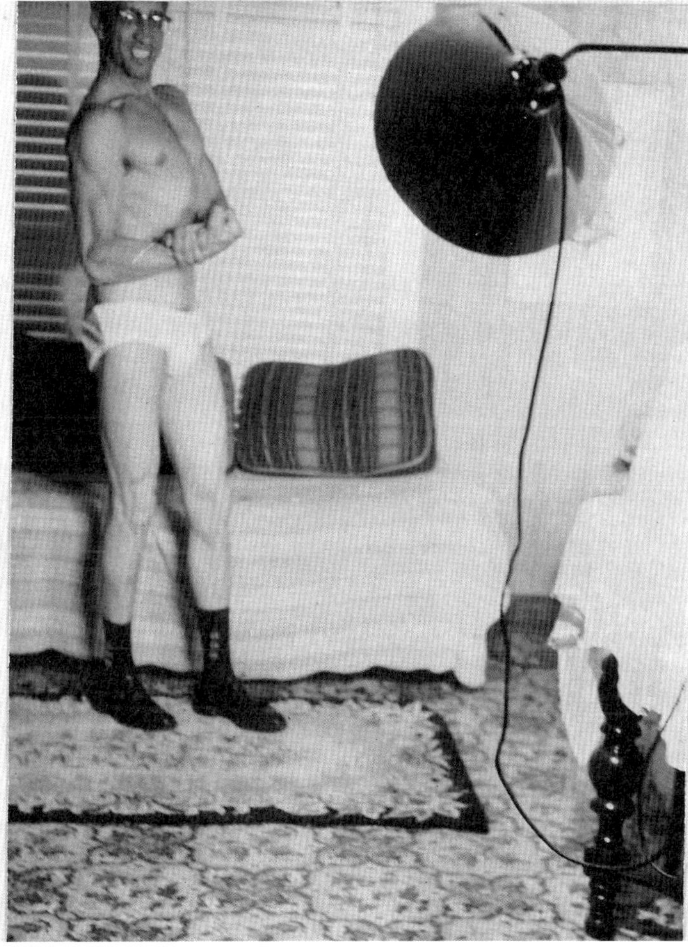

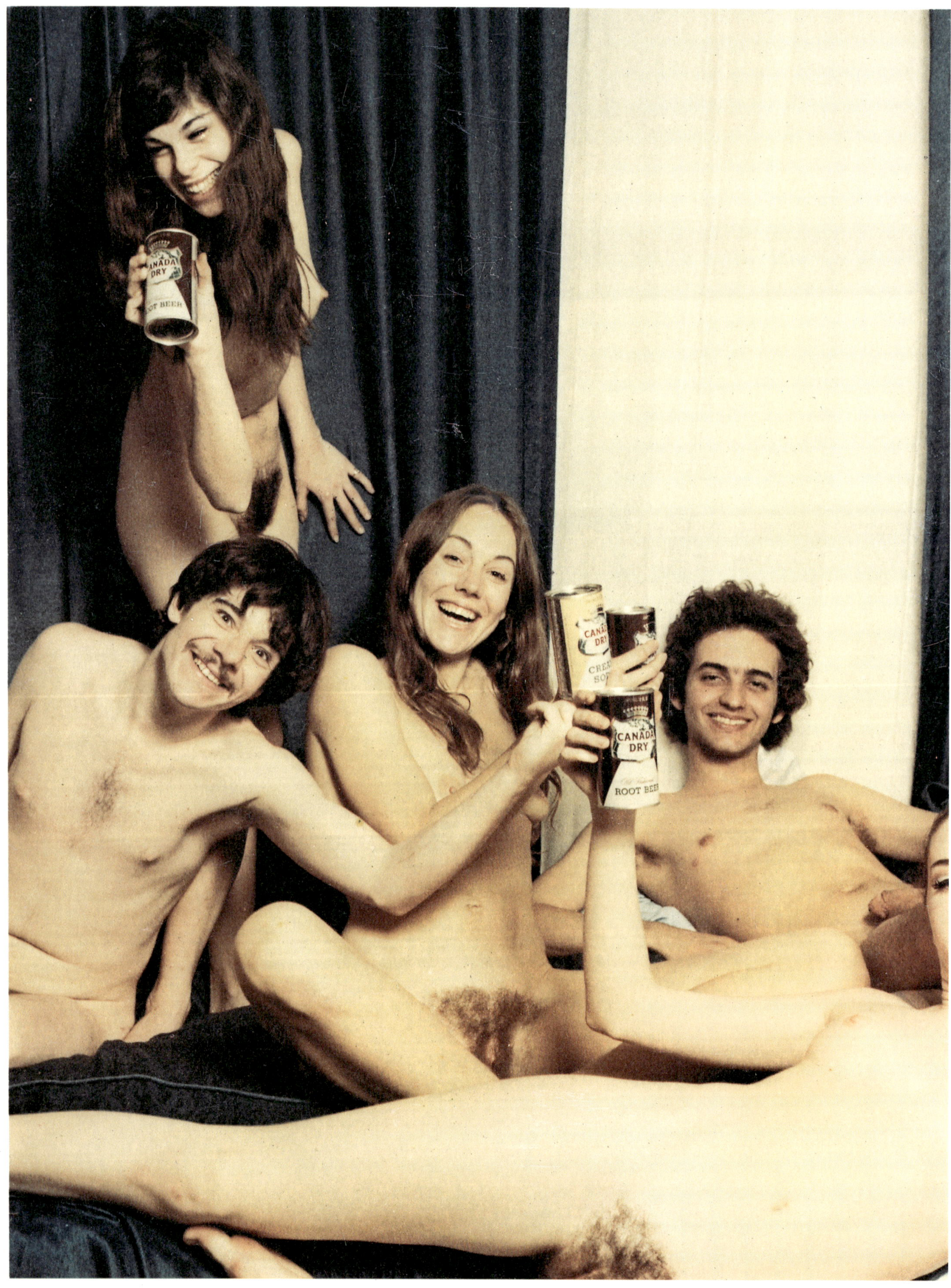
CANADA DRY
ROOT BEER
CANADA DRY
CREAM SODA
CANADA DRY
ROOT BEER

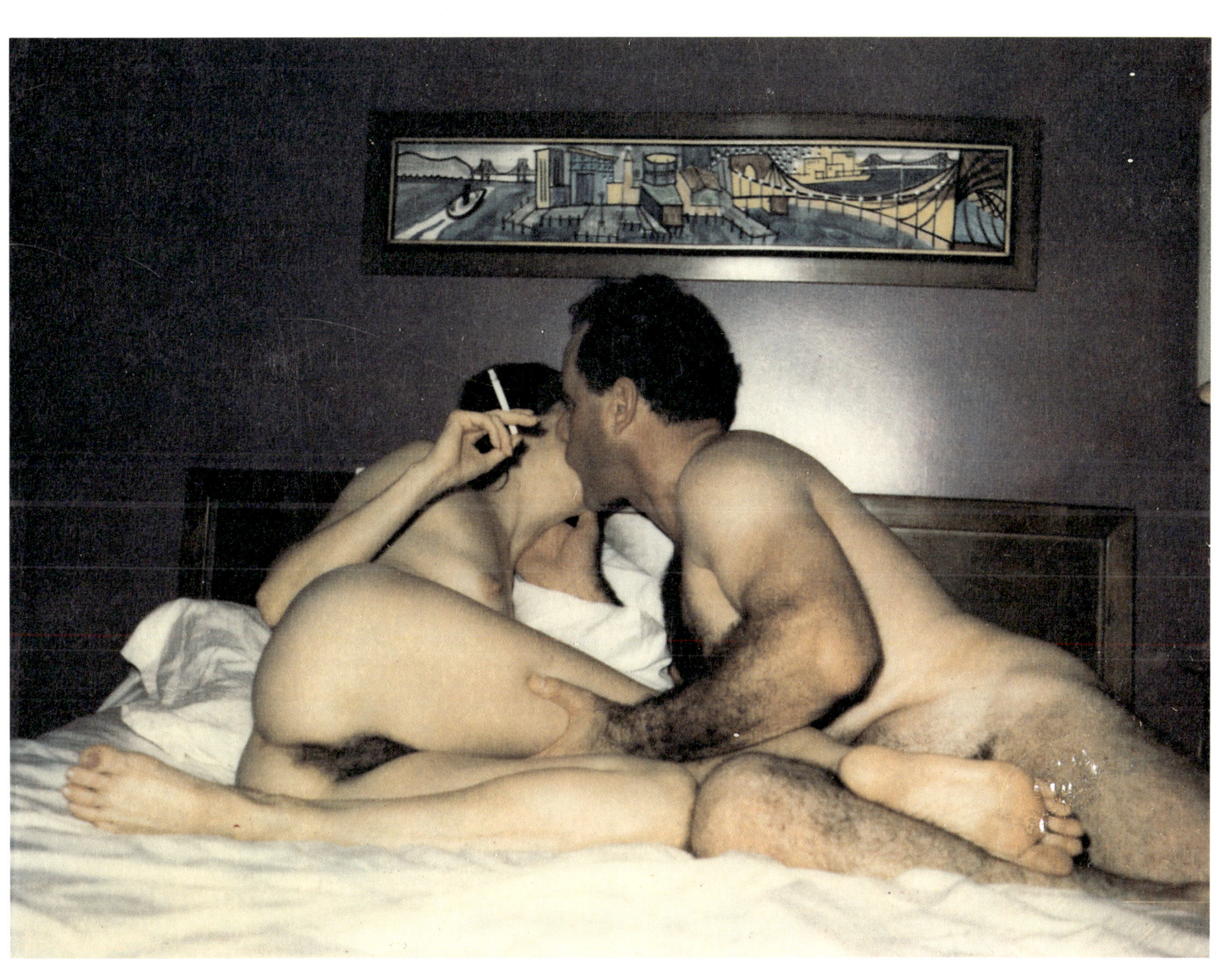

Close-up of a
Leaning Tower.

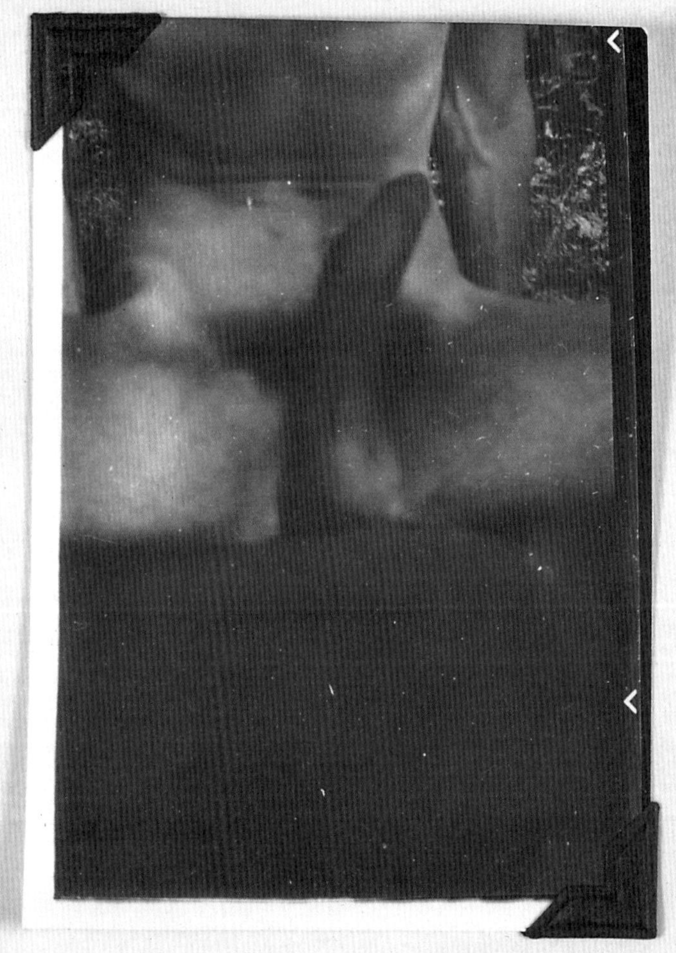

June 1936

A virgin loveland
except for being
seen, Kissed, & Touched
by The hand of her
lover. Would That she
had let me lie on it.

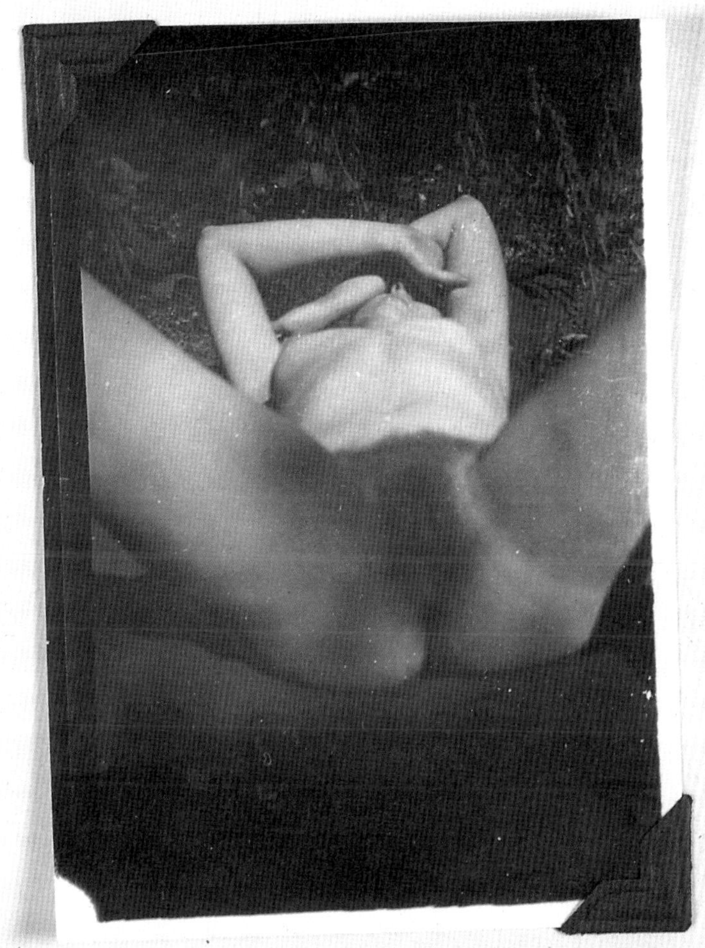

June   1936

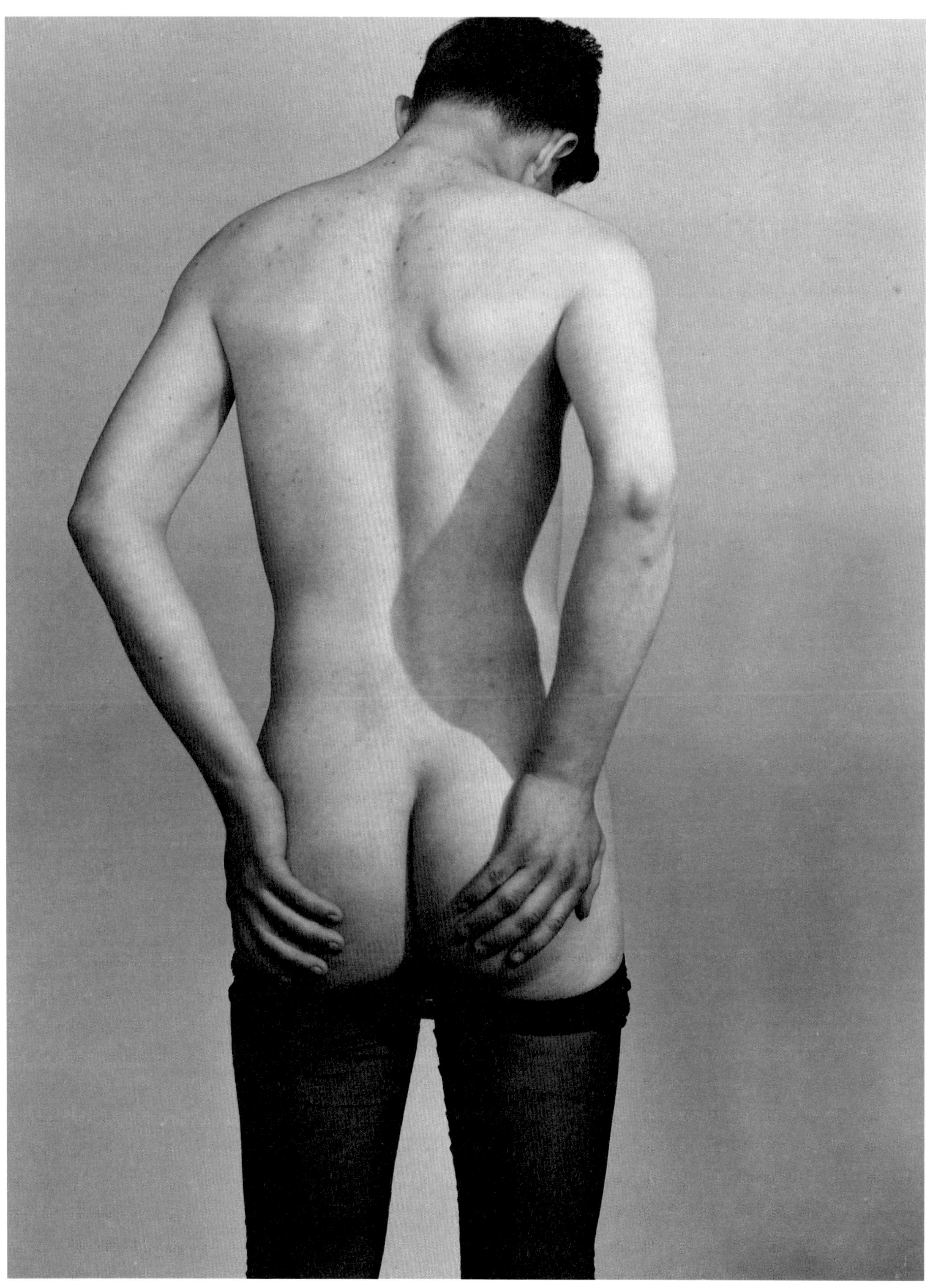

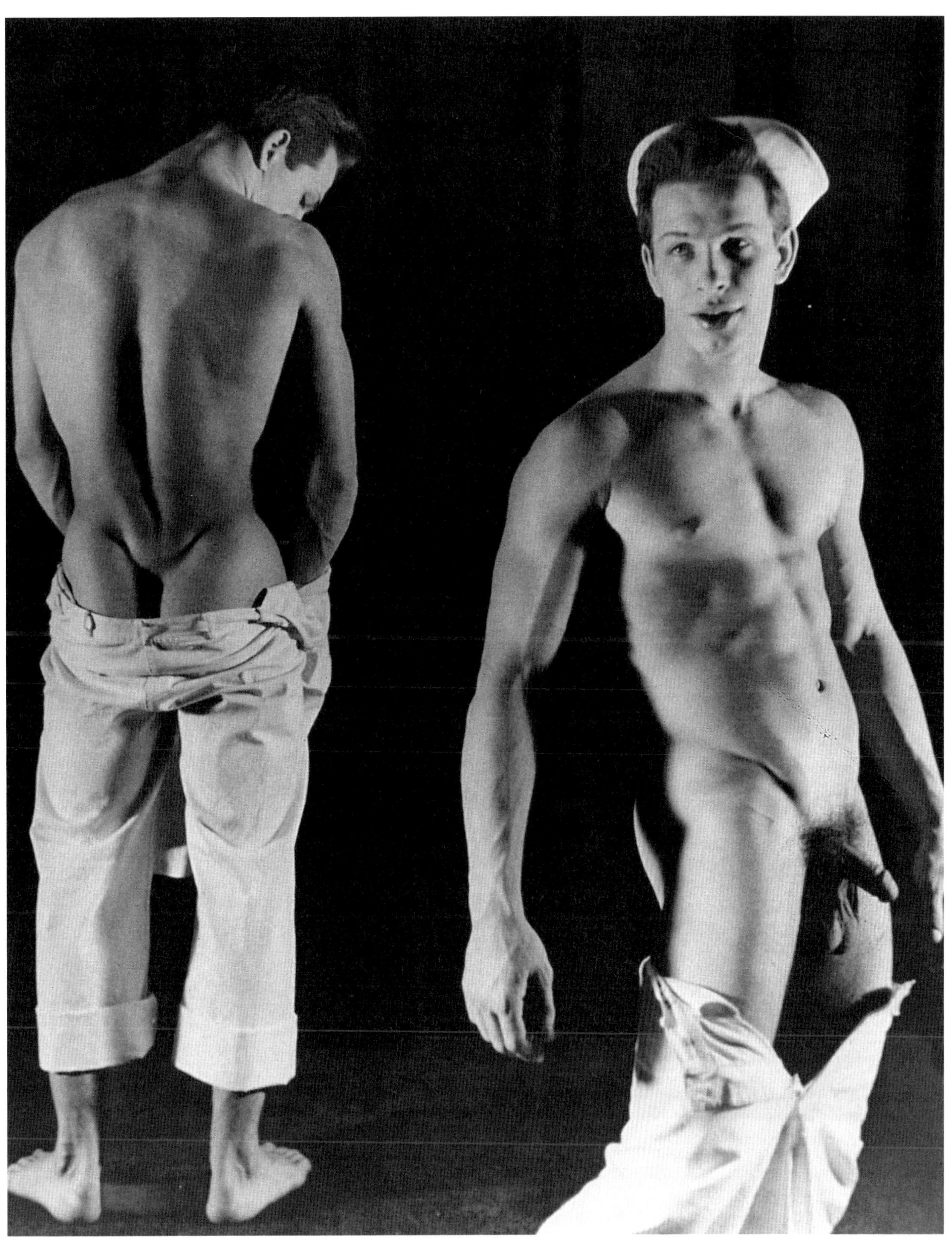

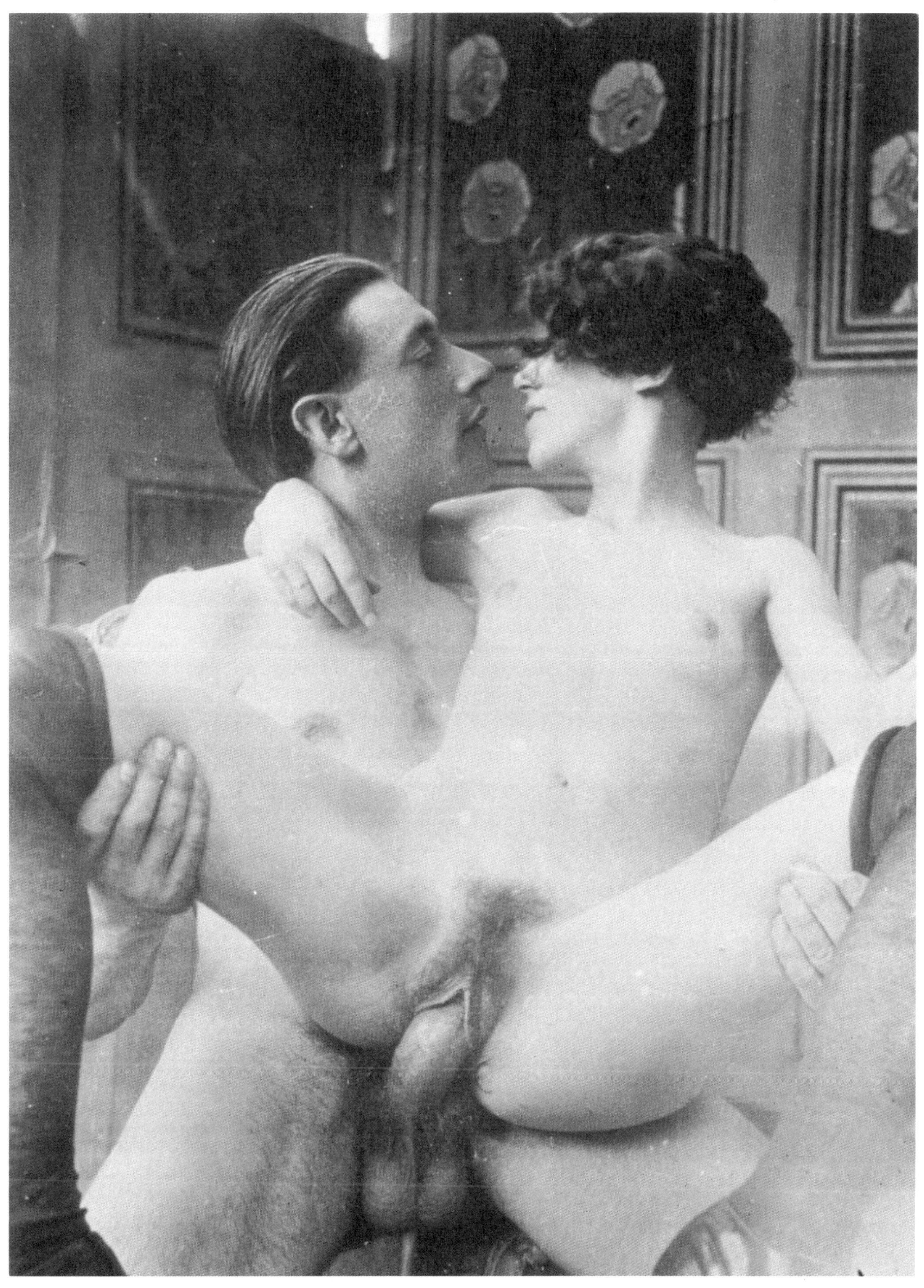

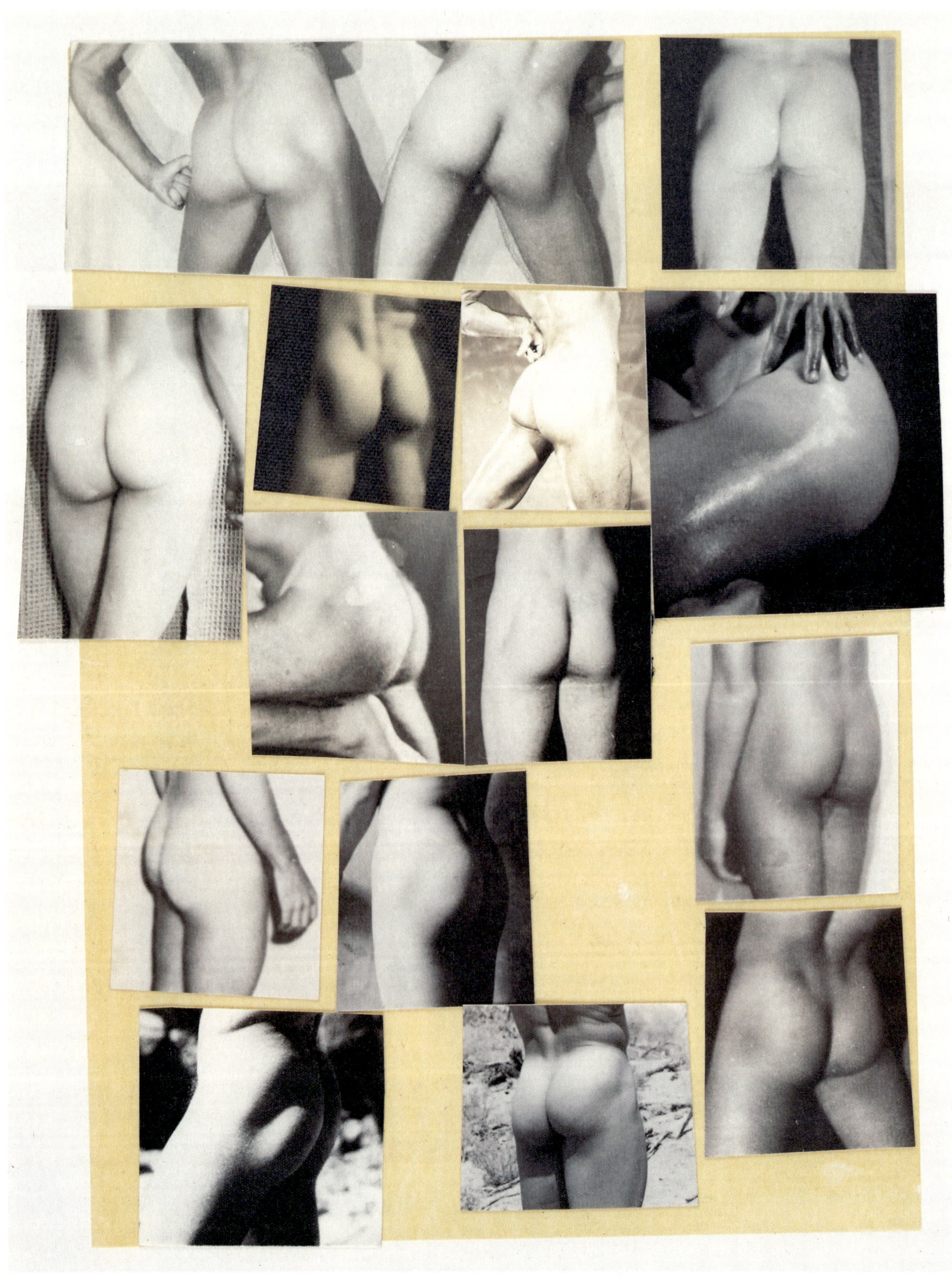

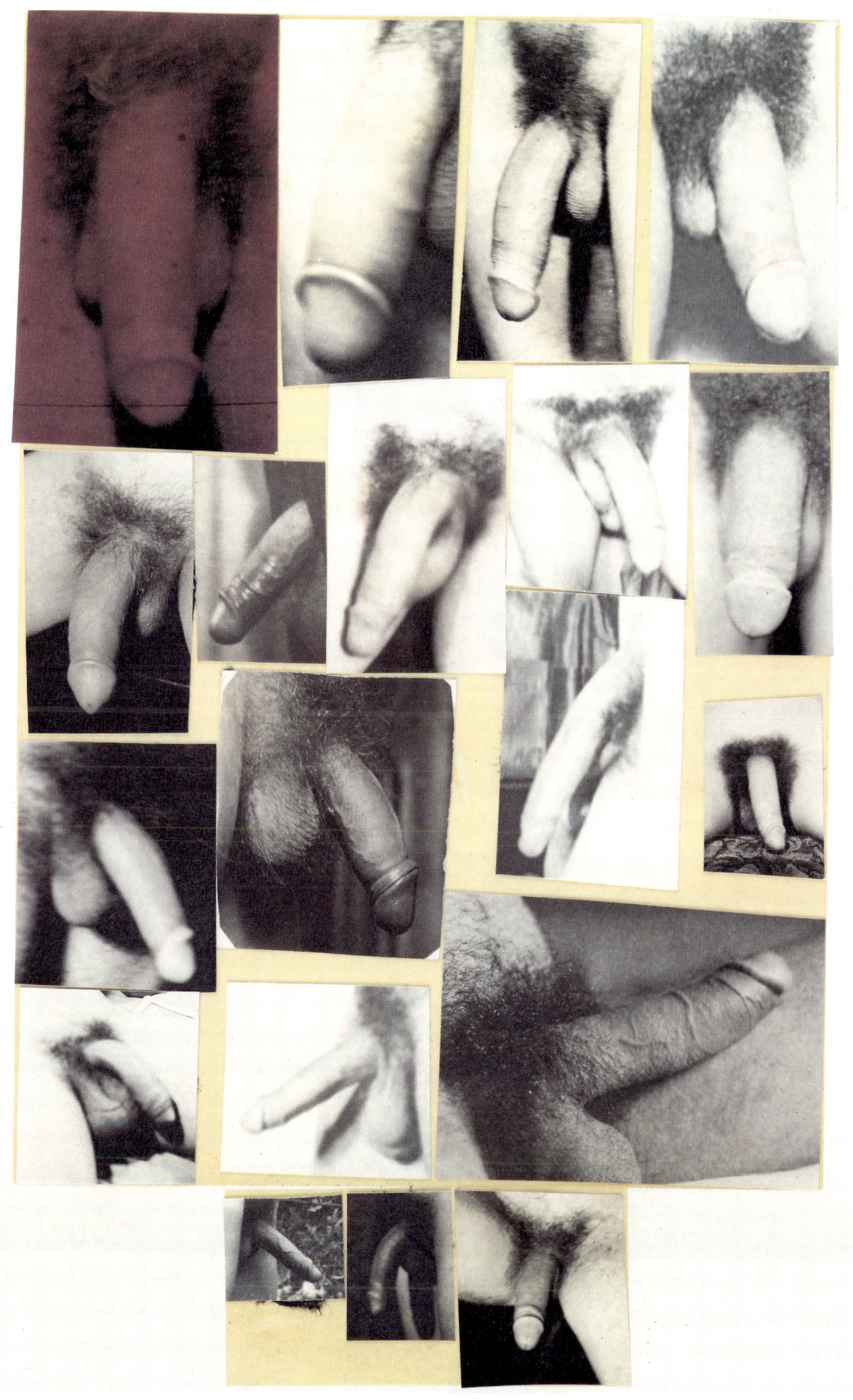

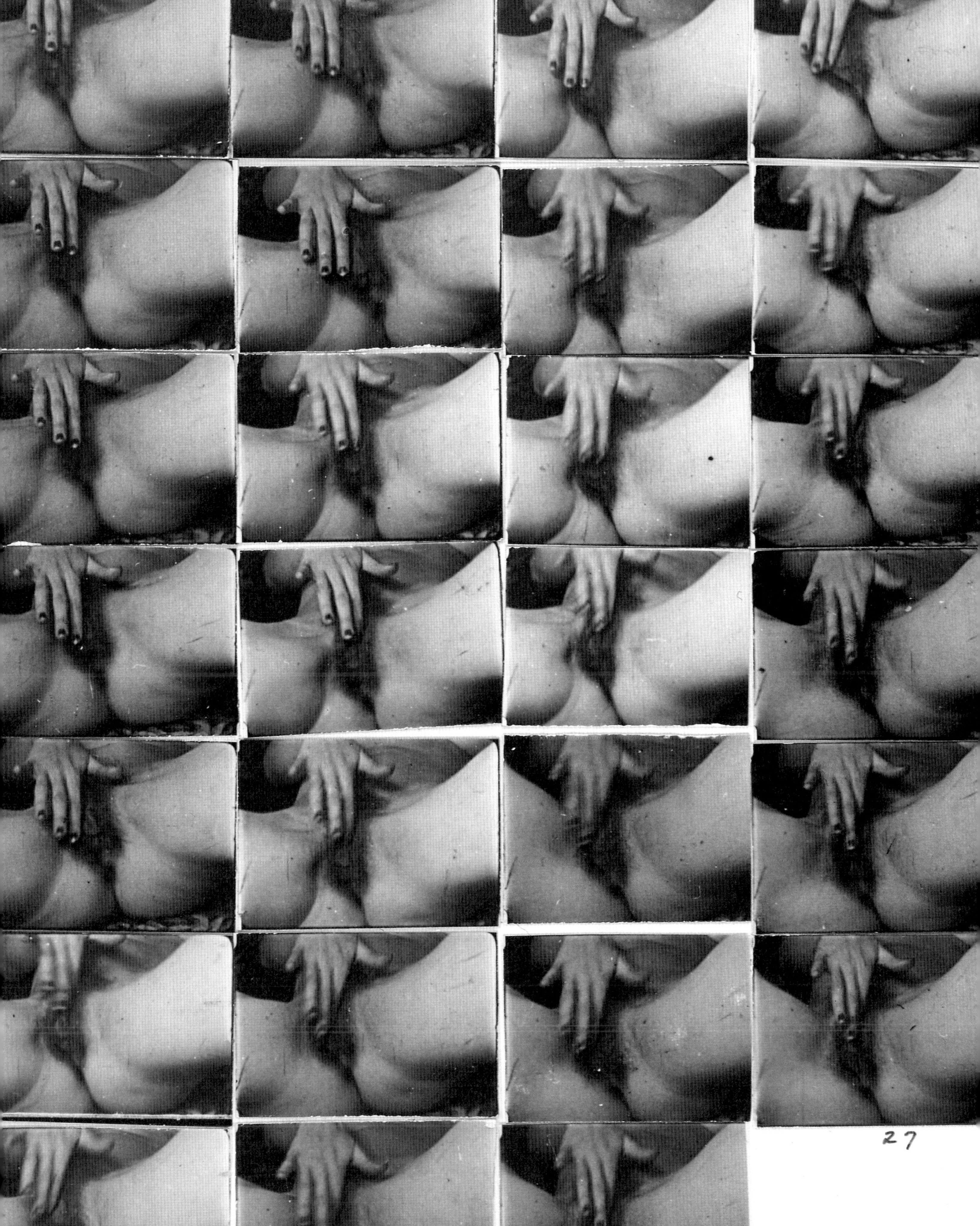

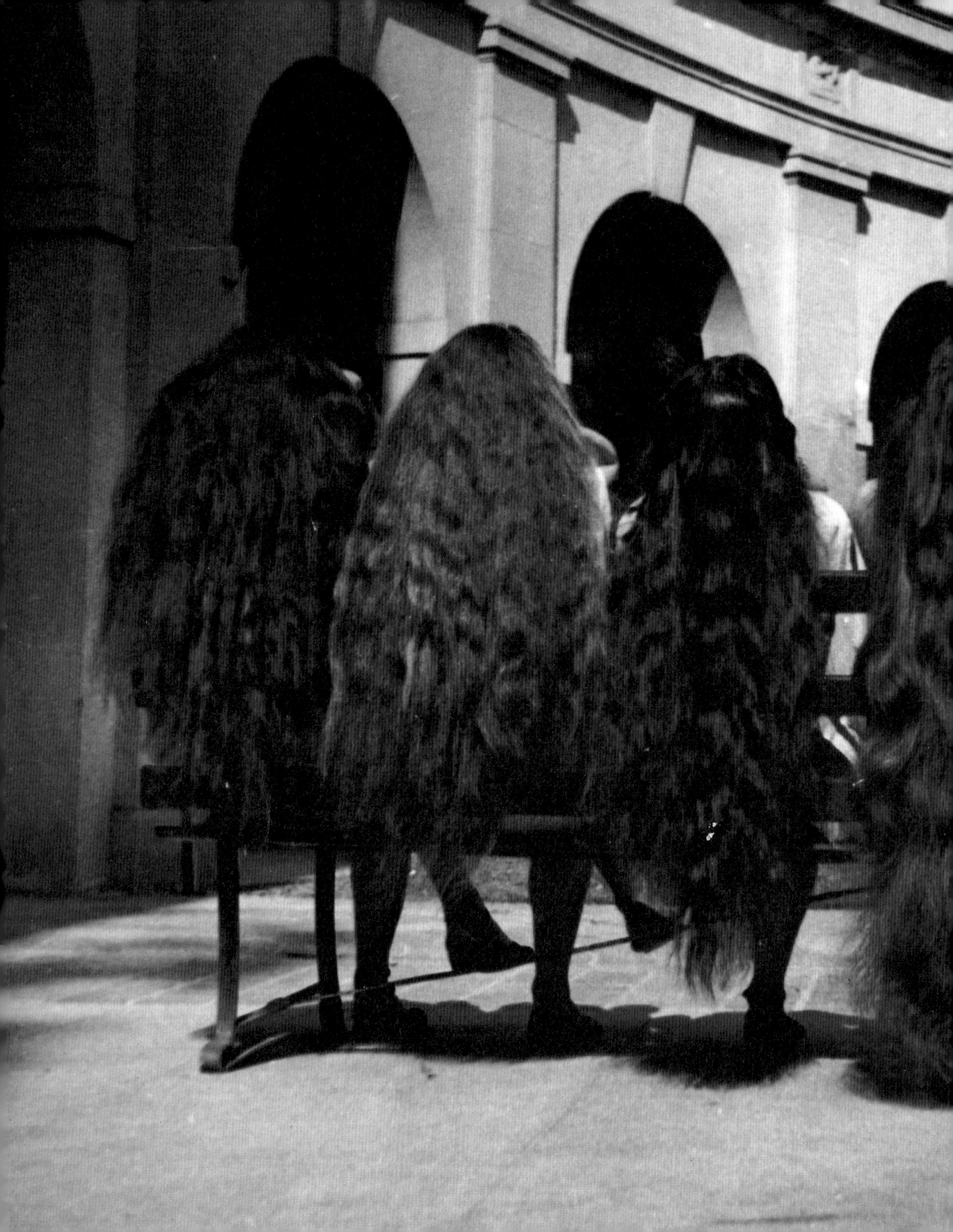

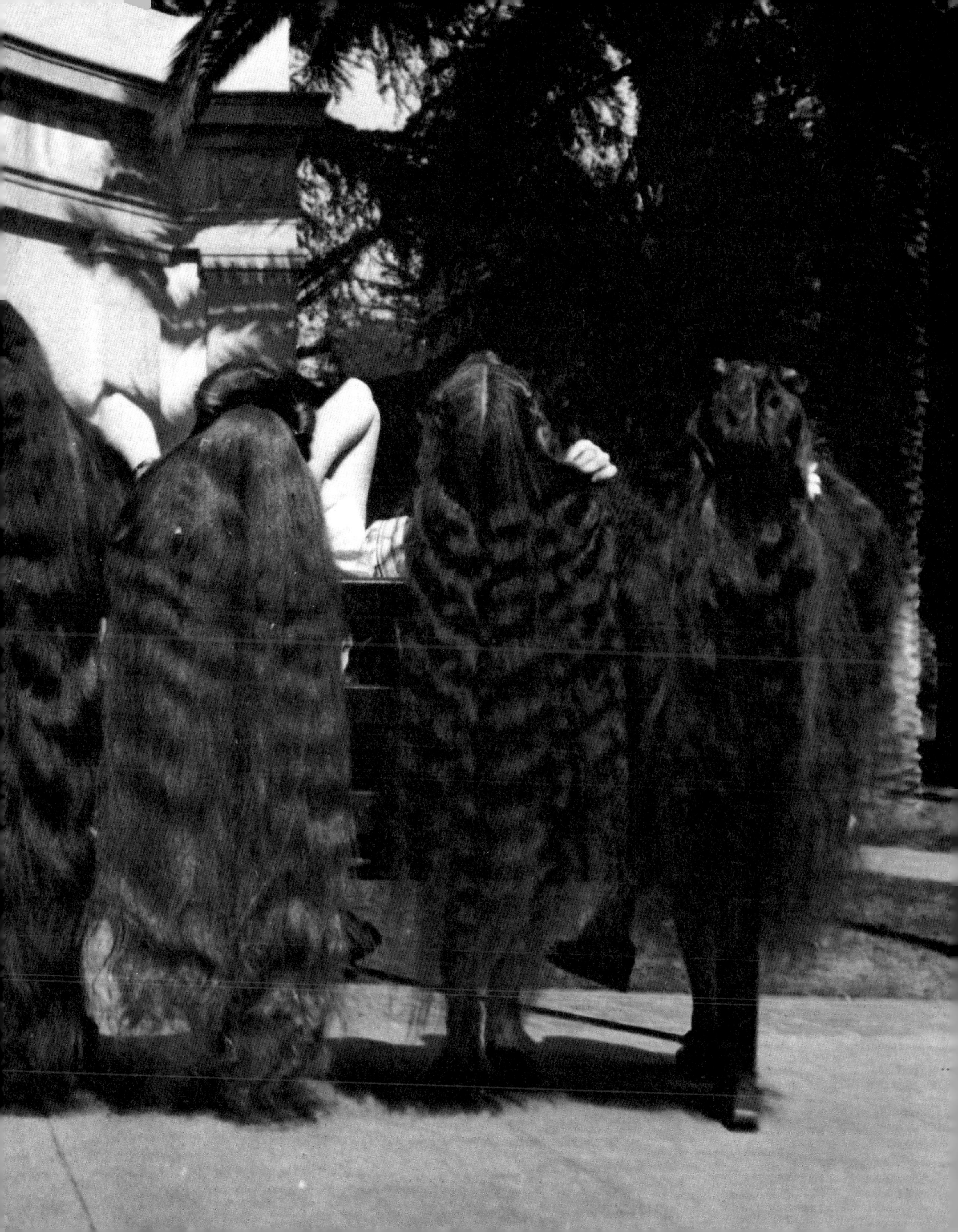

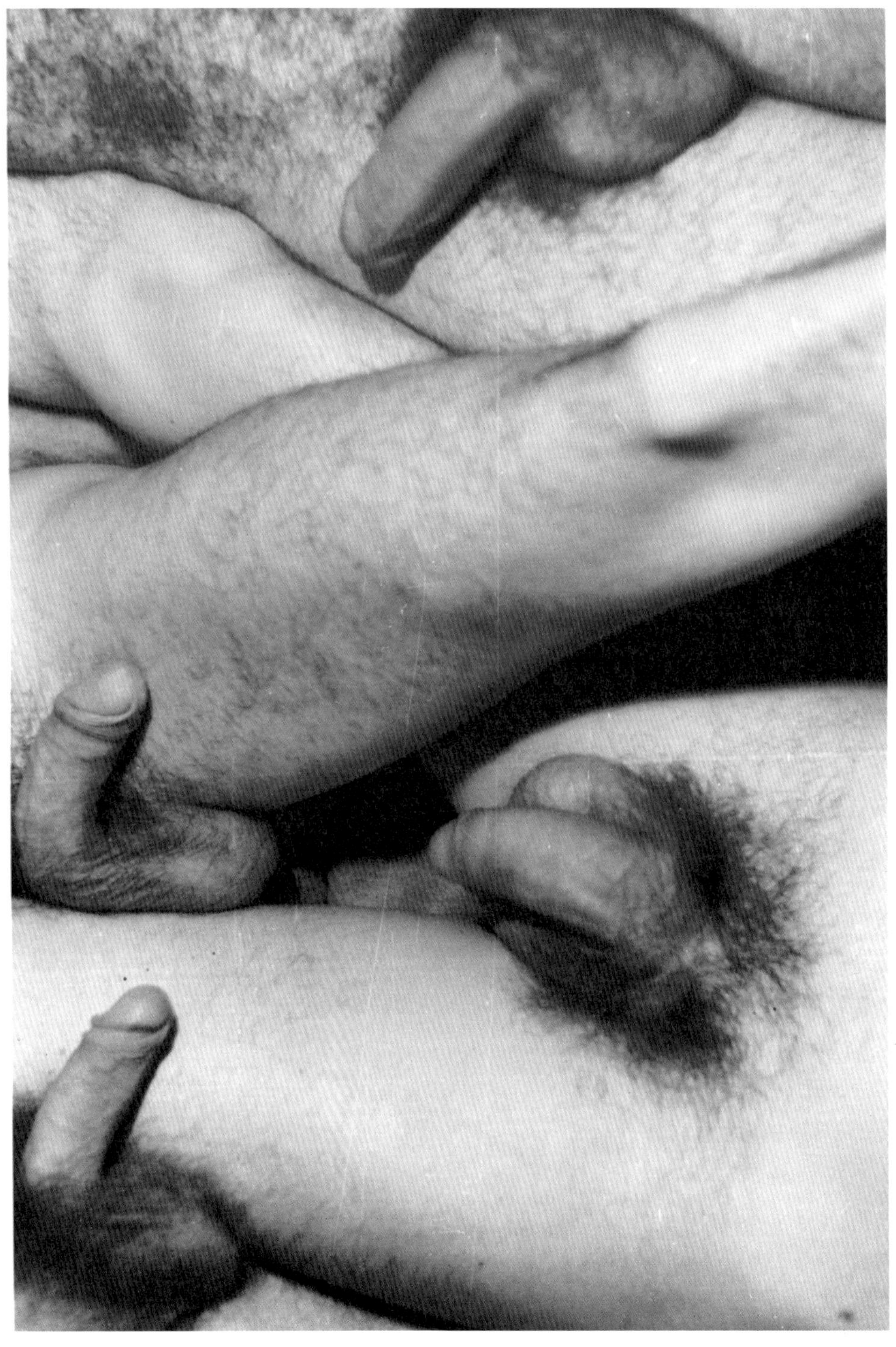

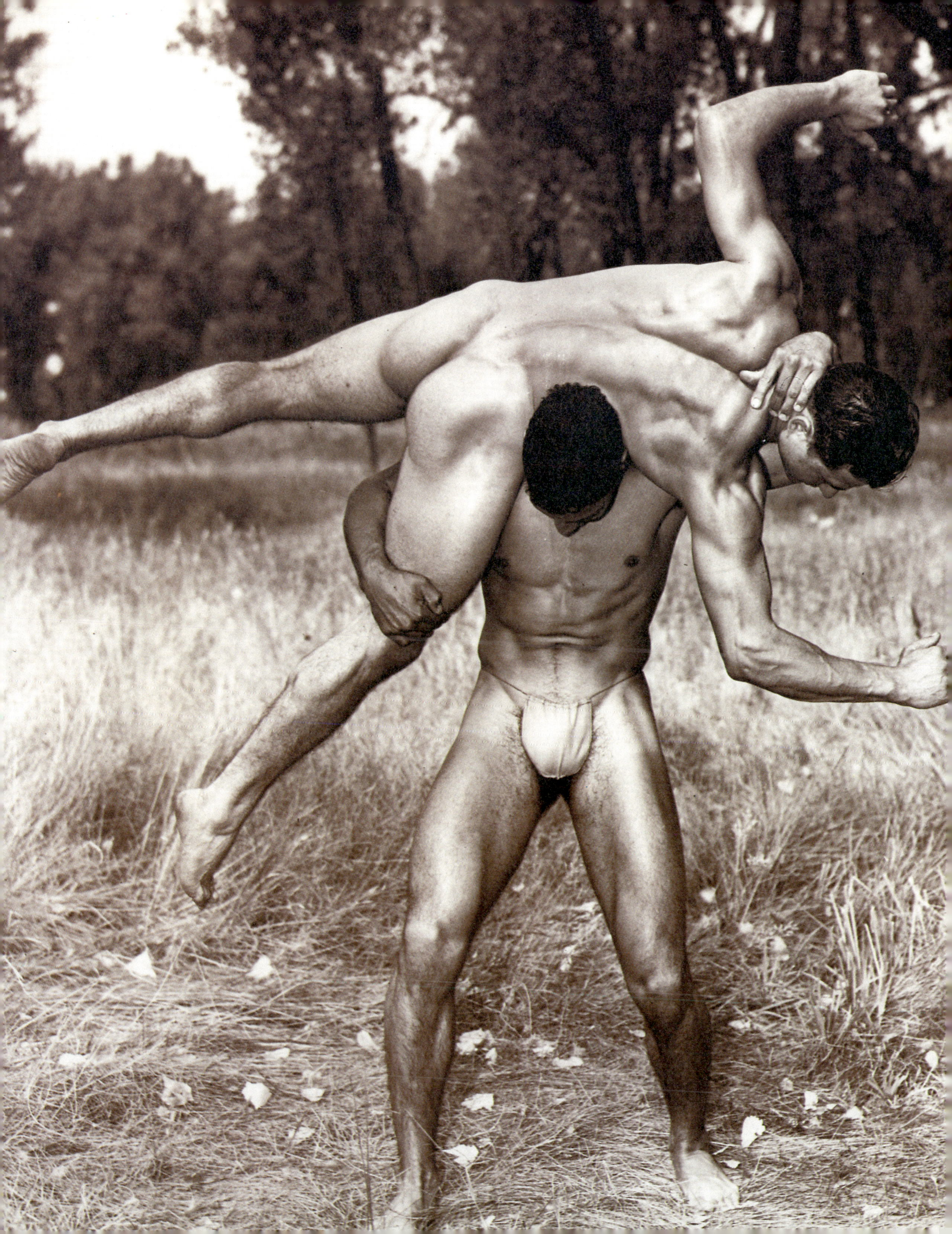

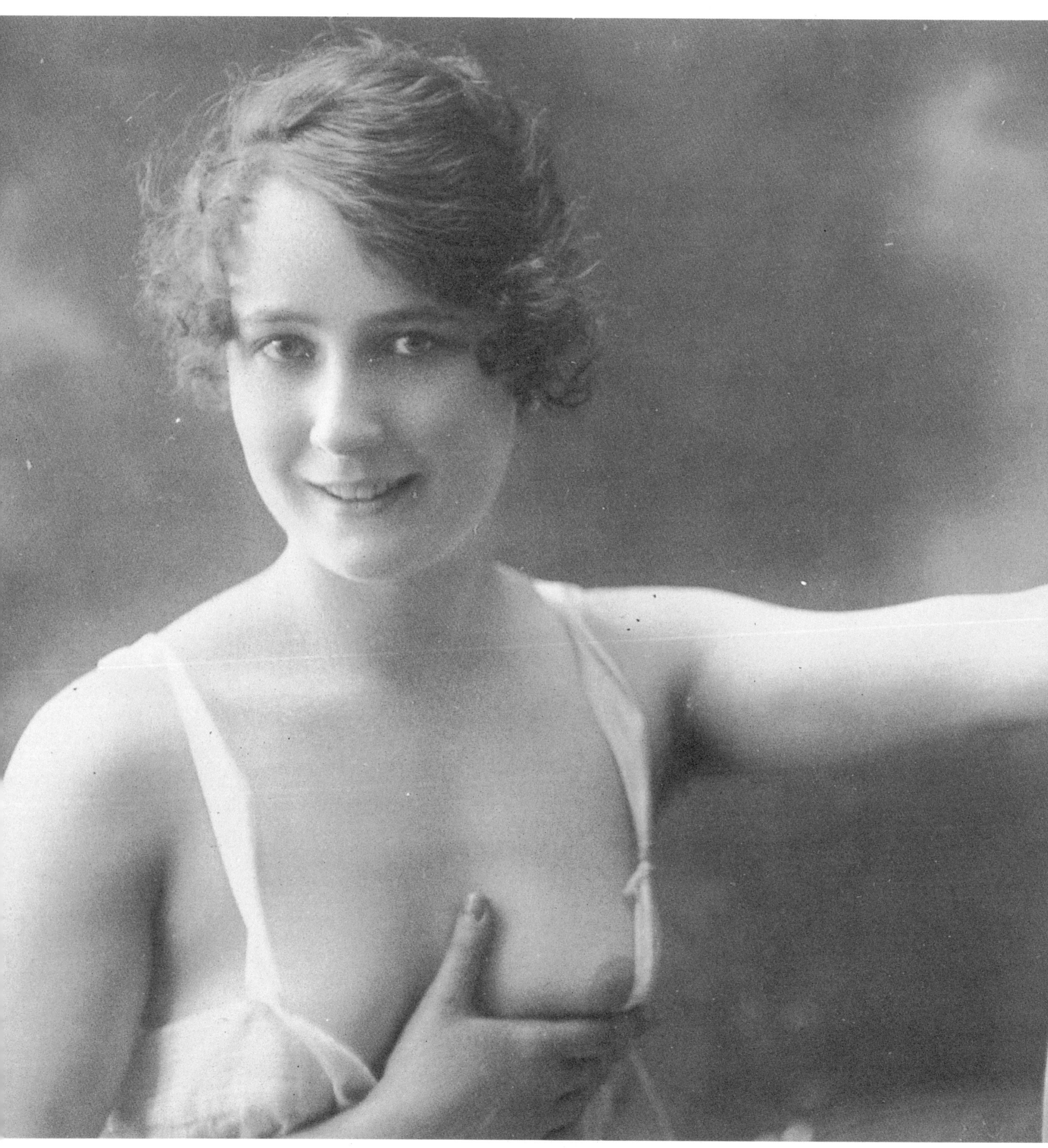

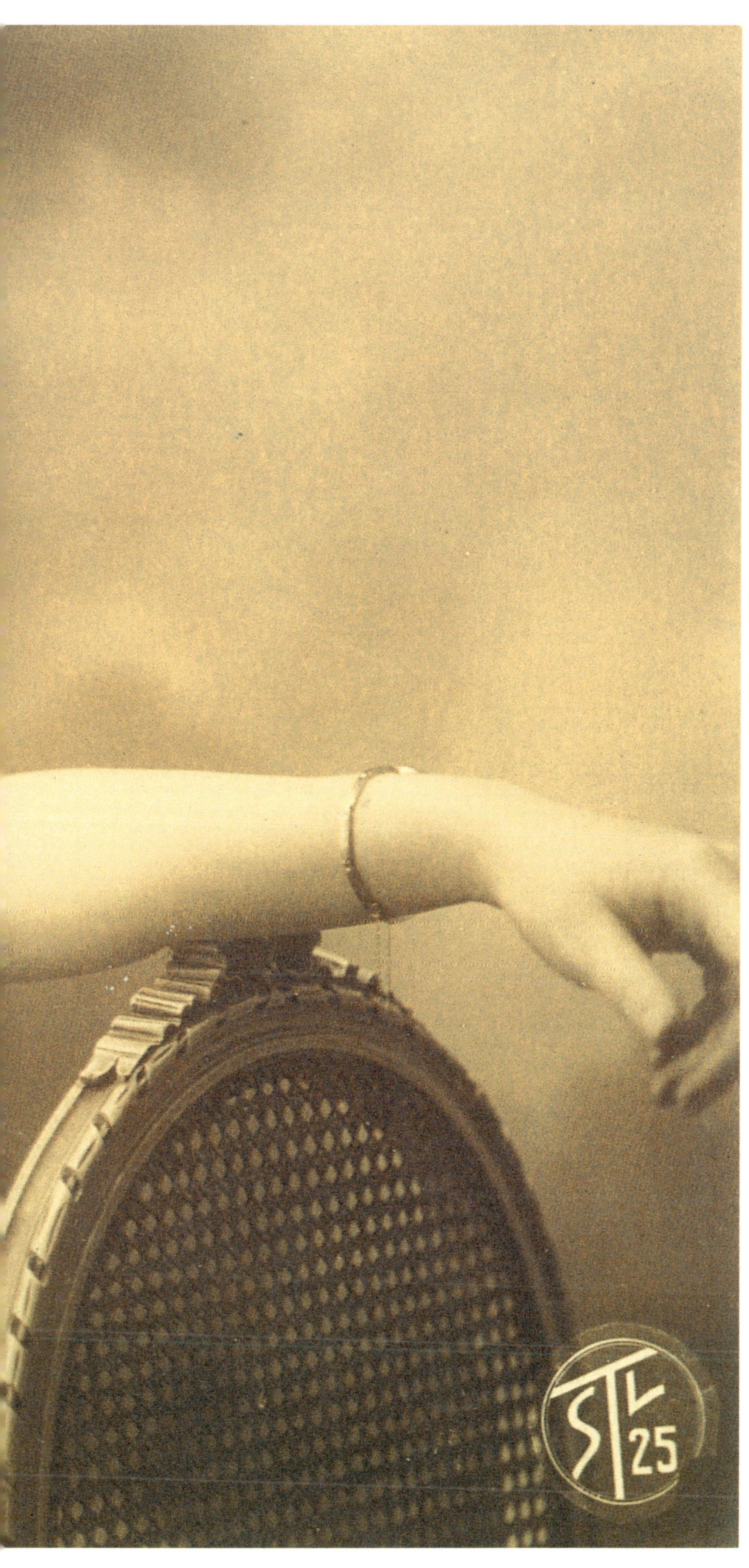

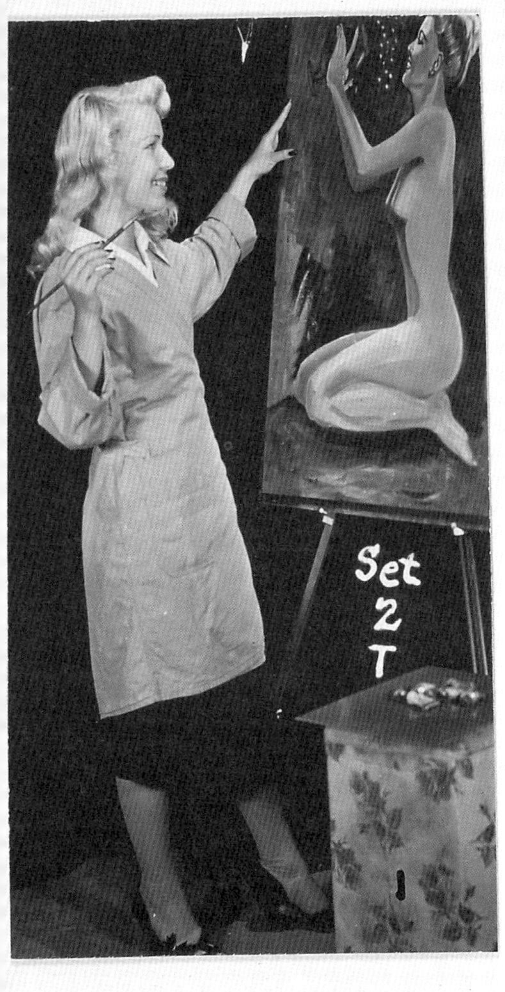
Set
2
T
1

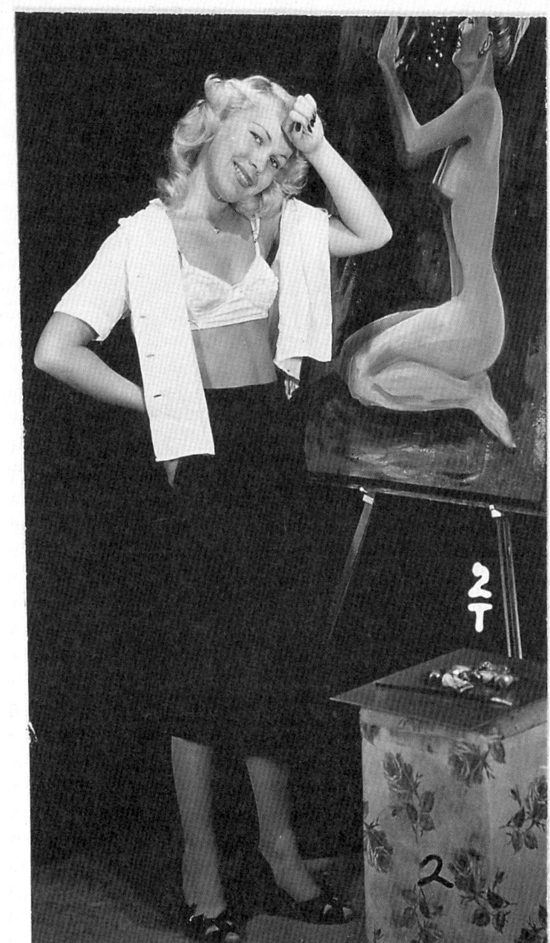
2
T
2

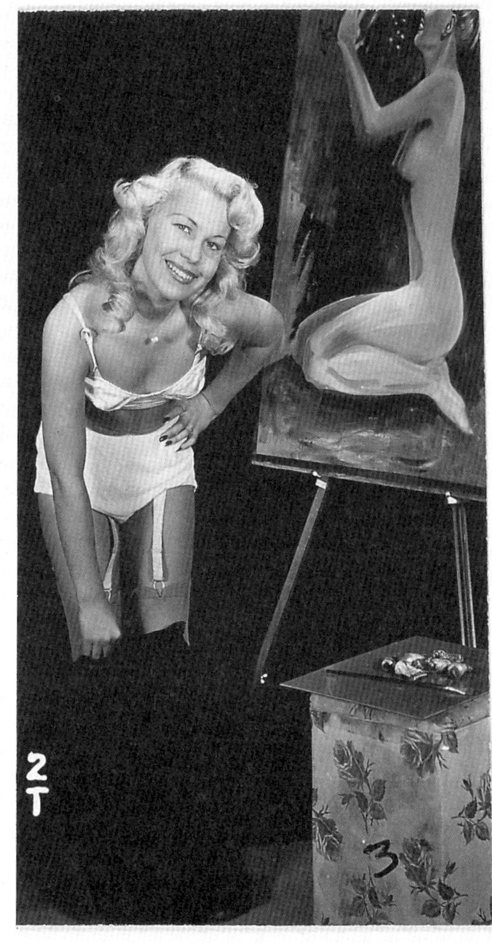
2
T
3

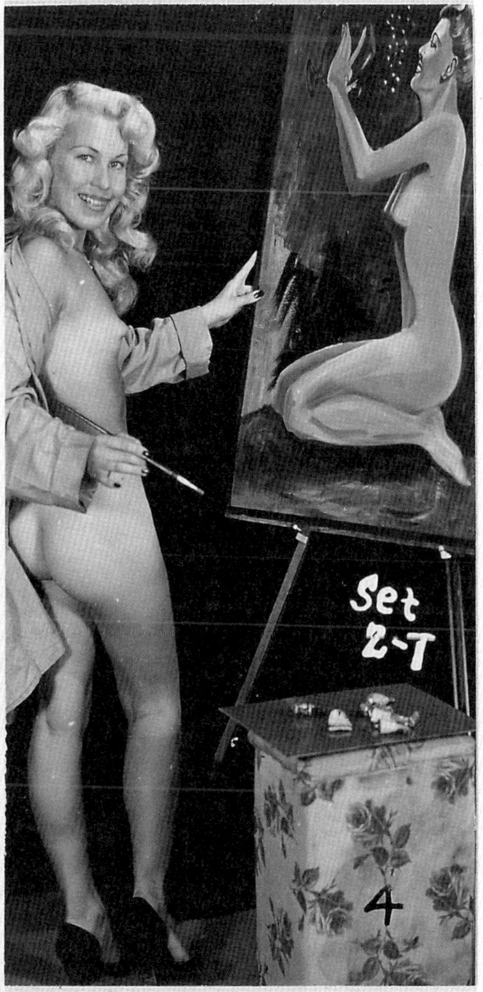
Set
2-T
4

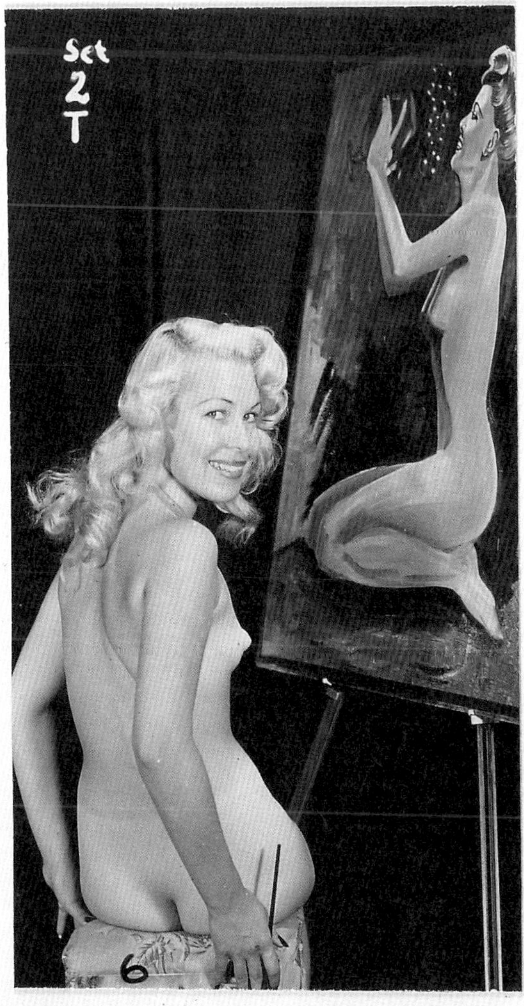
Set
2
T
6

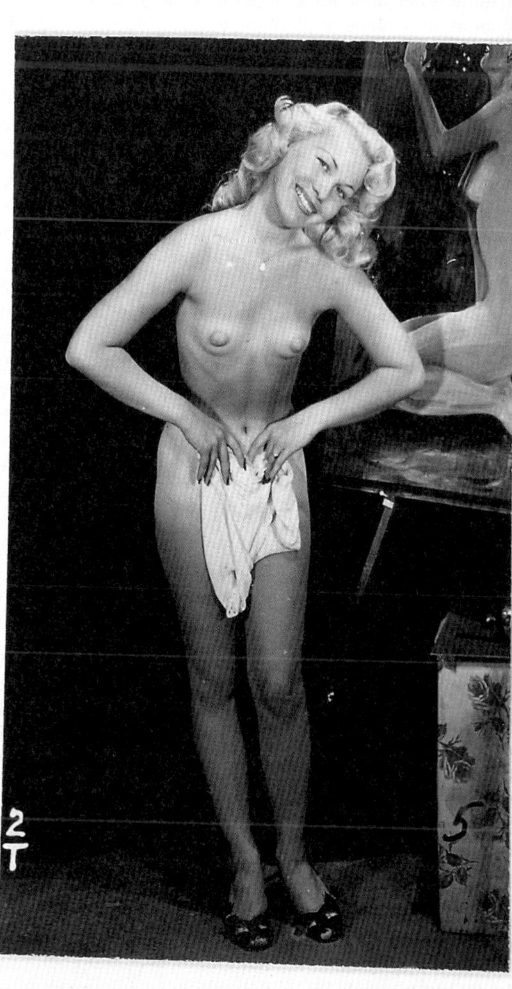
2
T
5

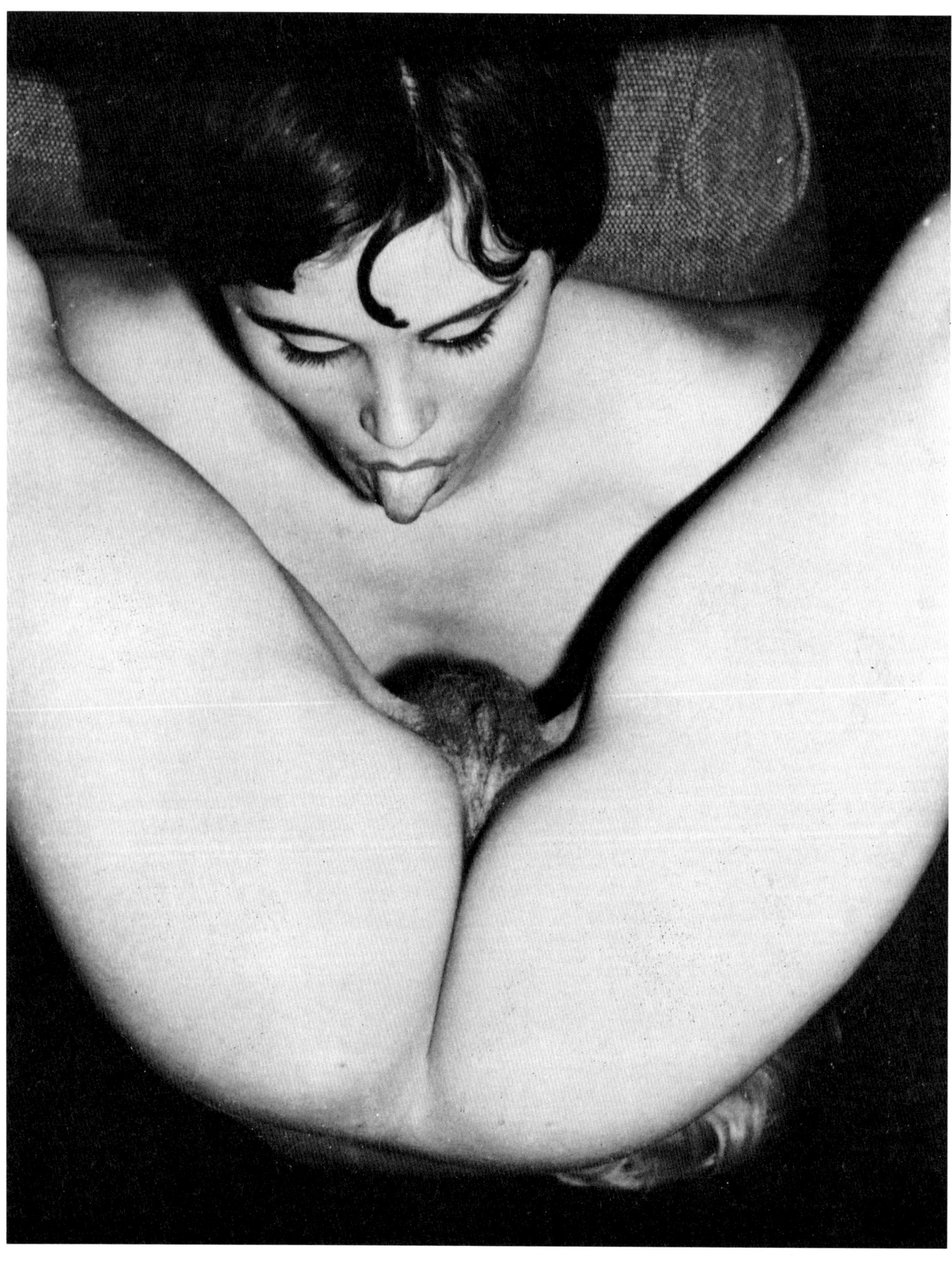

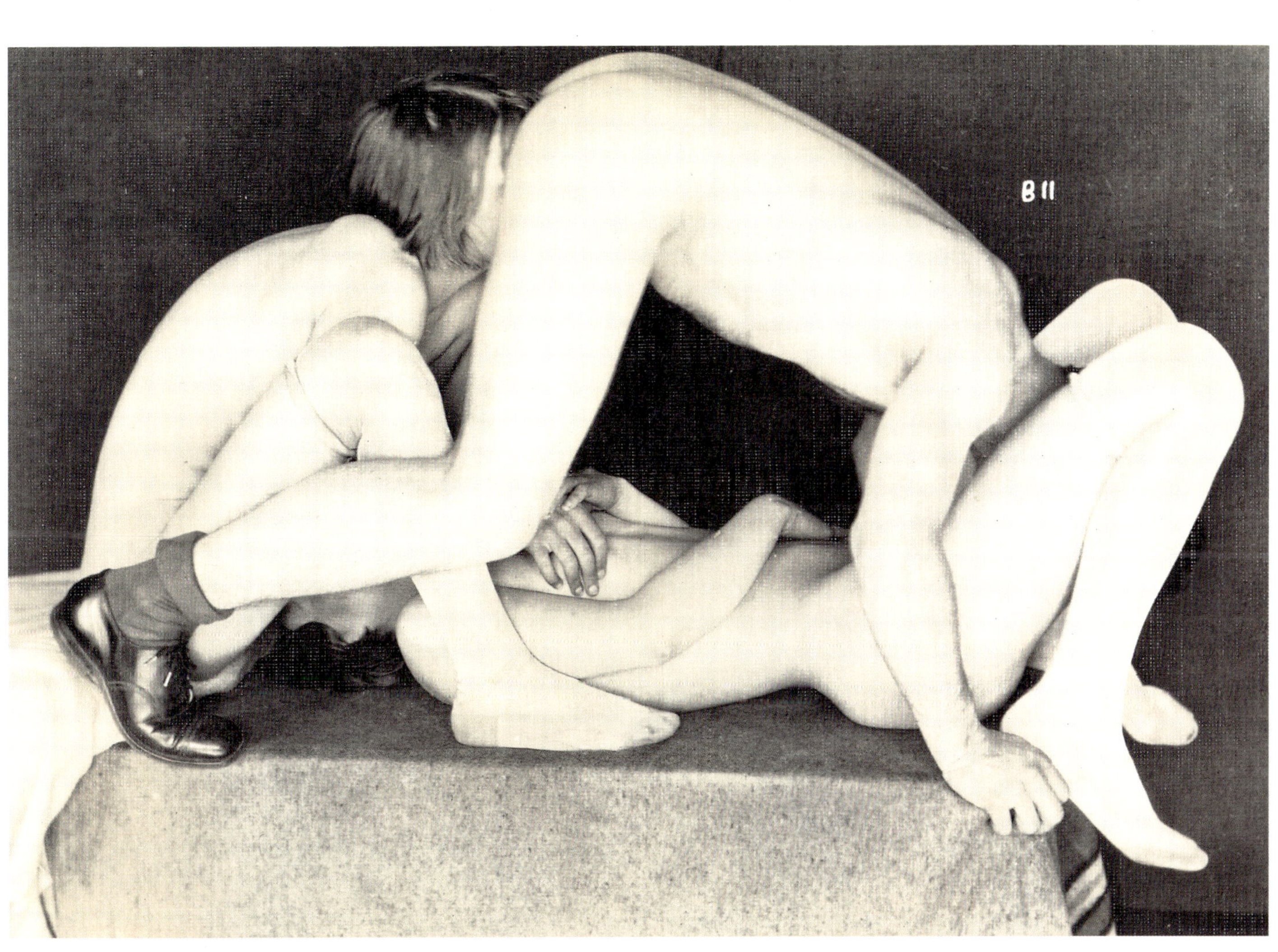
B 11

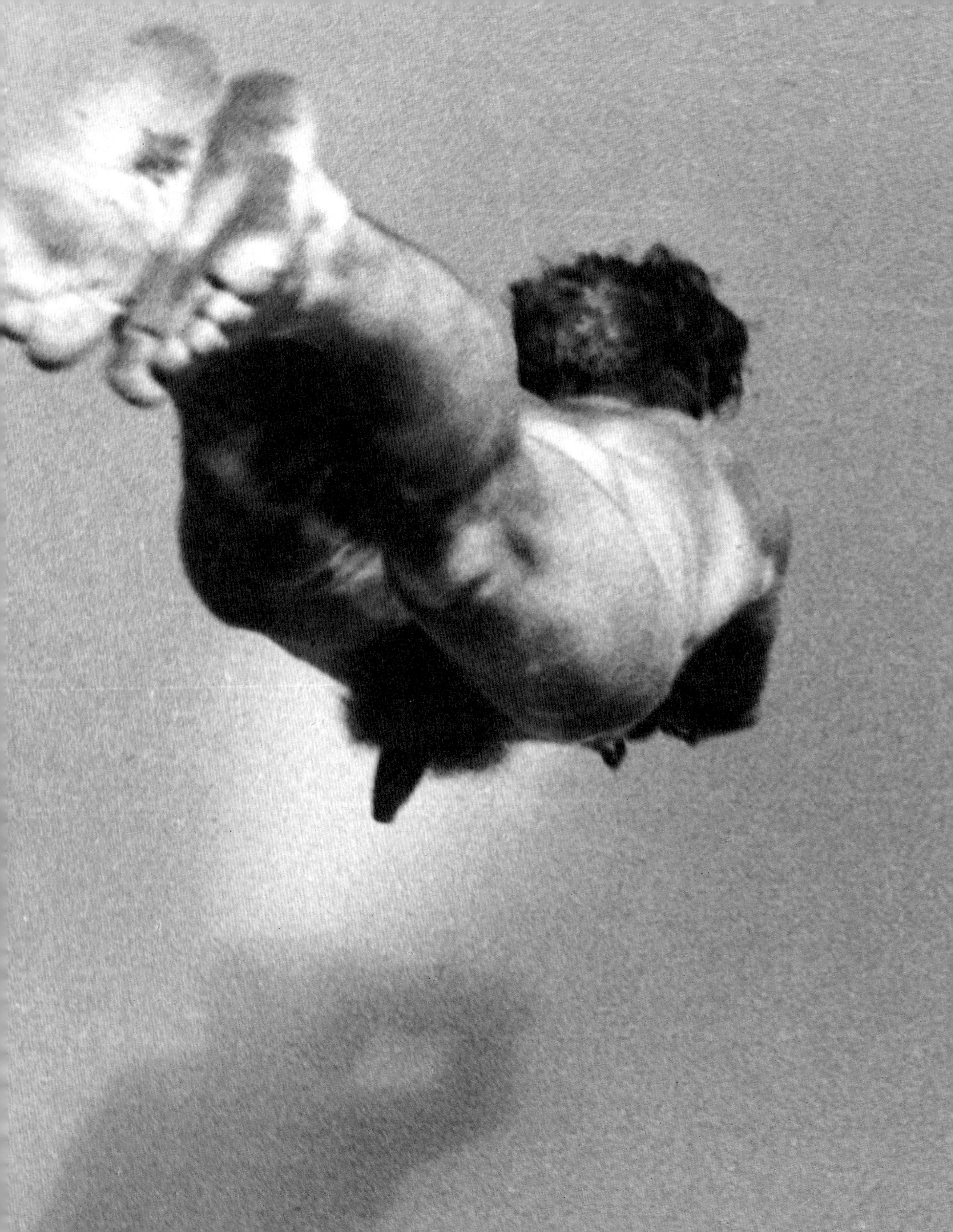

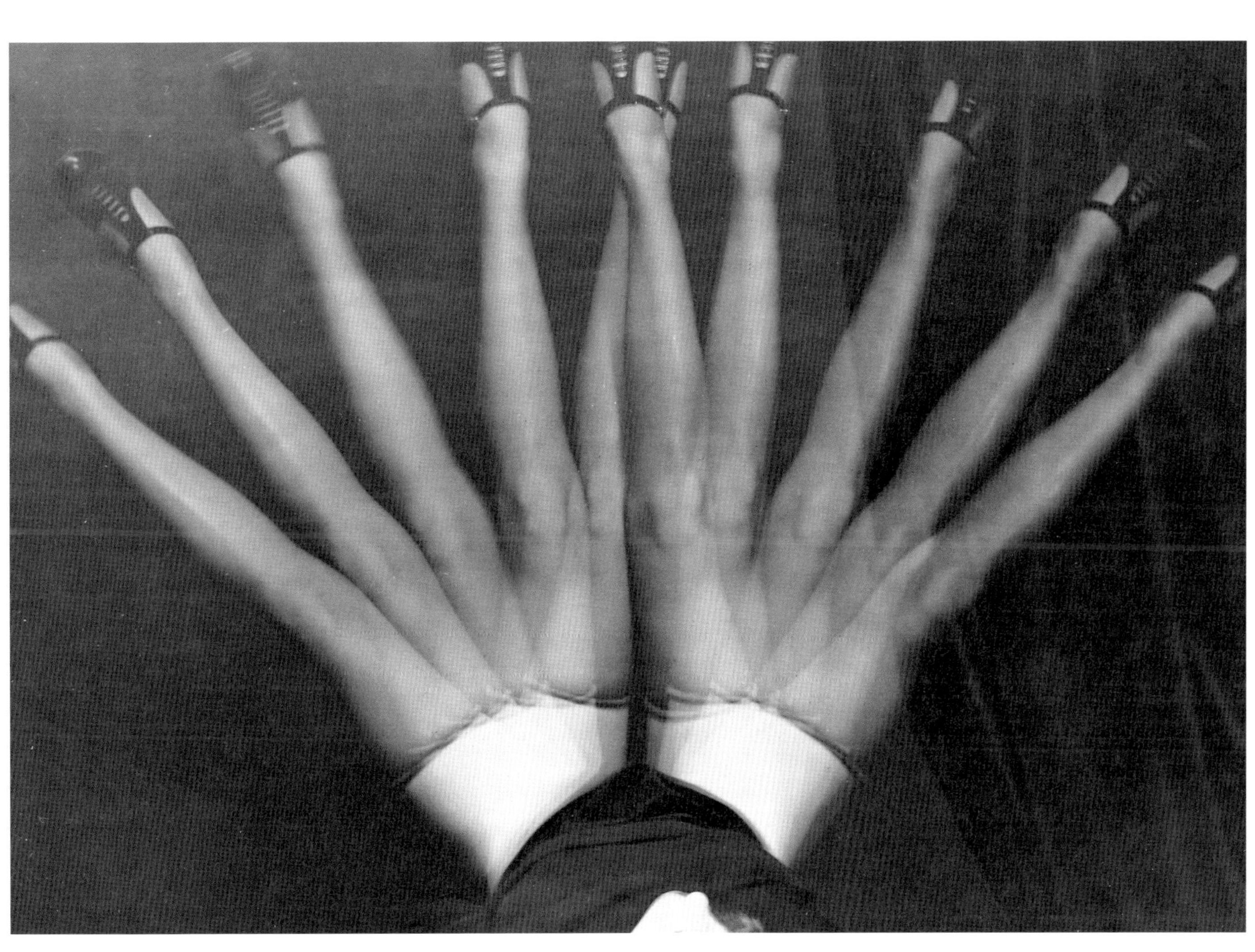

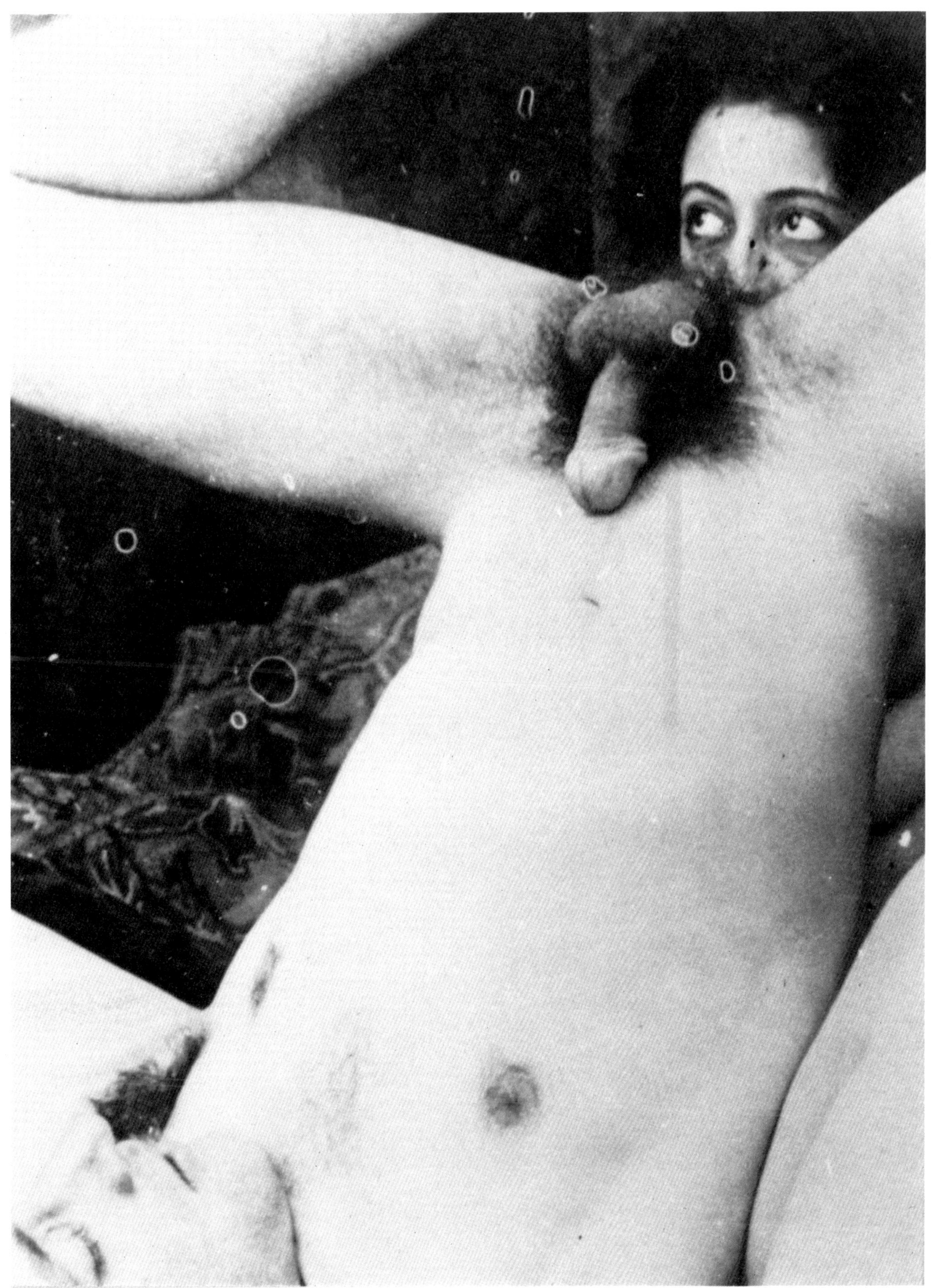

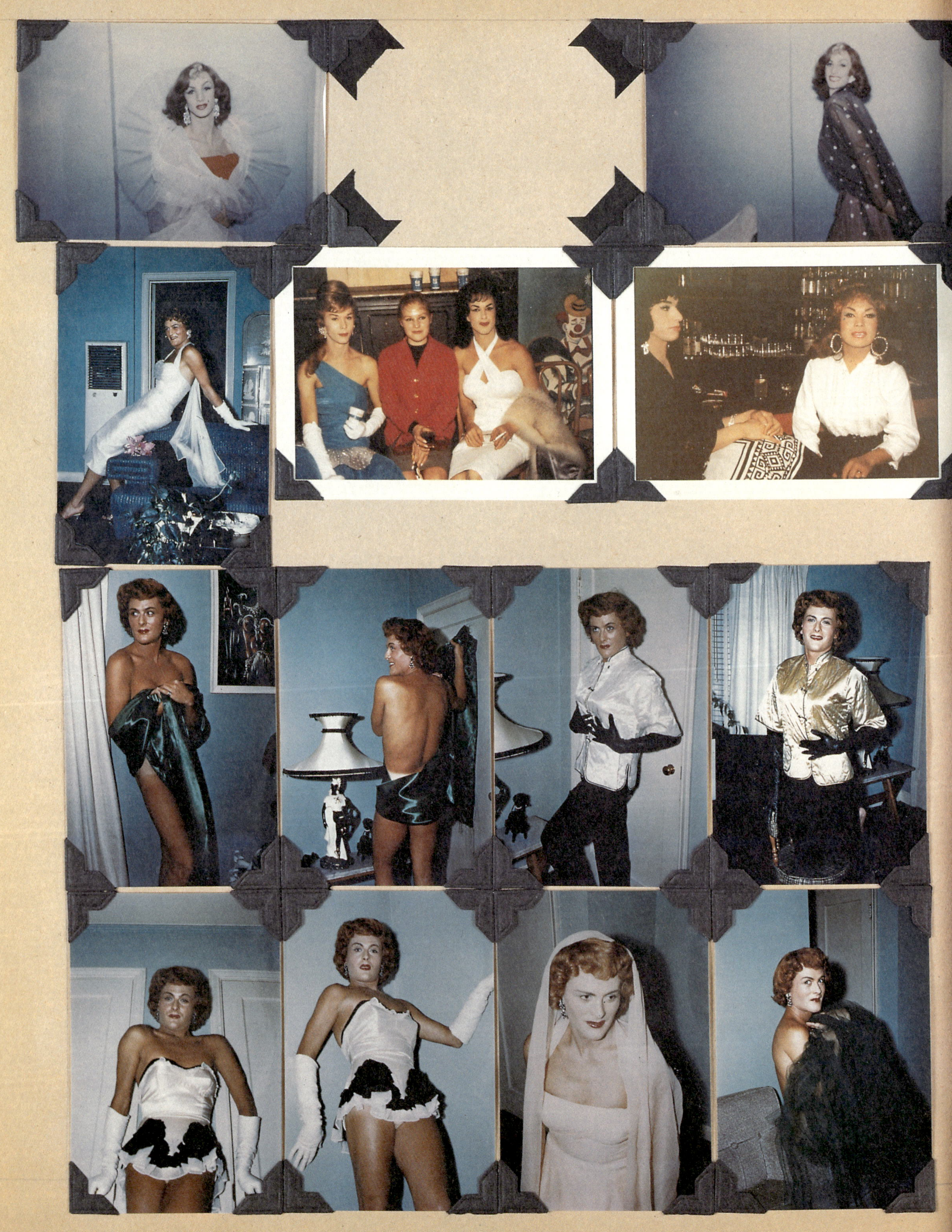

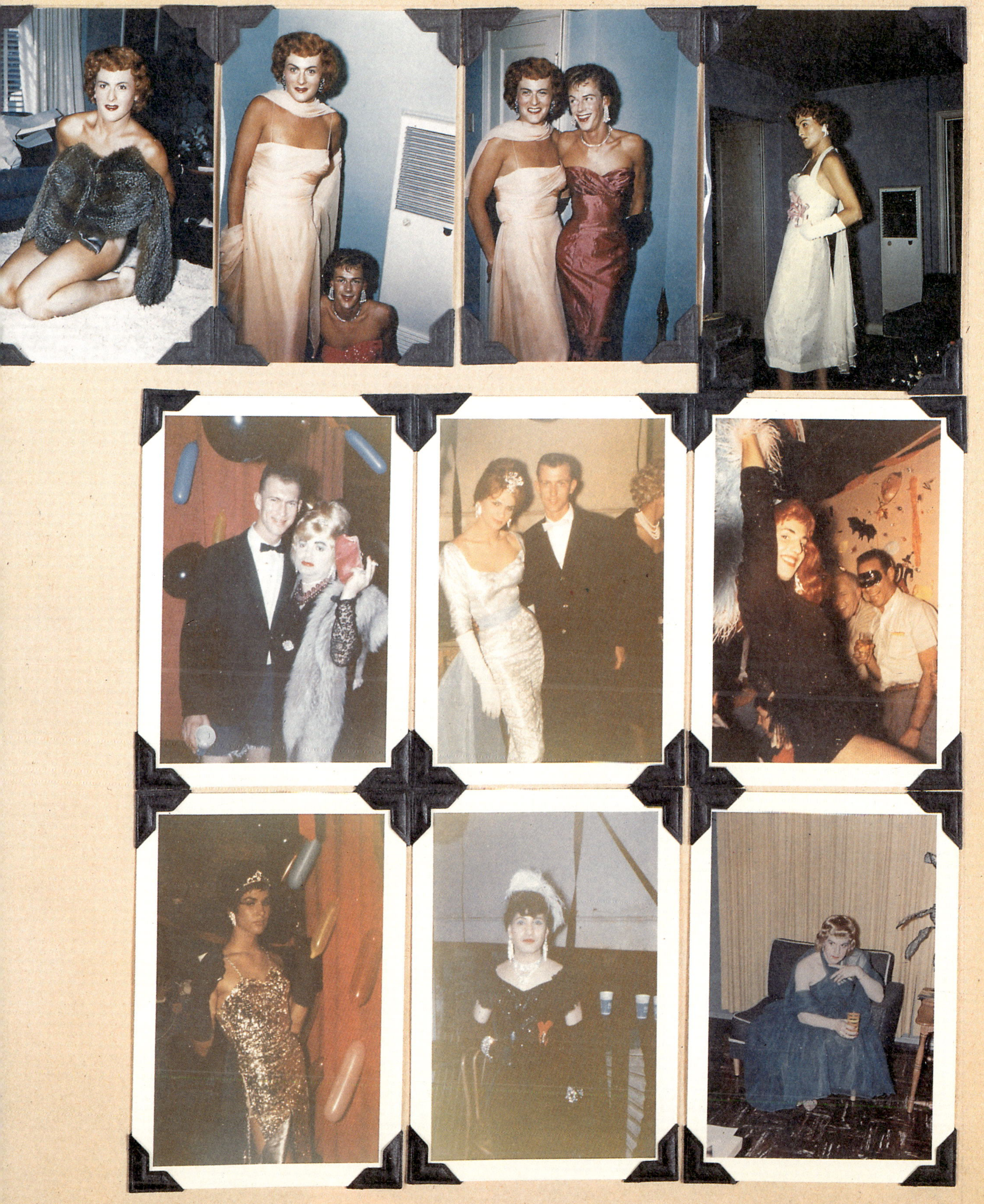

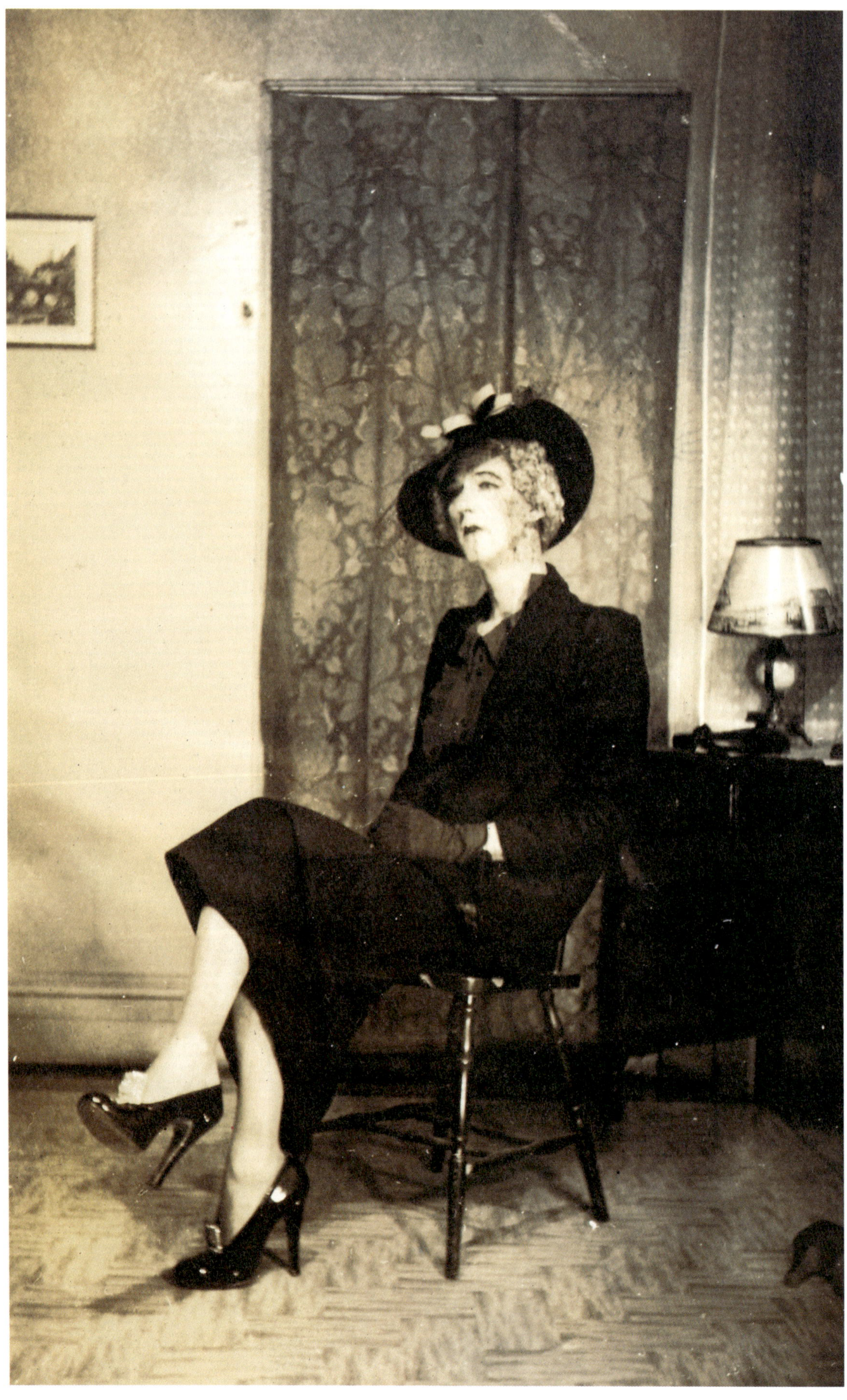

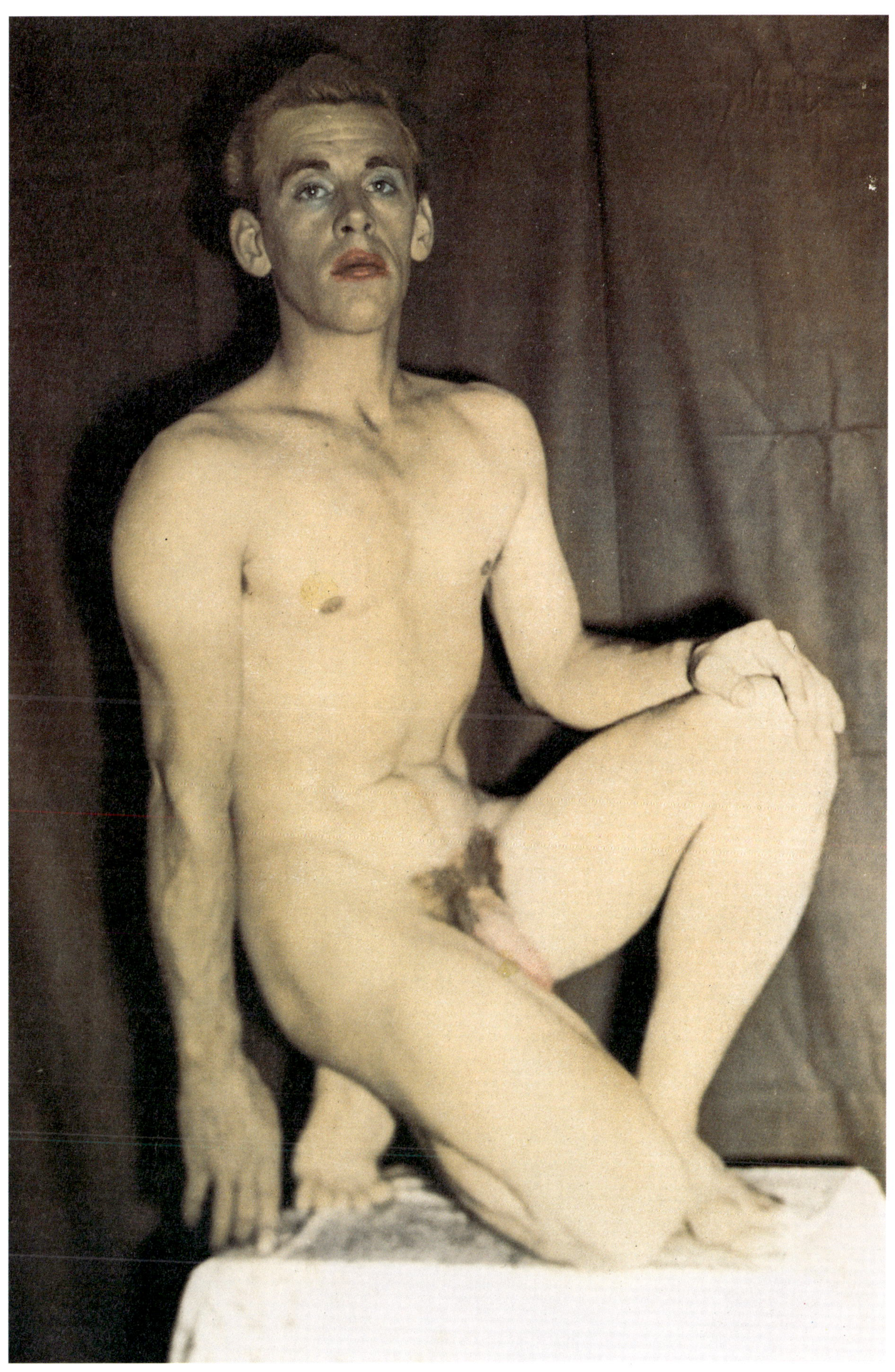

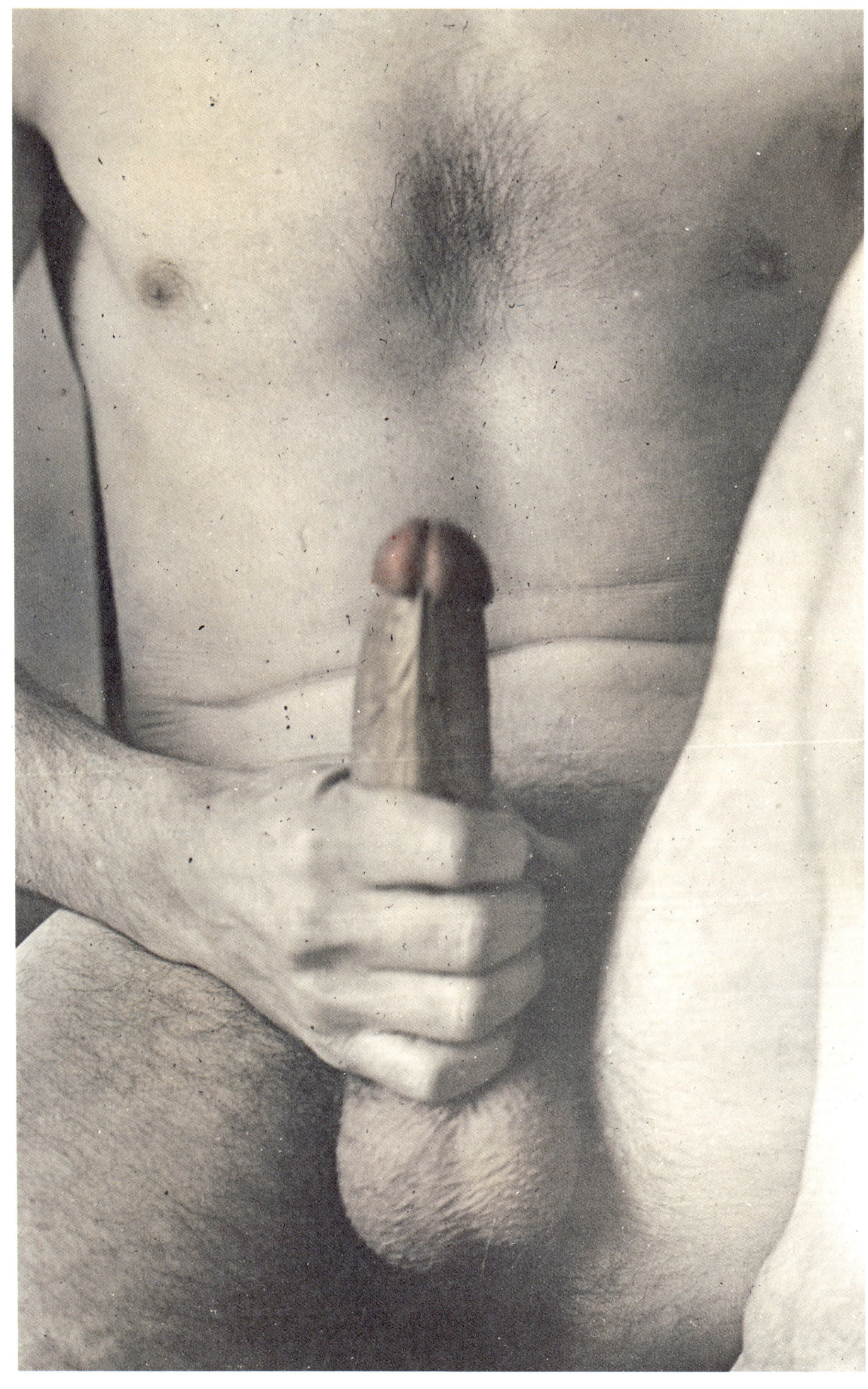

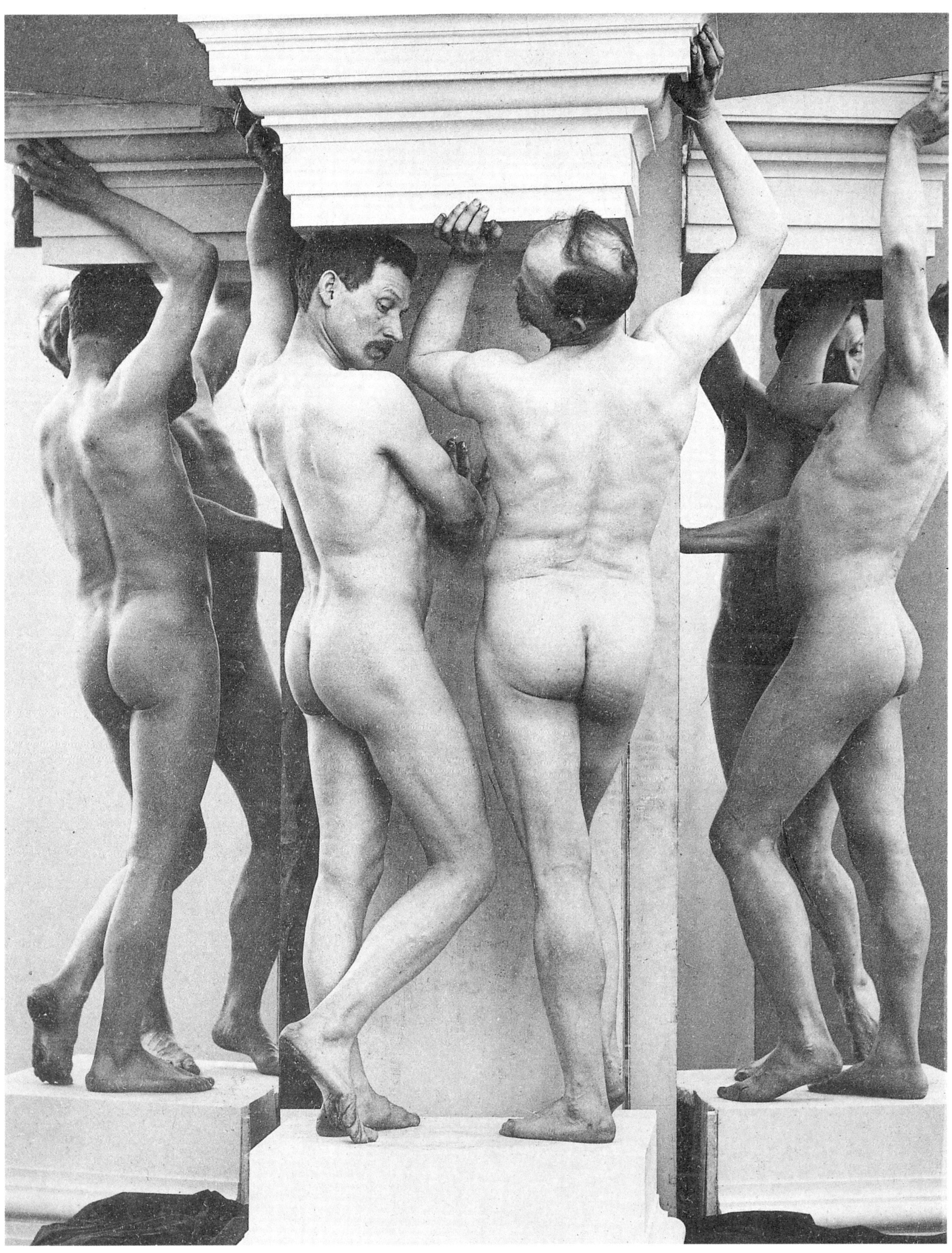

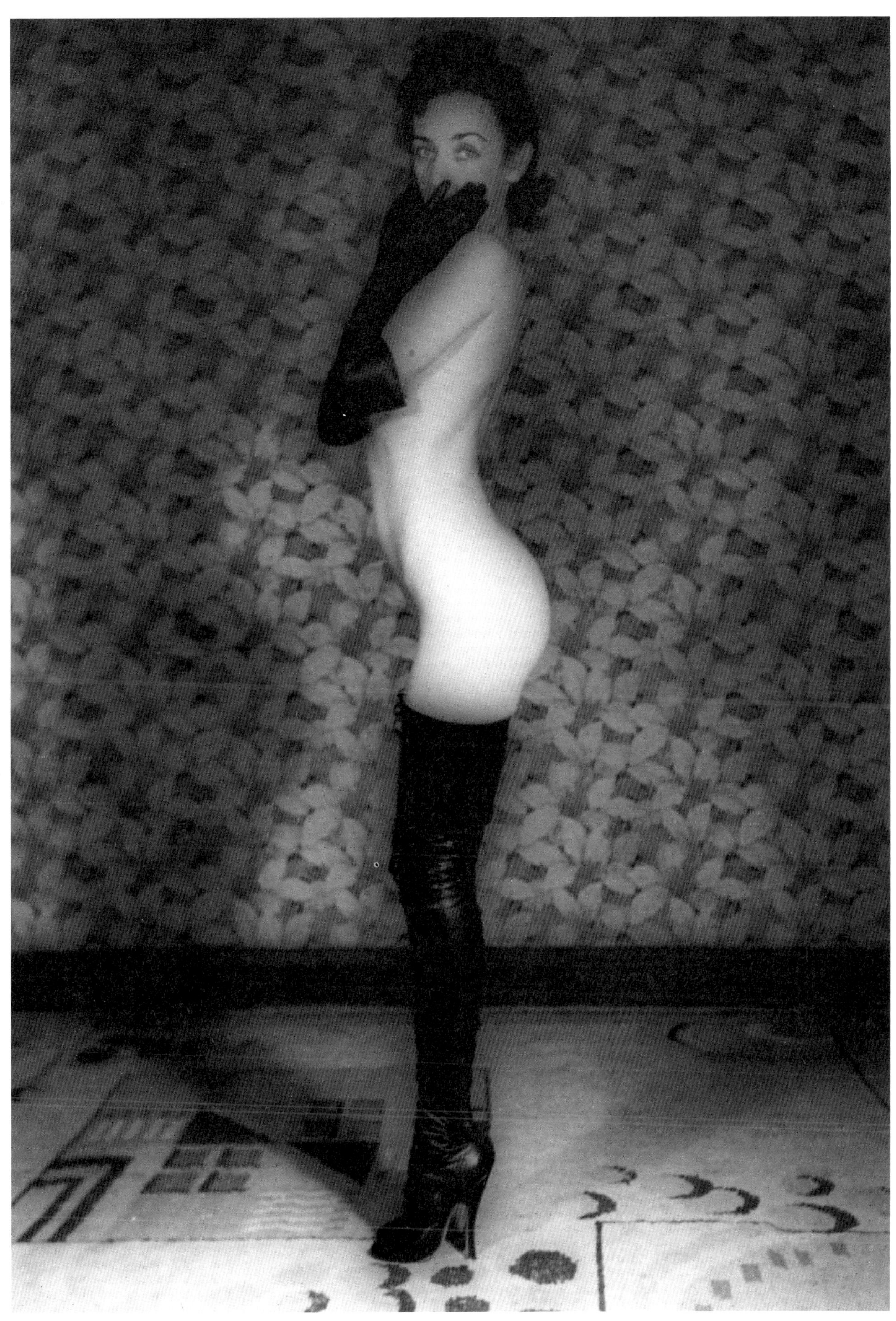

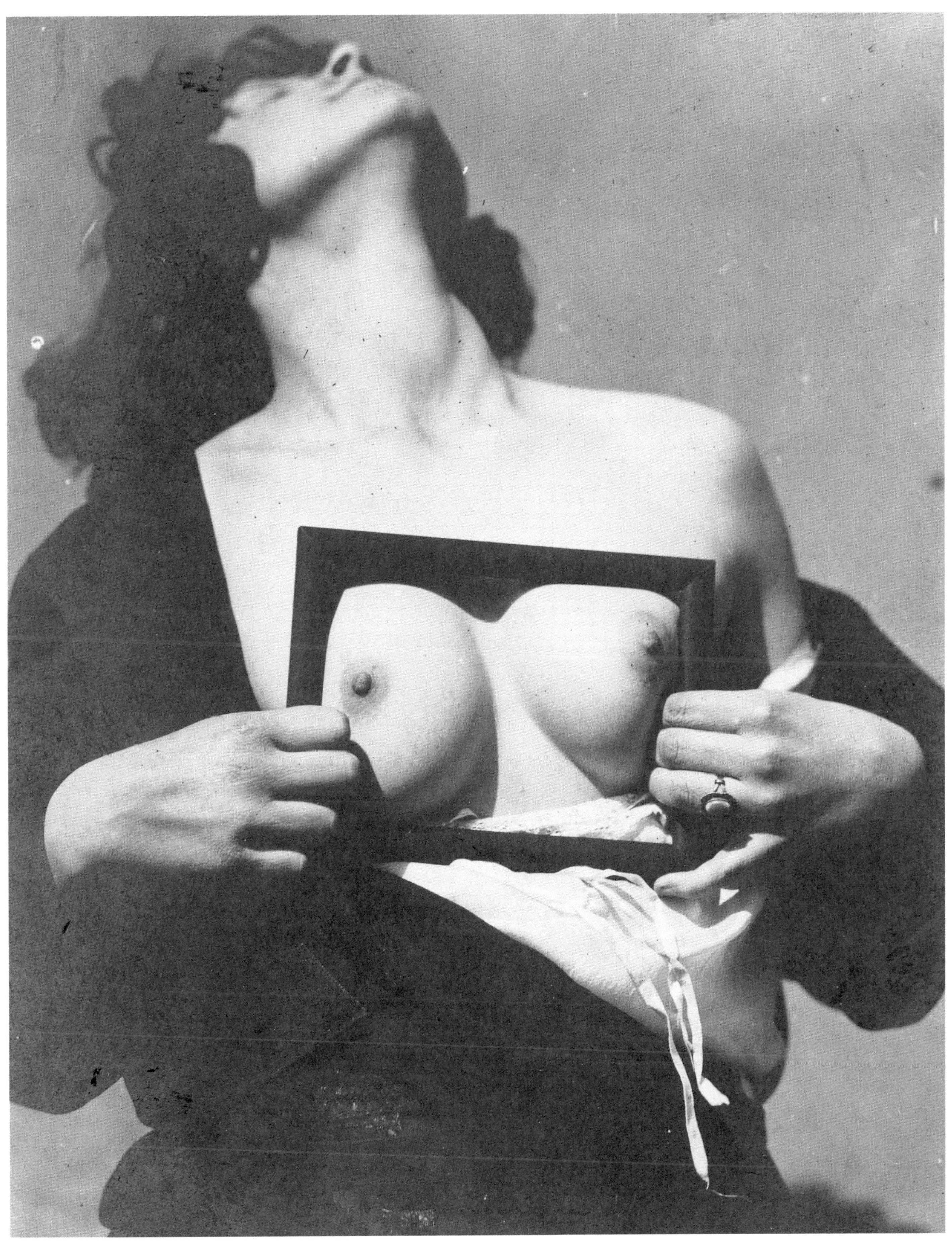

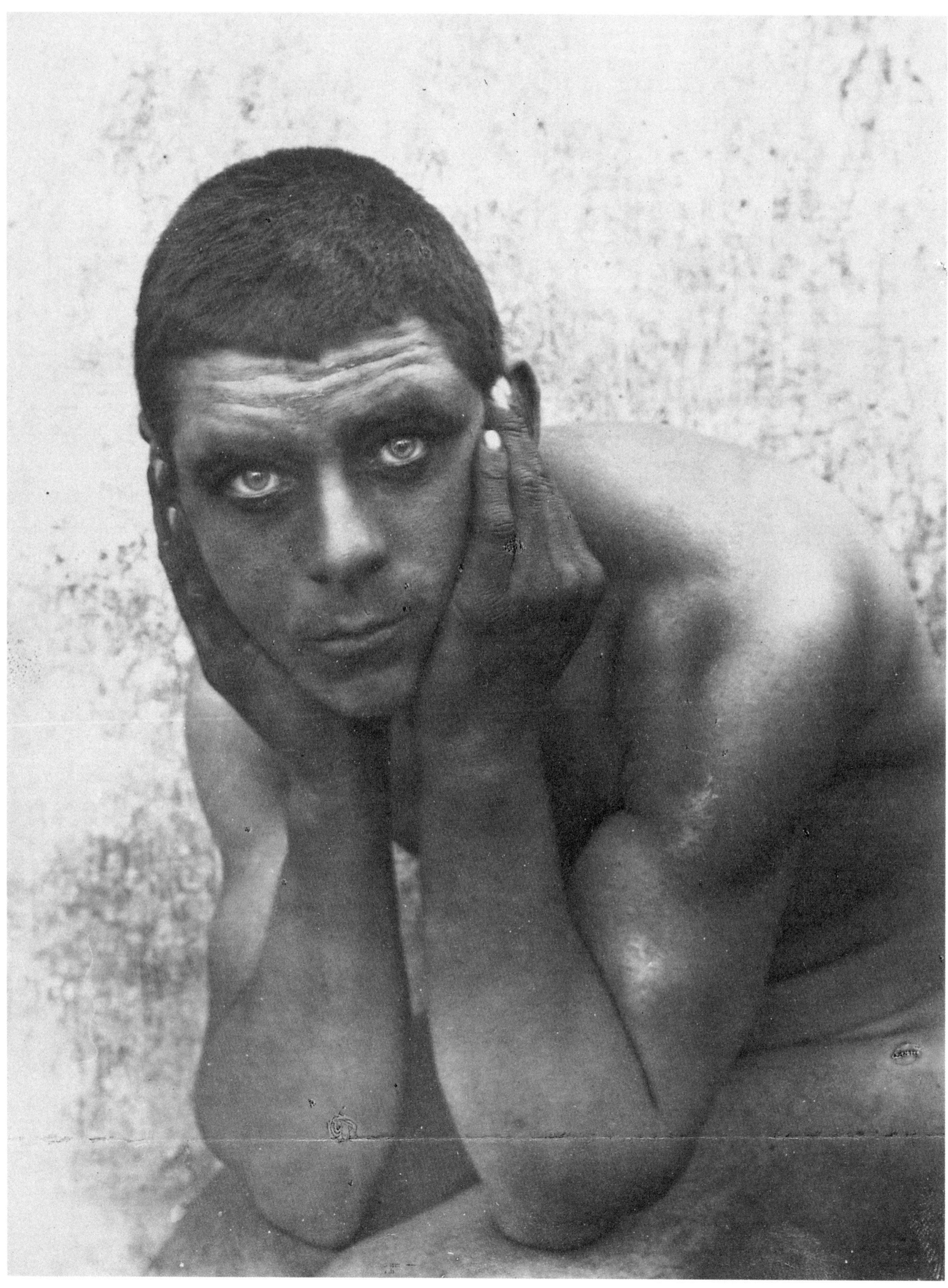

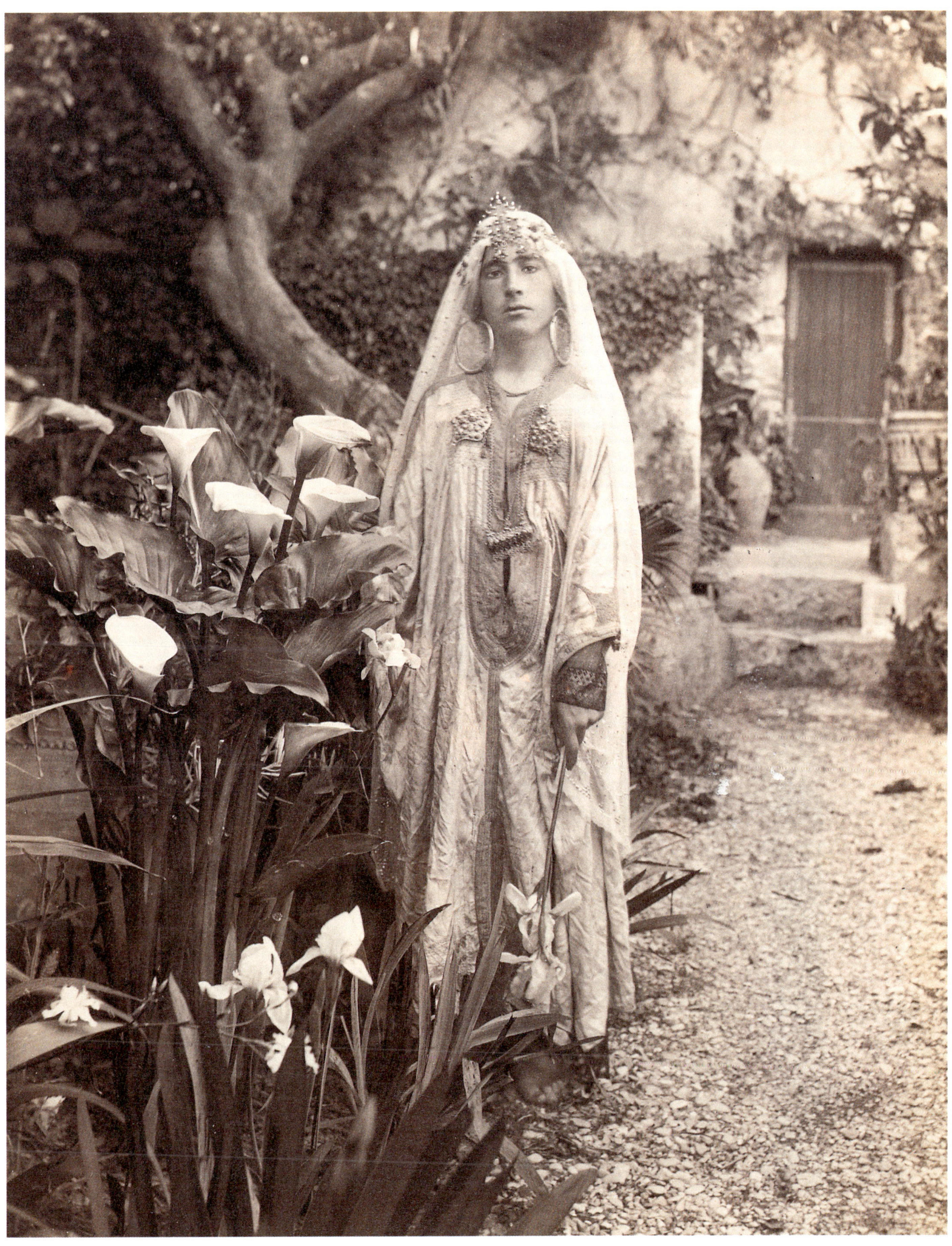

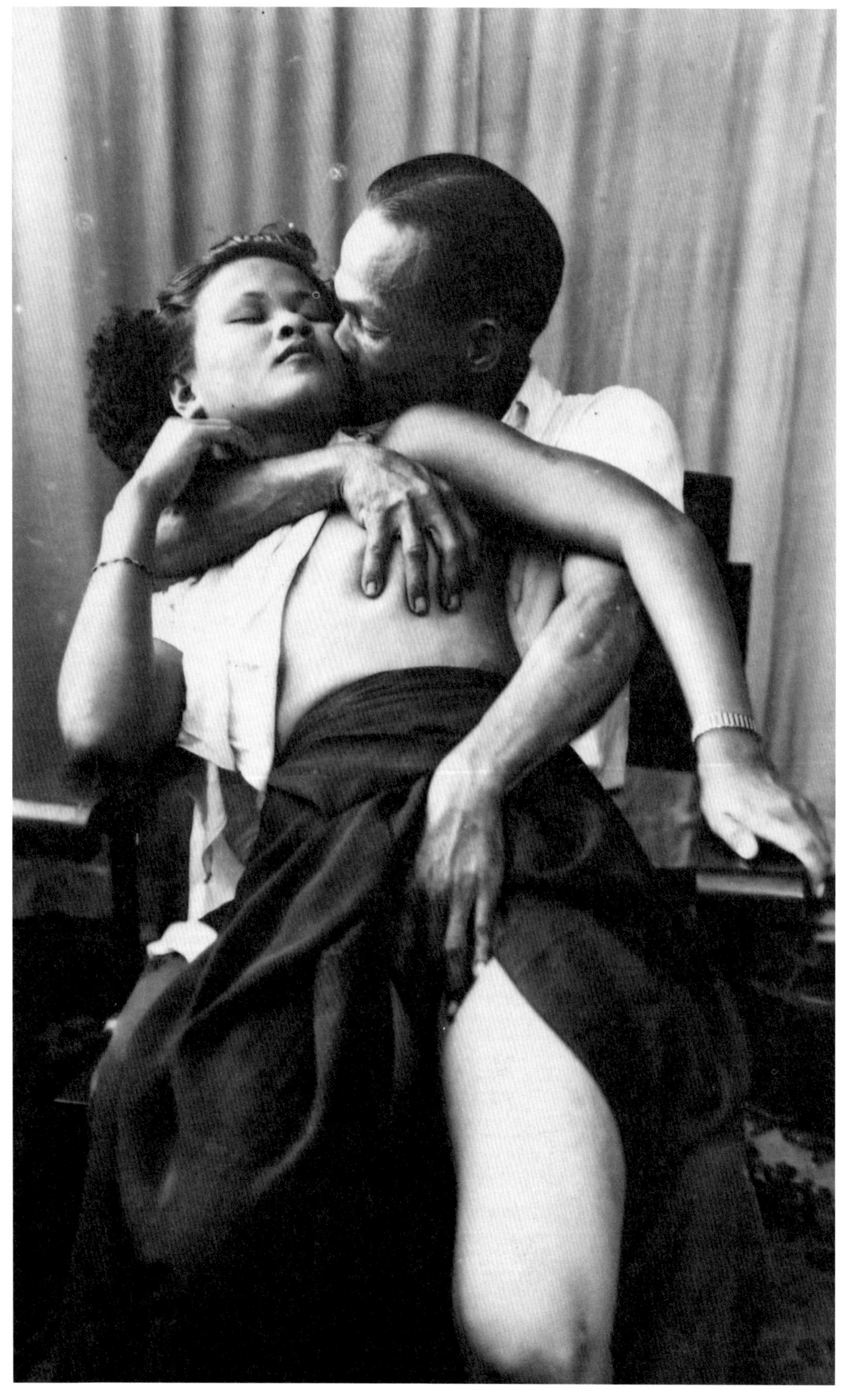

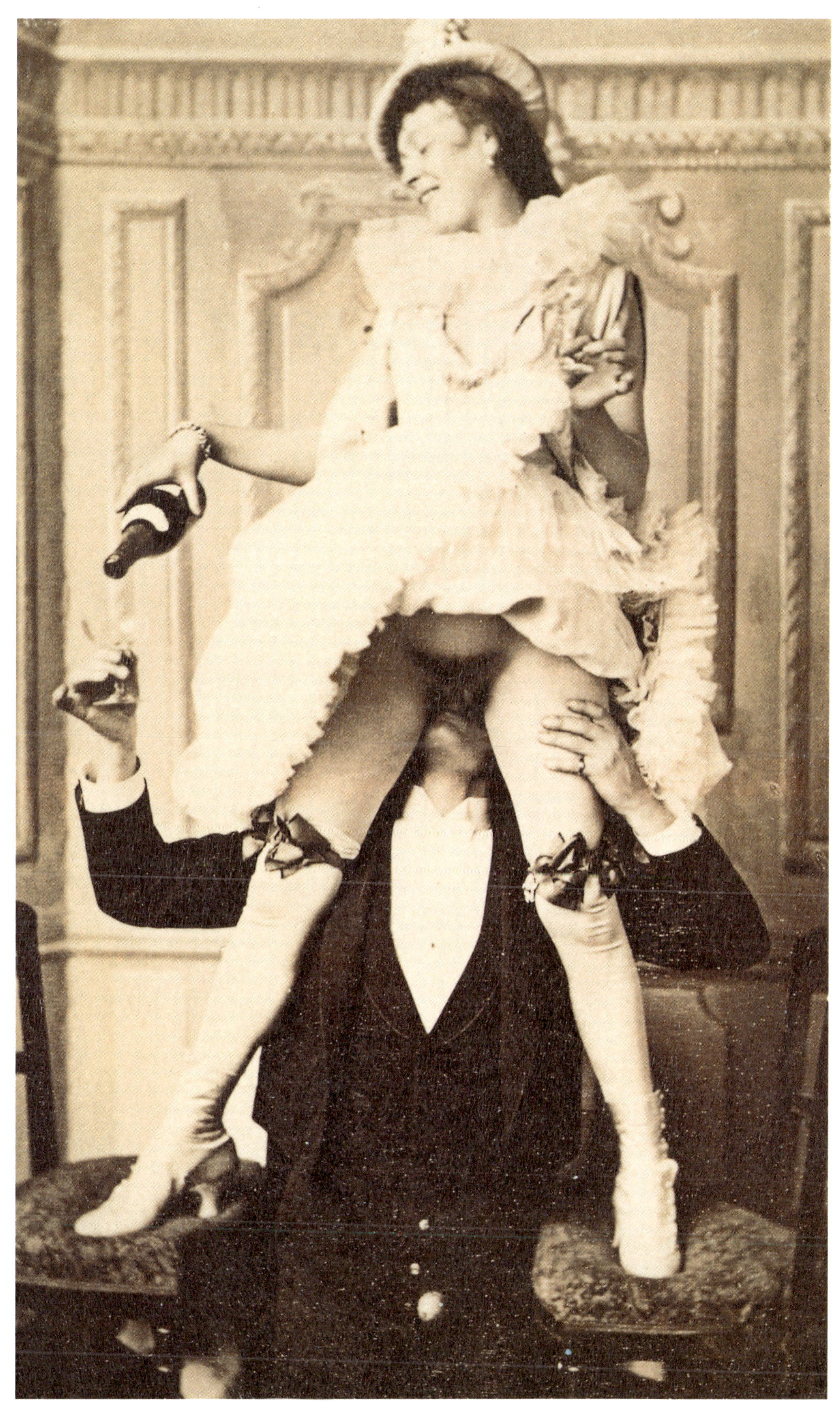

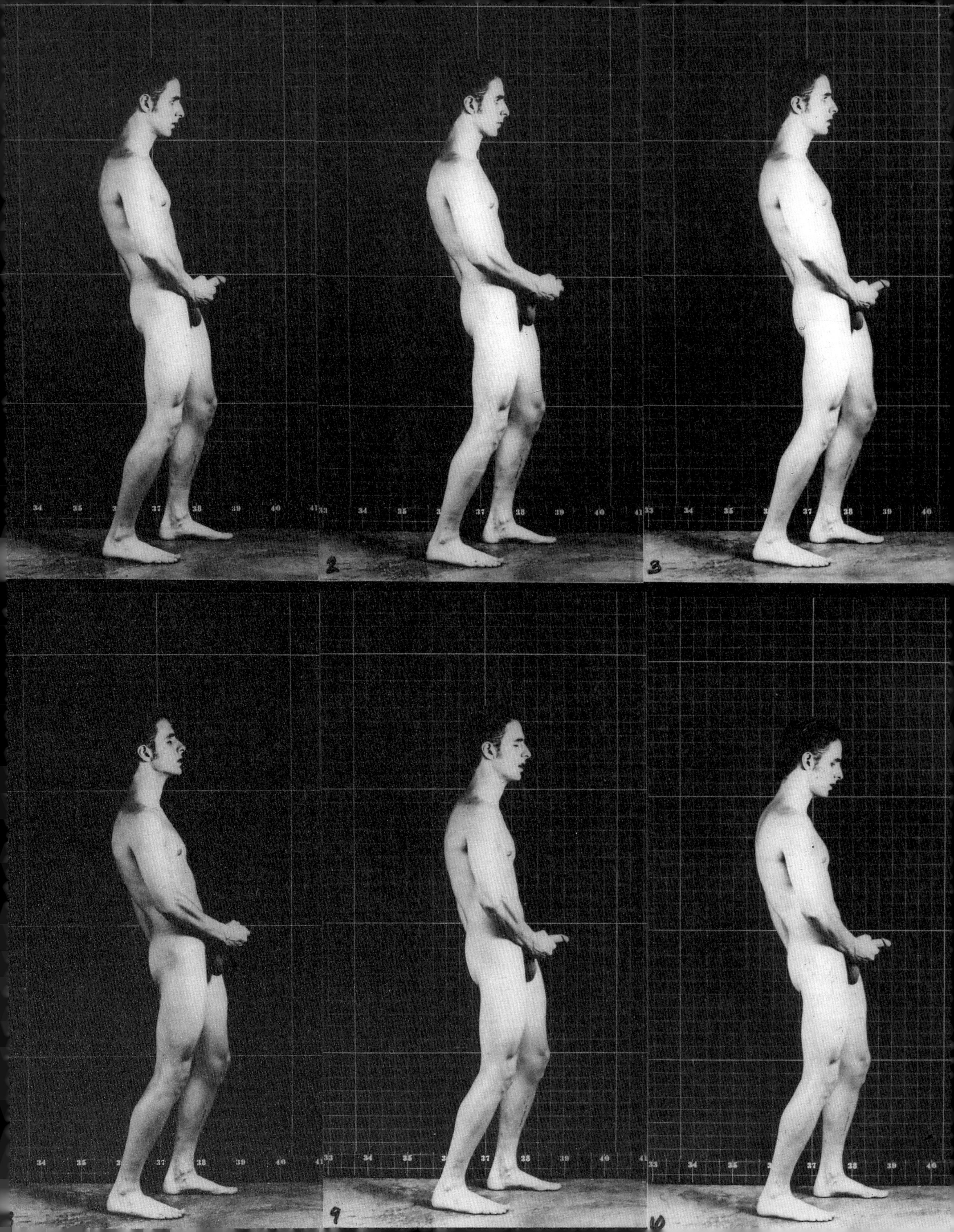

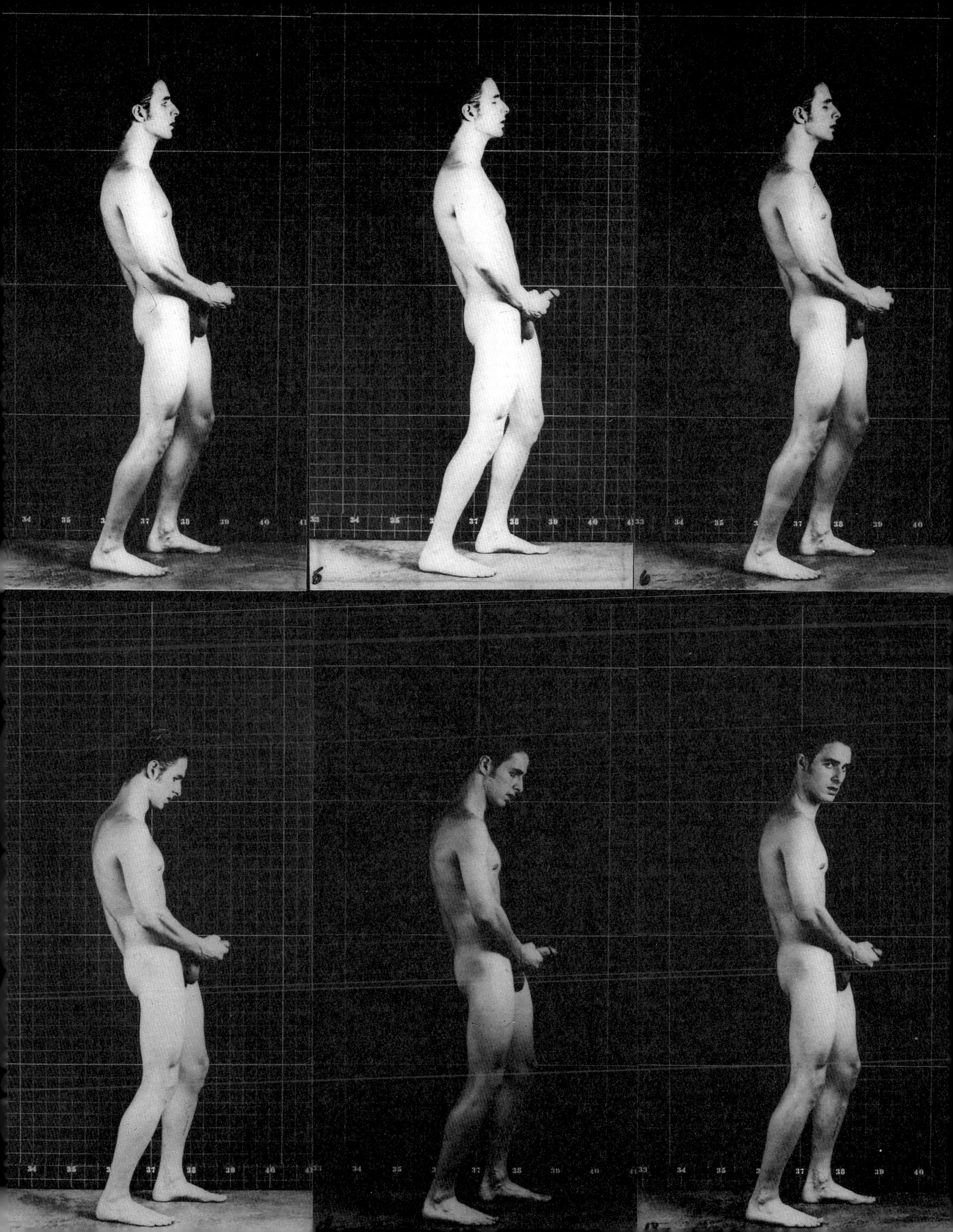

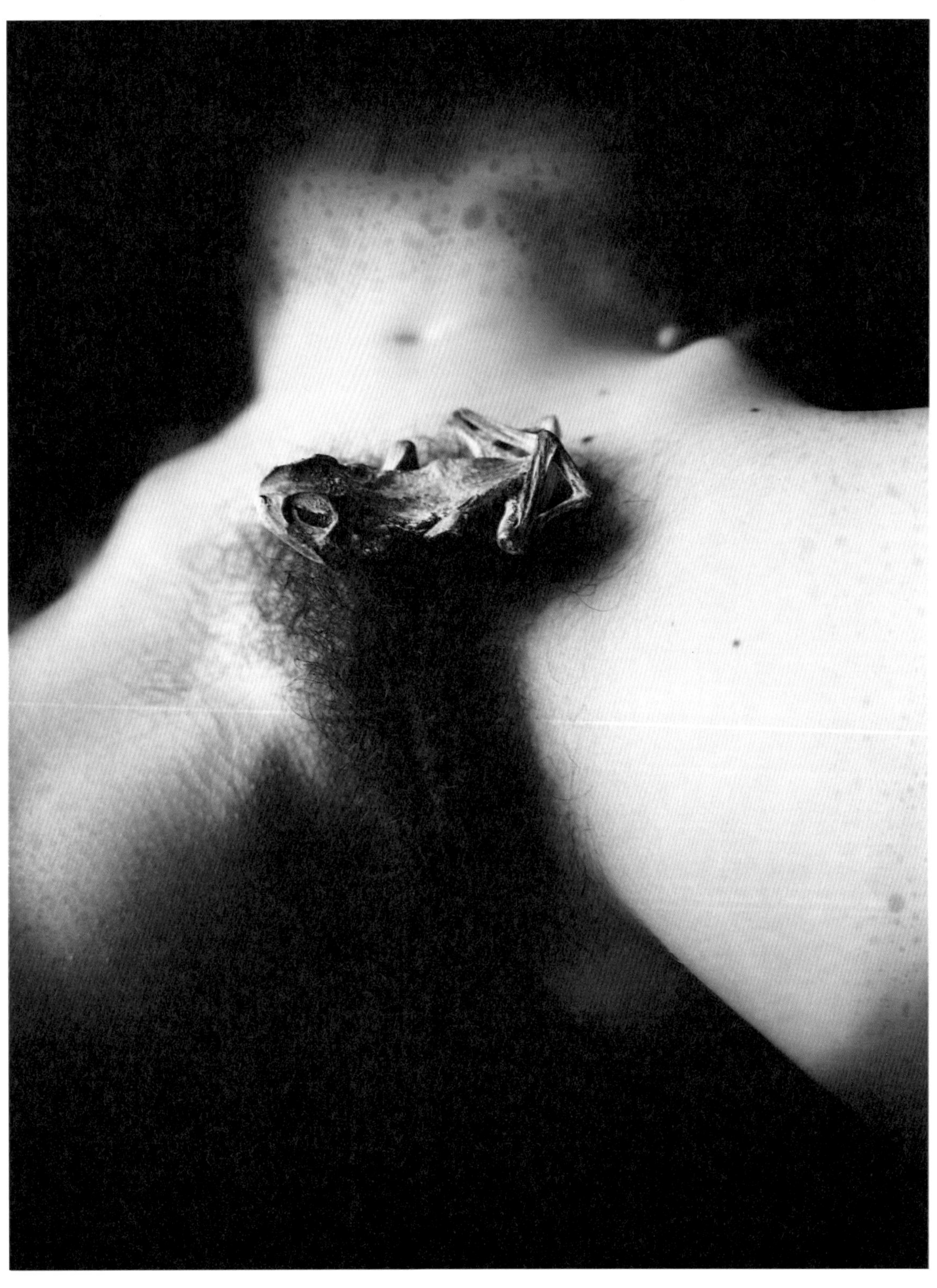

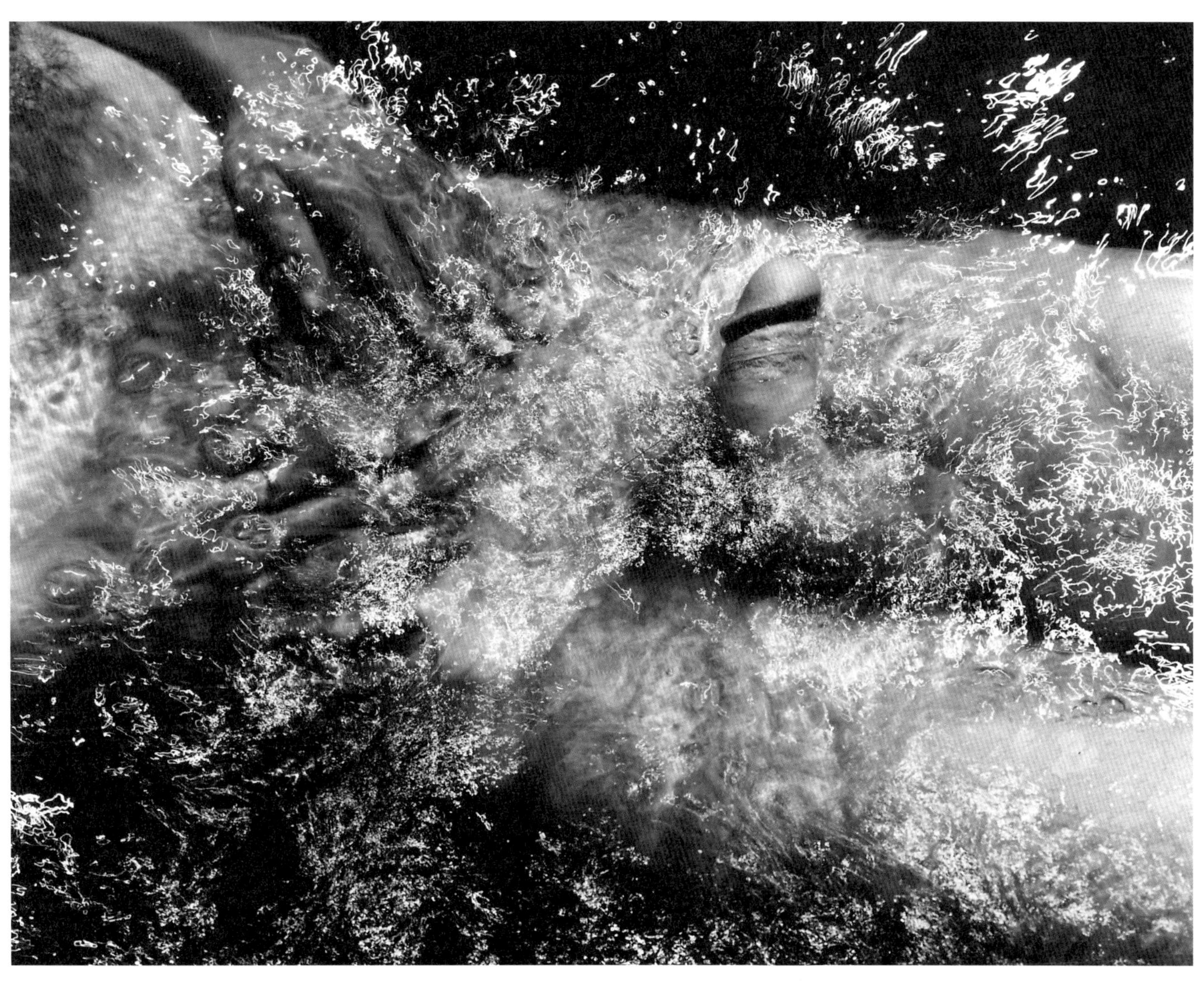

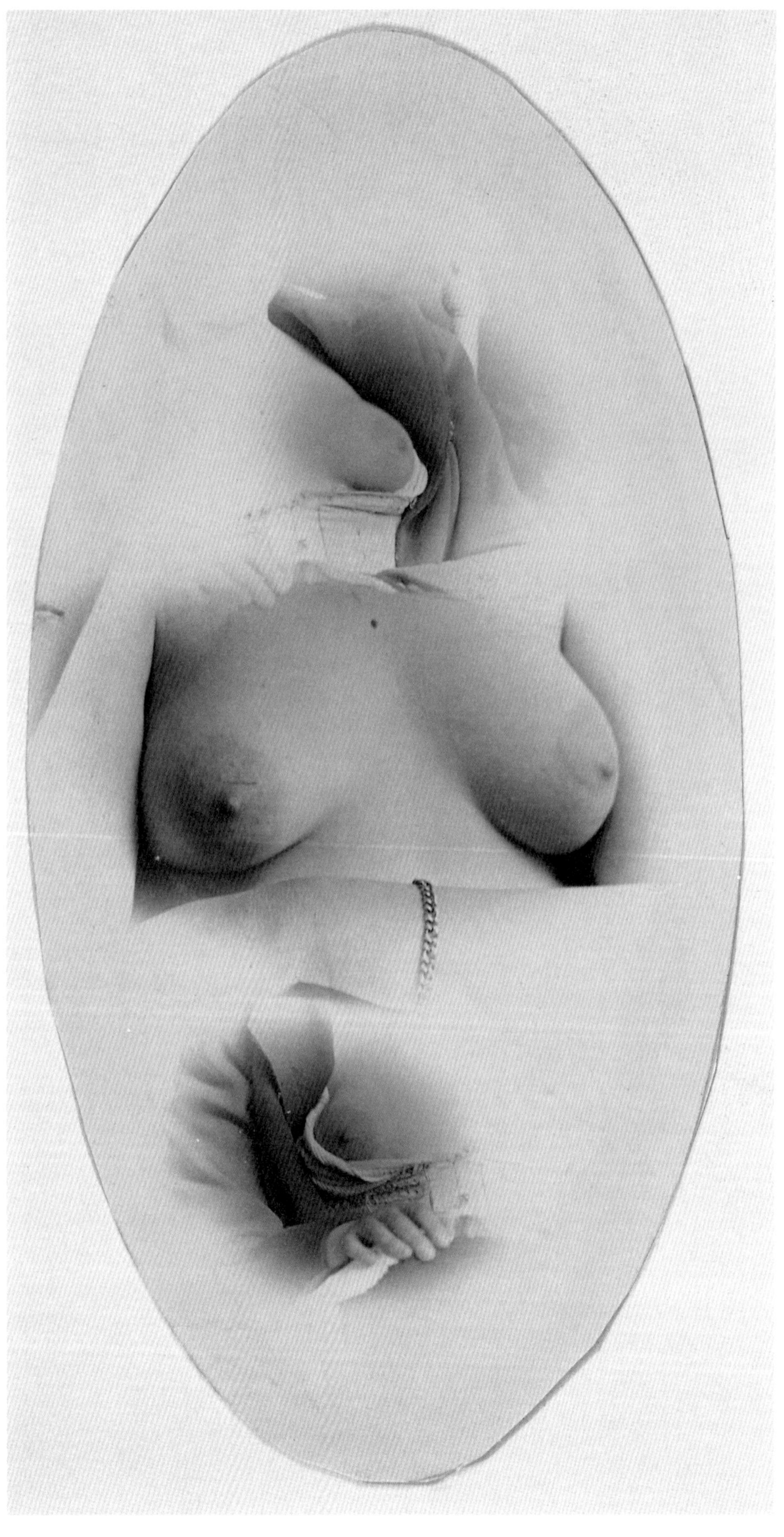

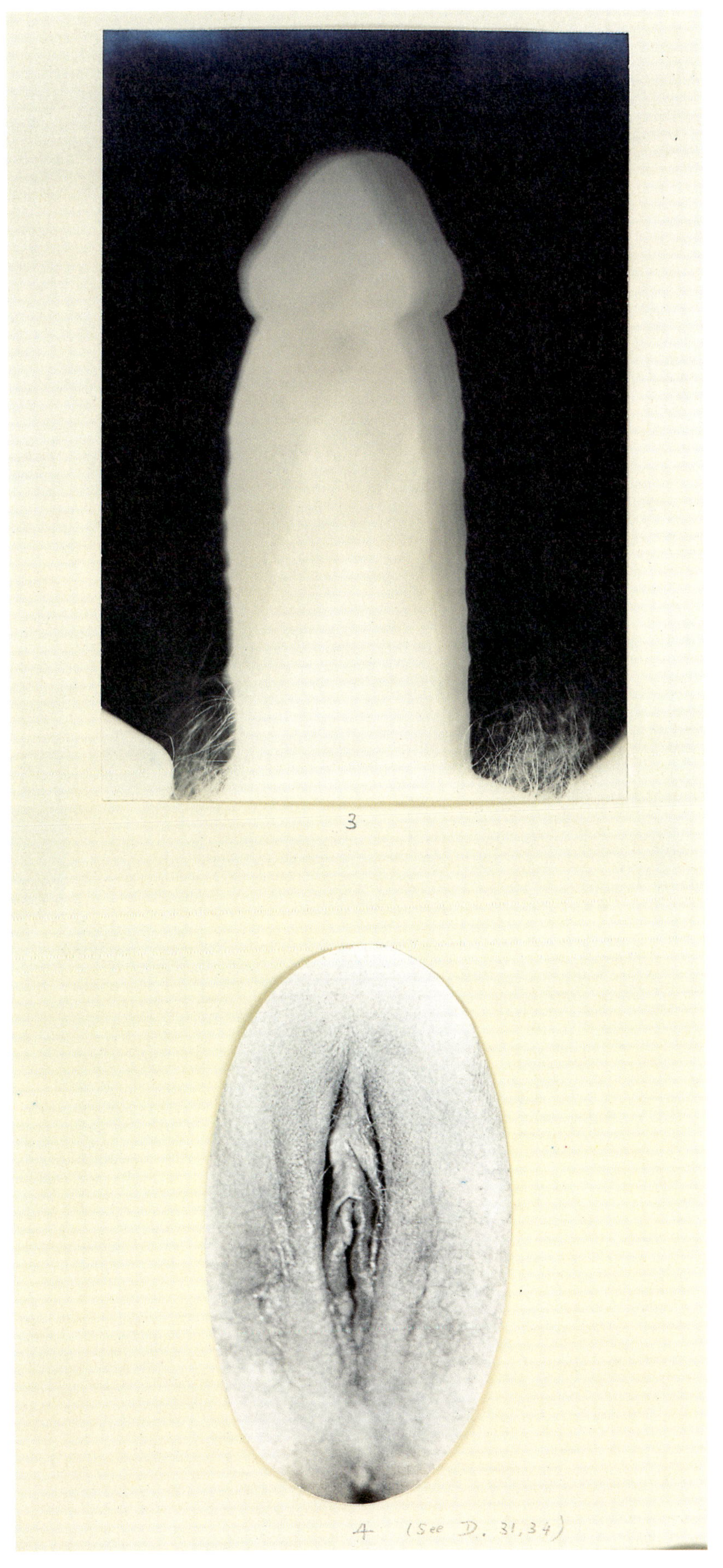

3

4 (see D. 31,34)

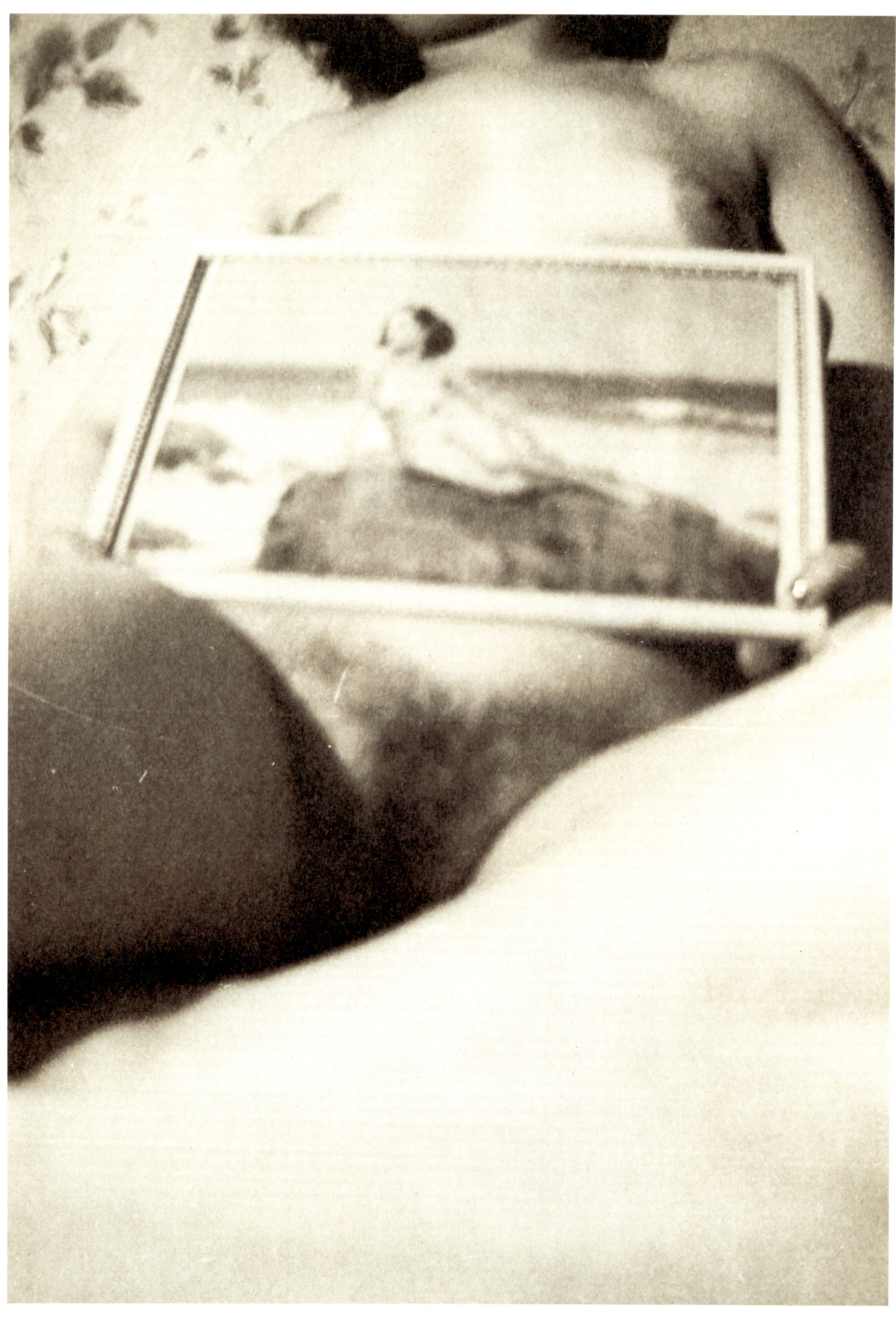

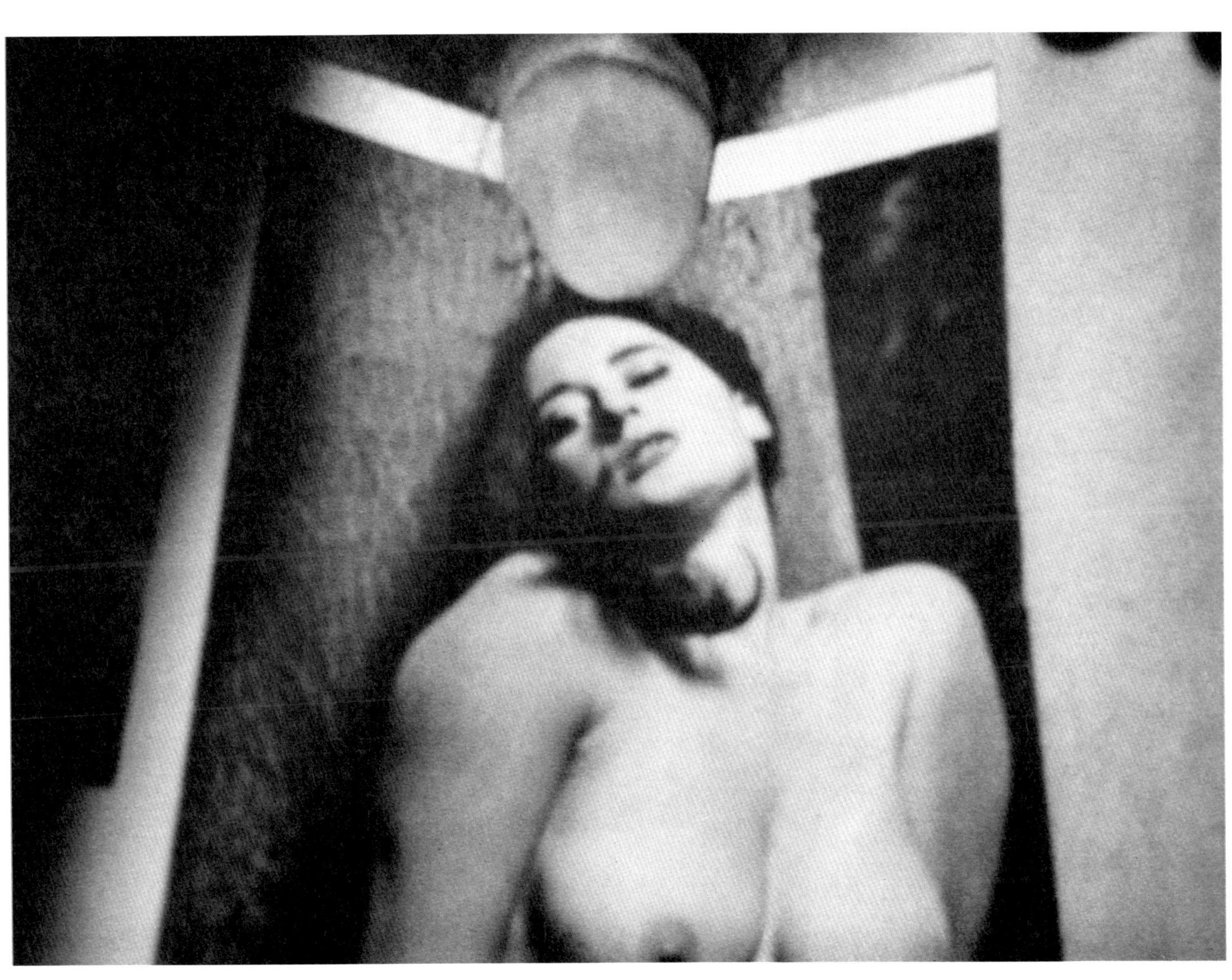

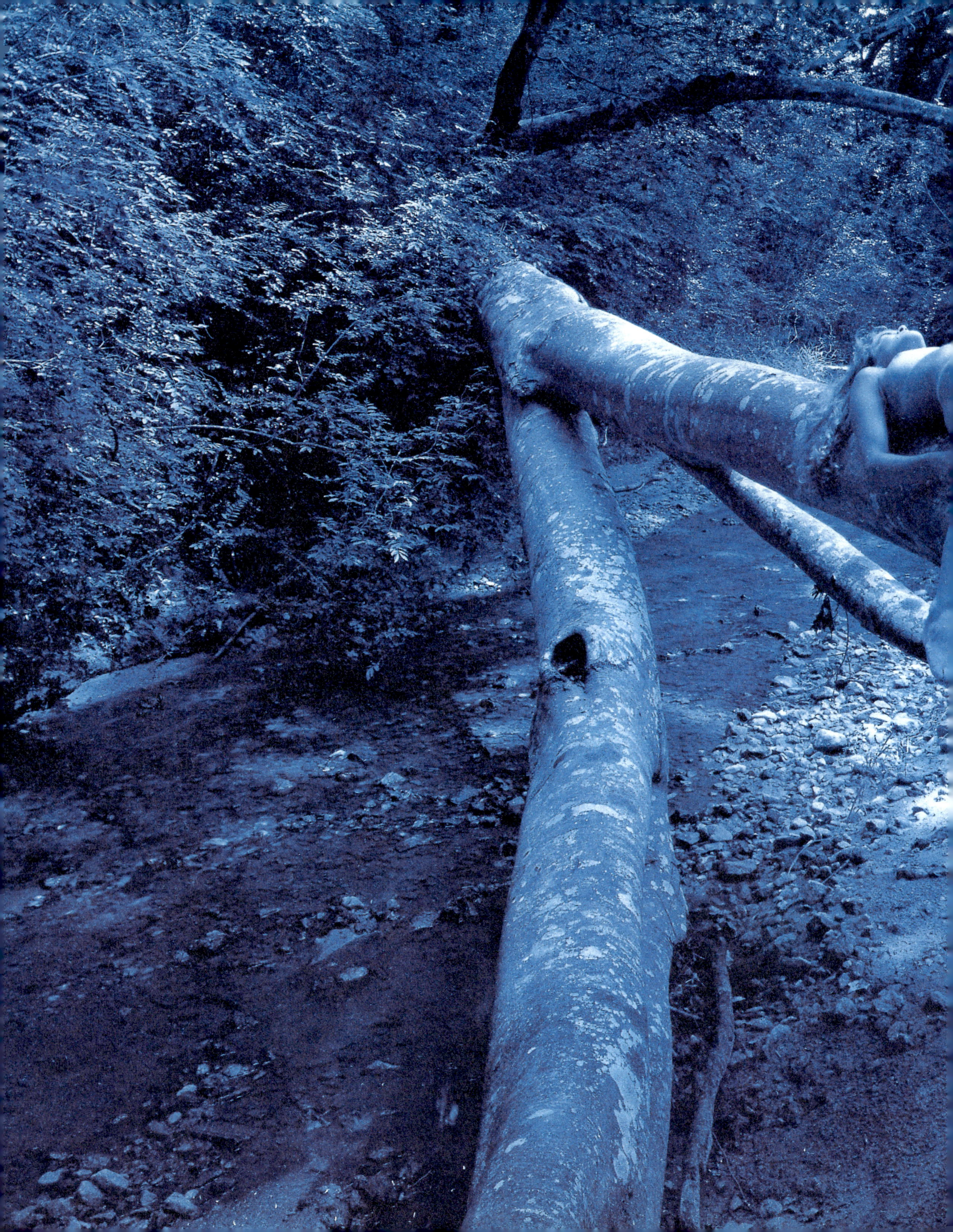

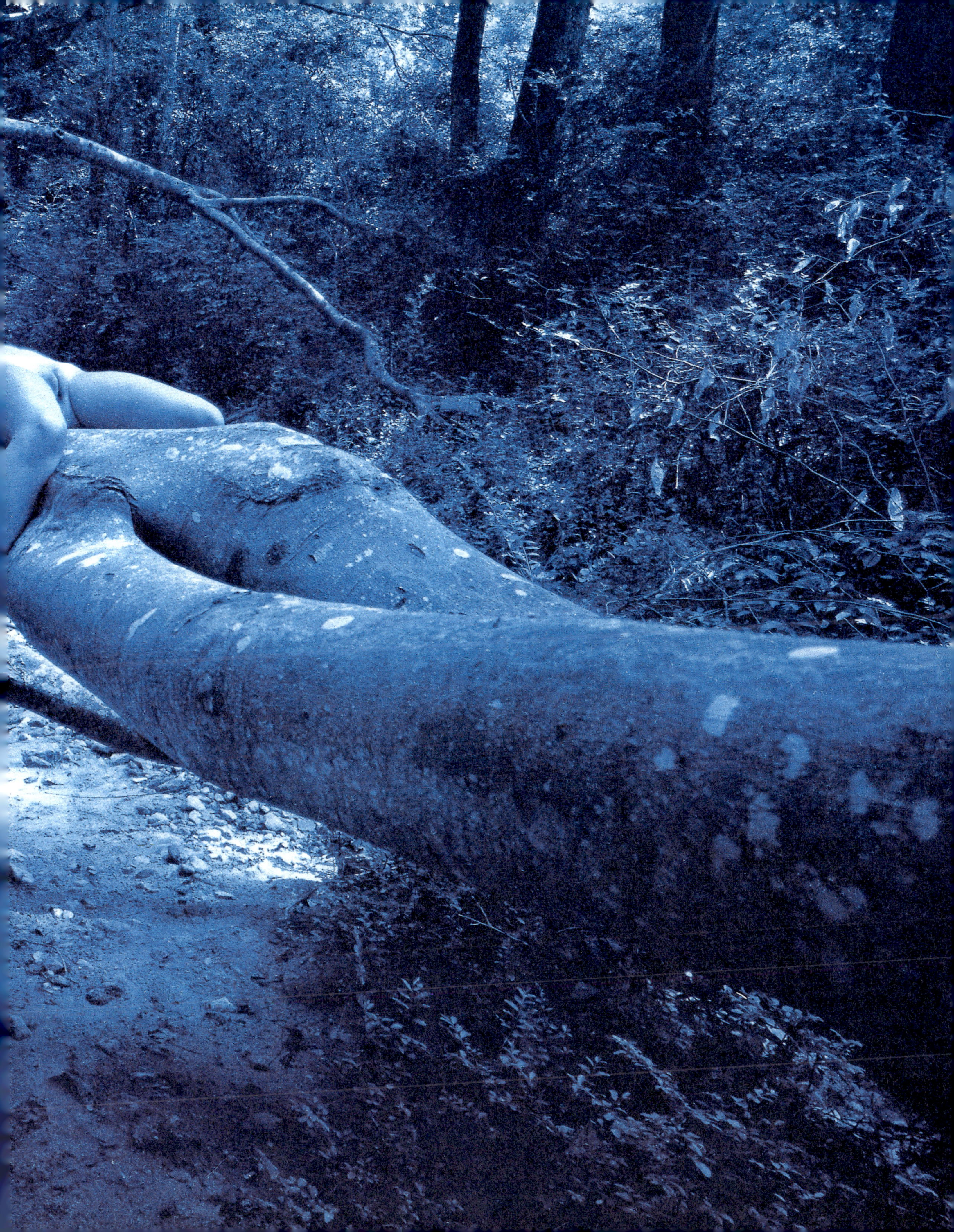

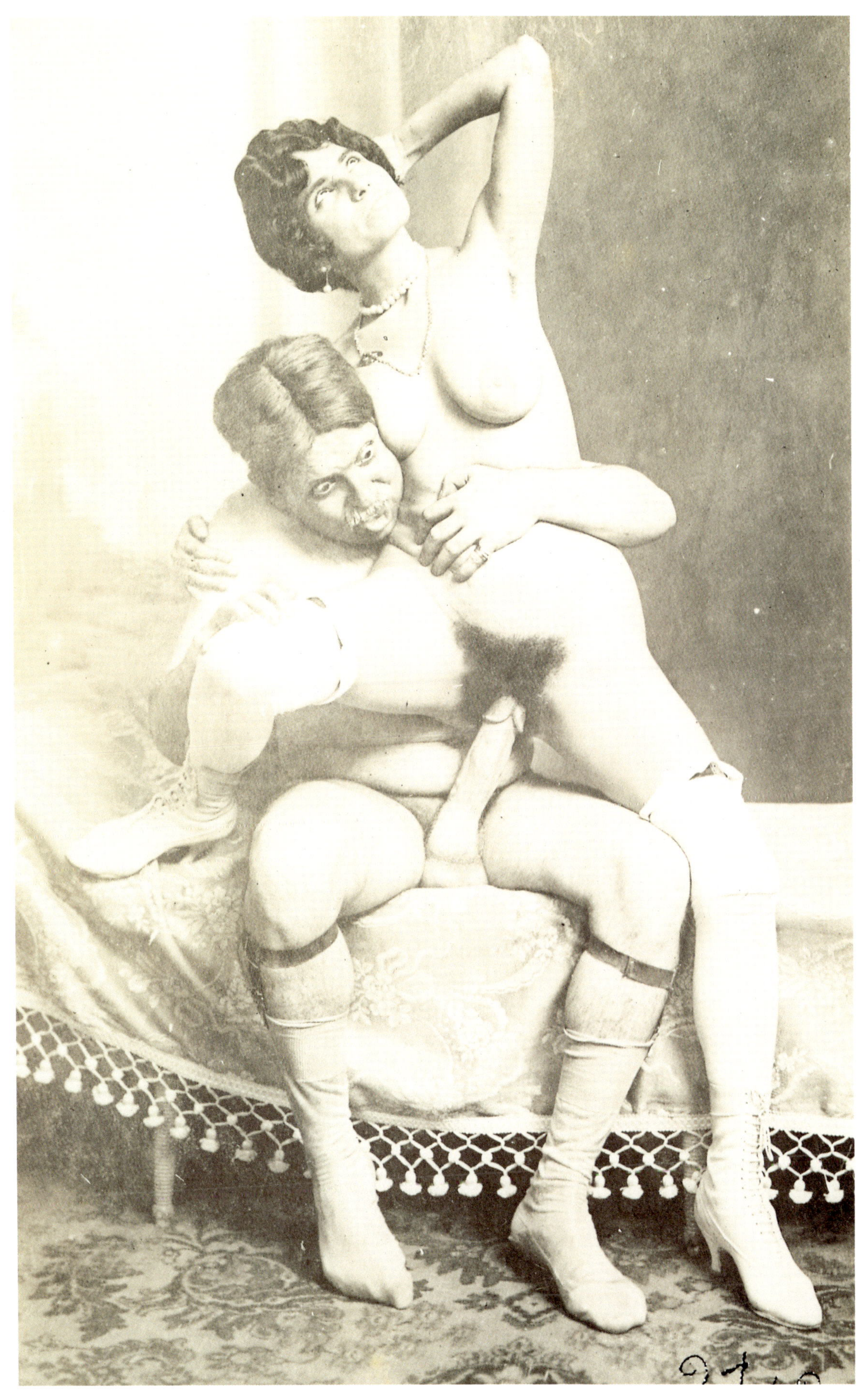

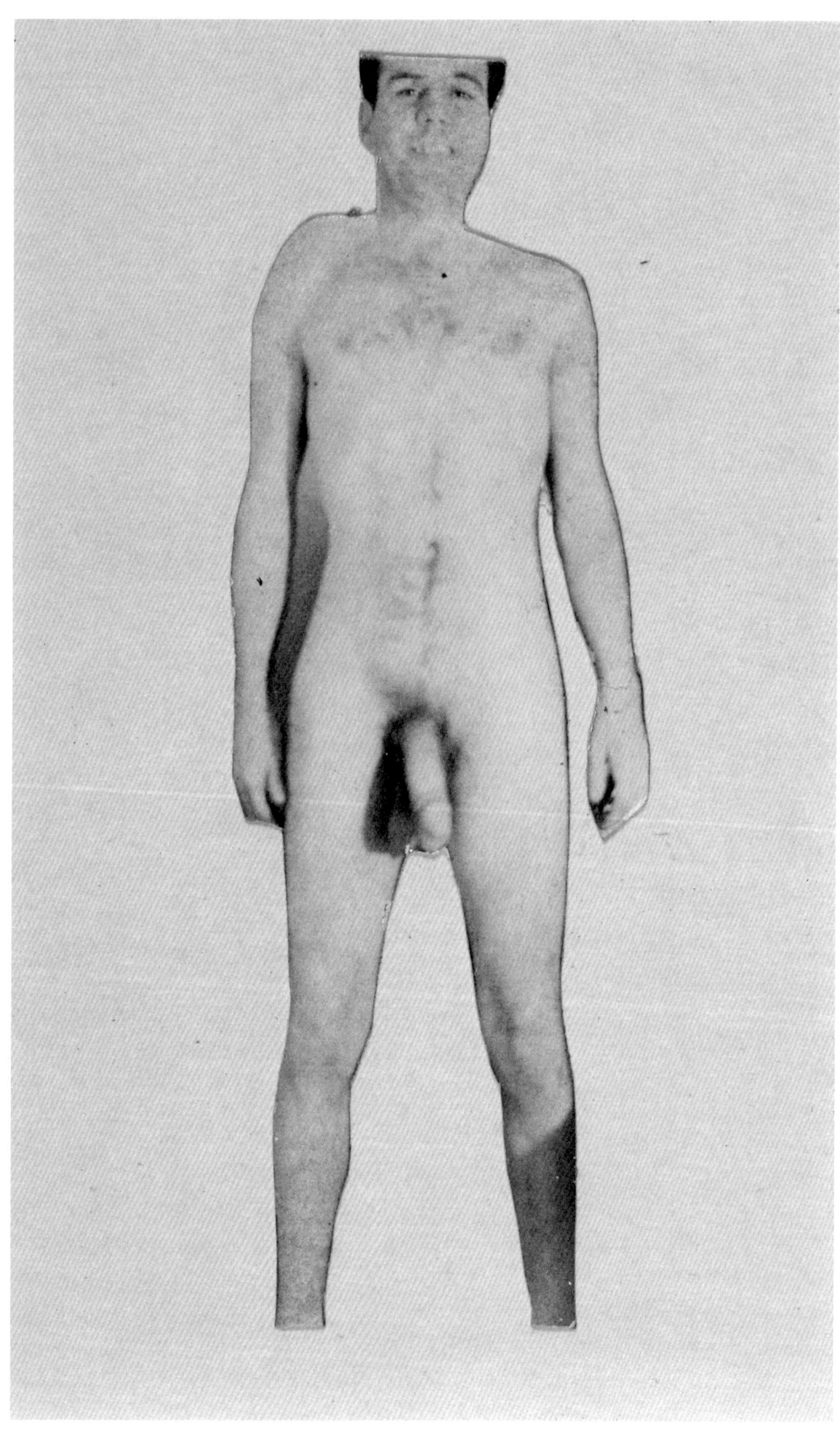

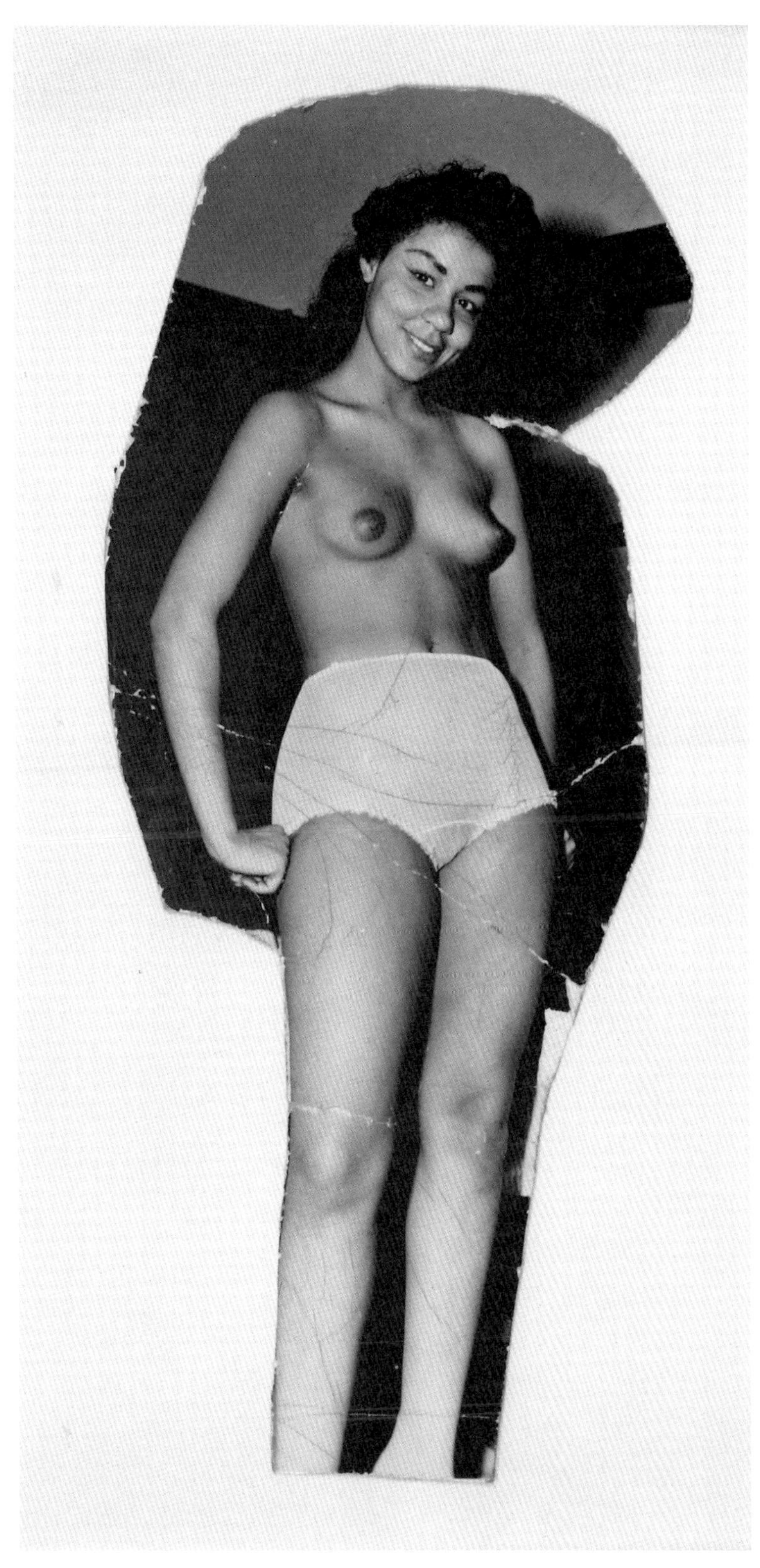

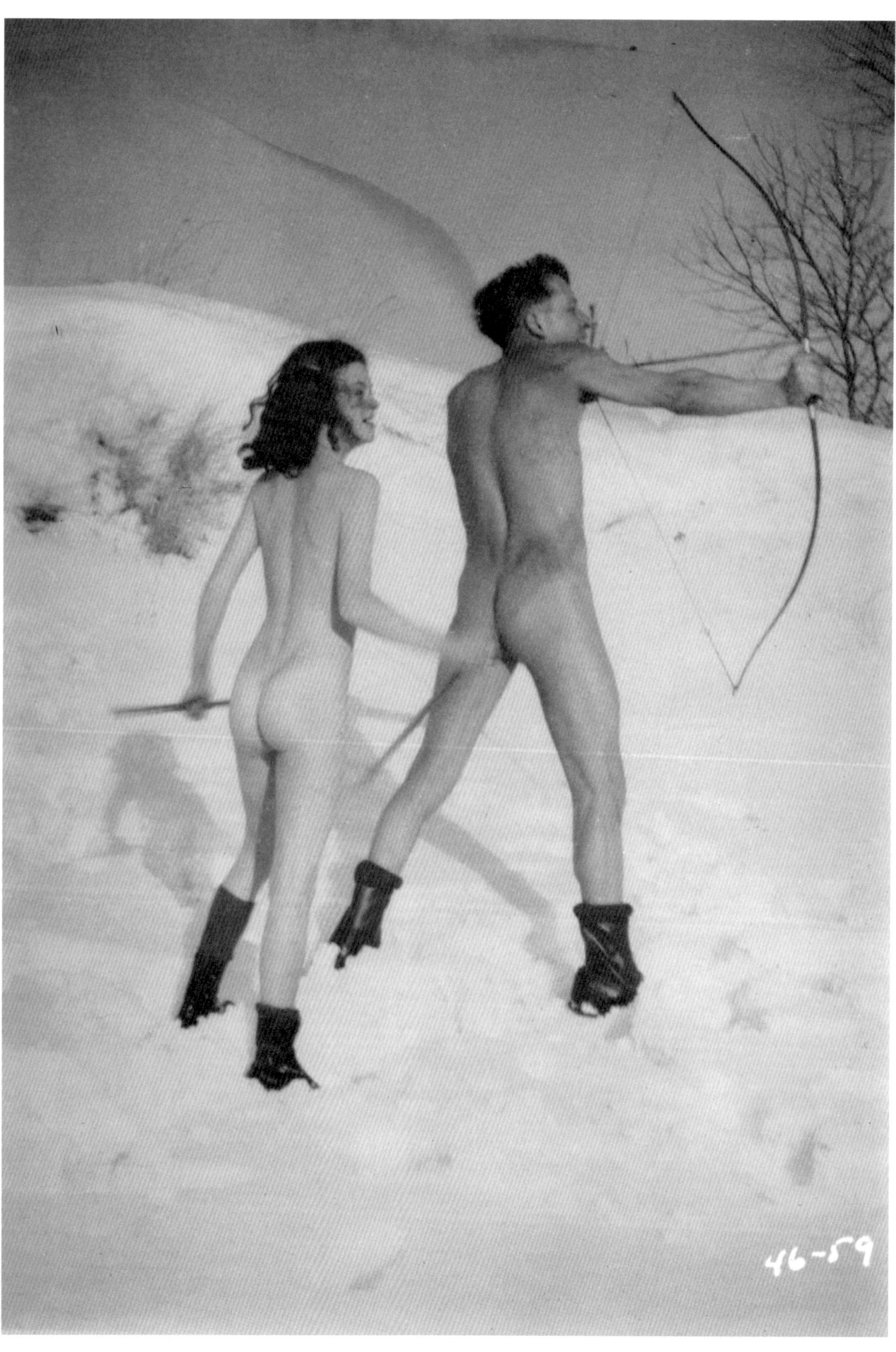

46-59

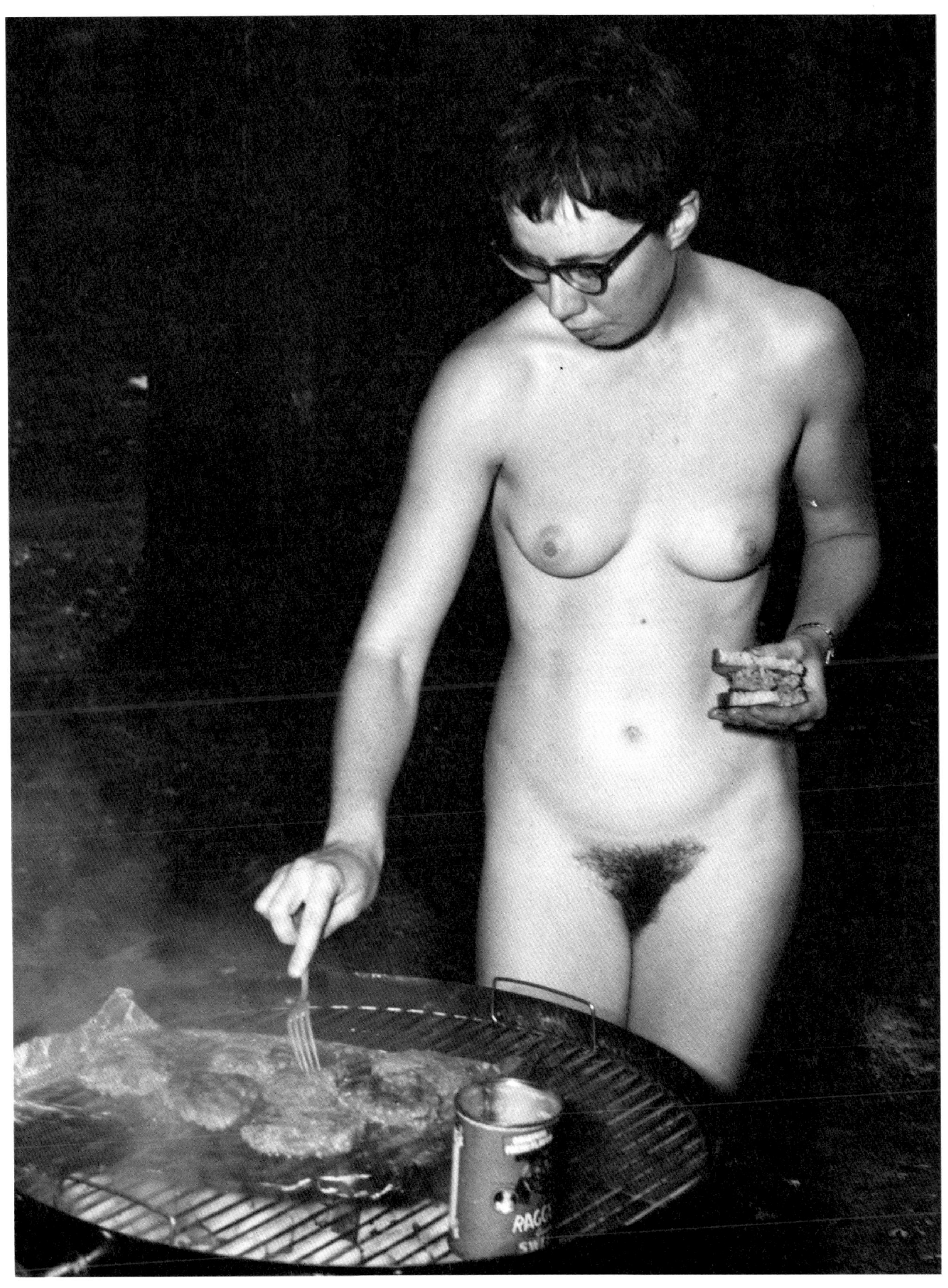

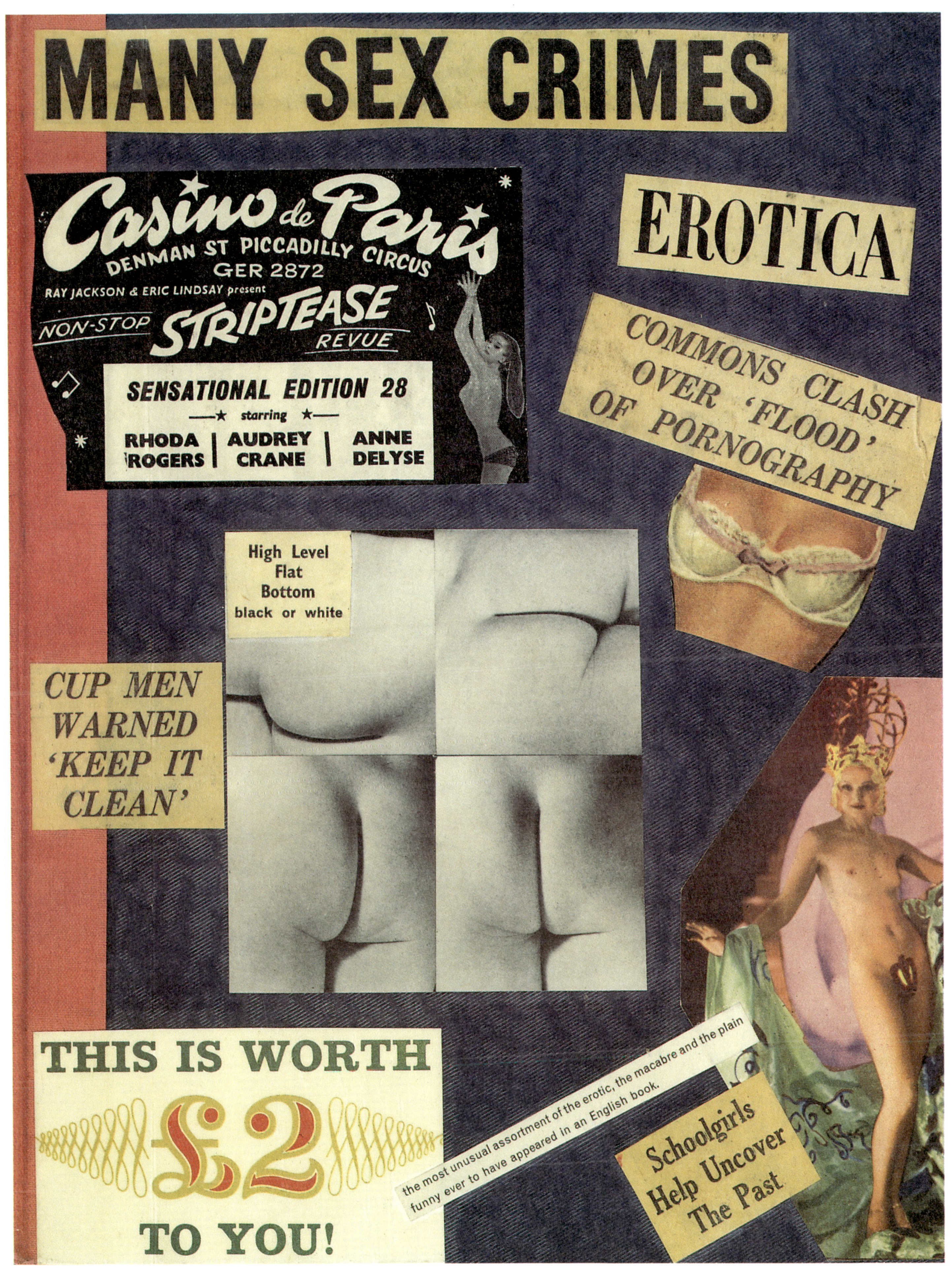
MANY SEX CRIMES
Casino de Paris
DENMAN ST PICCADILLY CIRCUS
GER 2872
RAY JACKSON & ERIC LINDSAY present
NON-STOP STRIPTEASE REVUE
SENSATIONAL EDITION 28
starring
RHODA ROGERS | AUDREY CRANE | ANNE DELYSE
EROTICA
COMMONS CLASH OVER 'FLOOD' OF PORNOGRAPHY
High Level
Flat
Bottom
black or white
CUP MEN WARNED 'KEEP IT CLEAN'
THIS IS WORTH £2 TO YOU!
the most unusual assortment of the erotic, the macabre and the plain
funny ever to have appeared in an English book.
Schoolgirls Help Uncover The Past

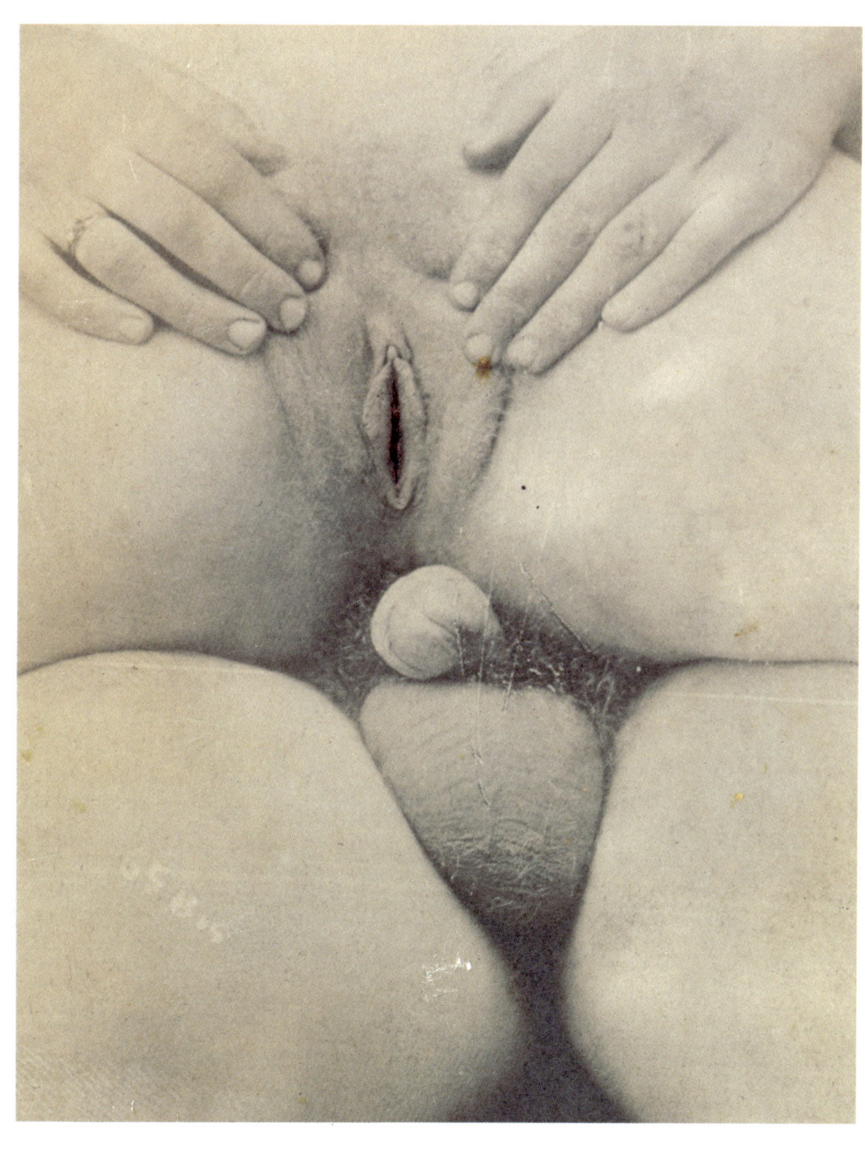

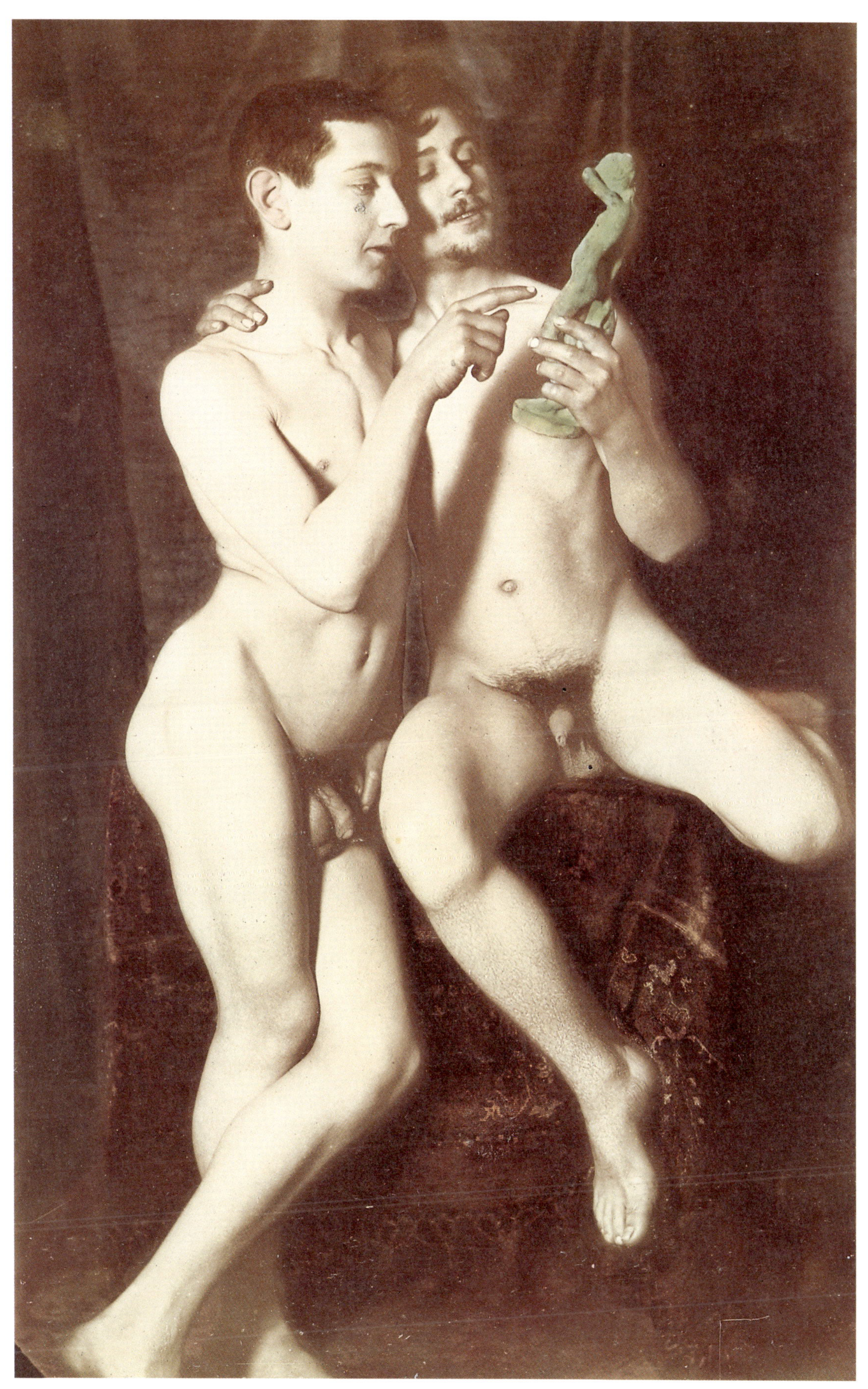

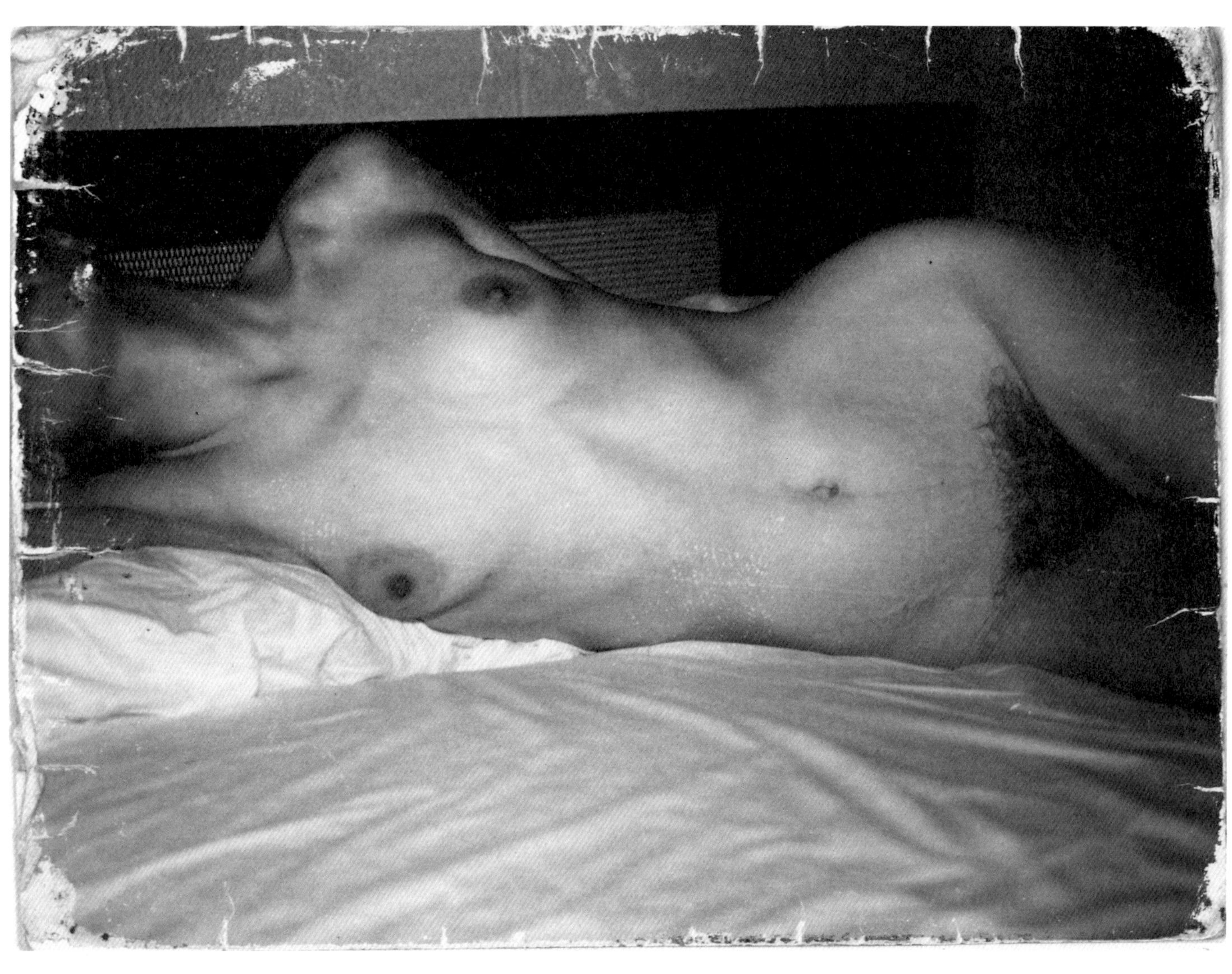

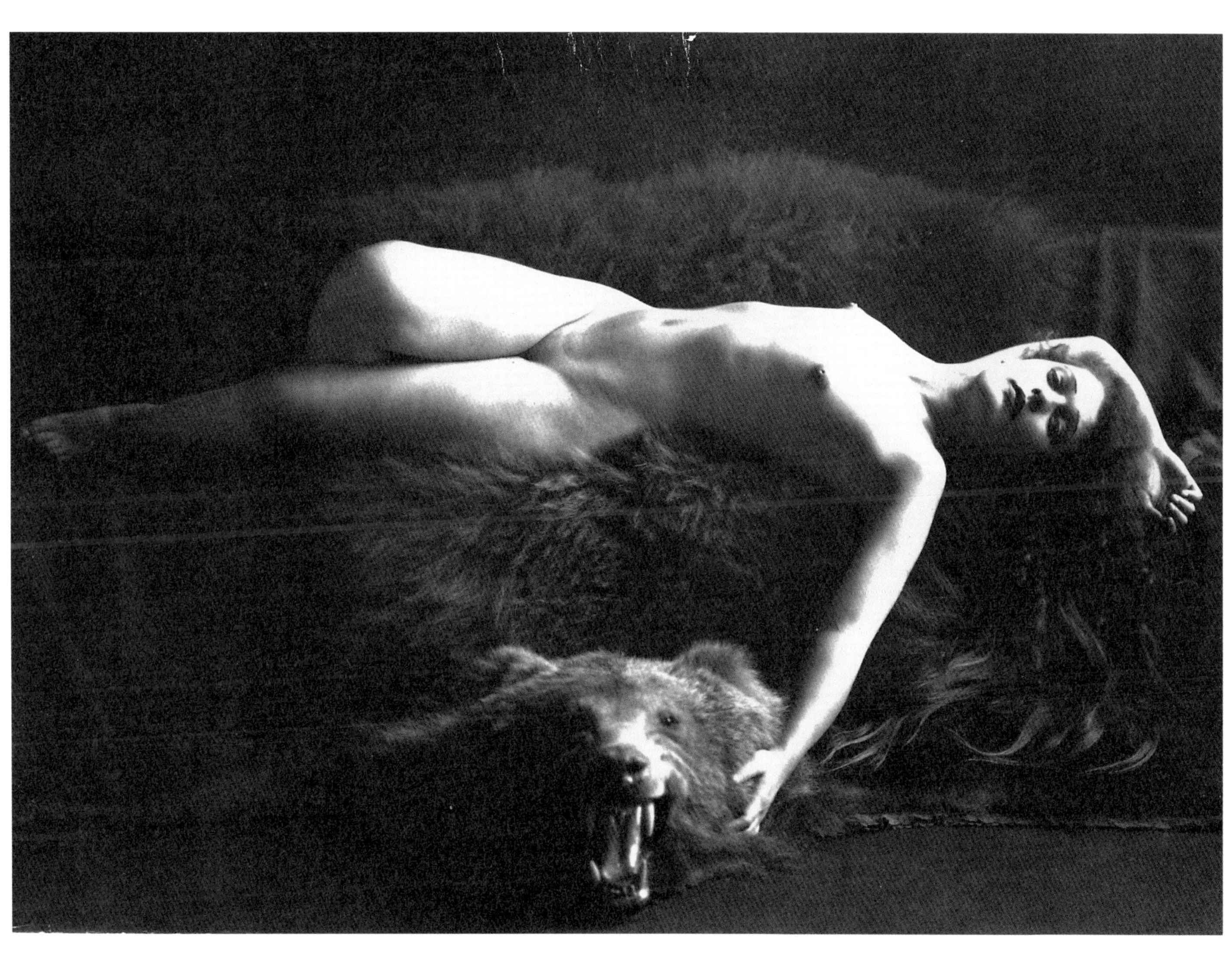

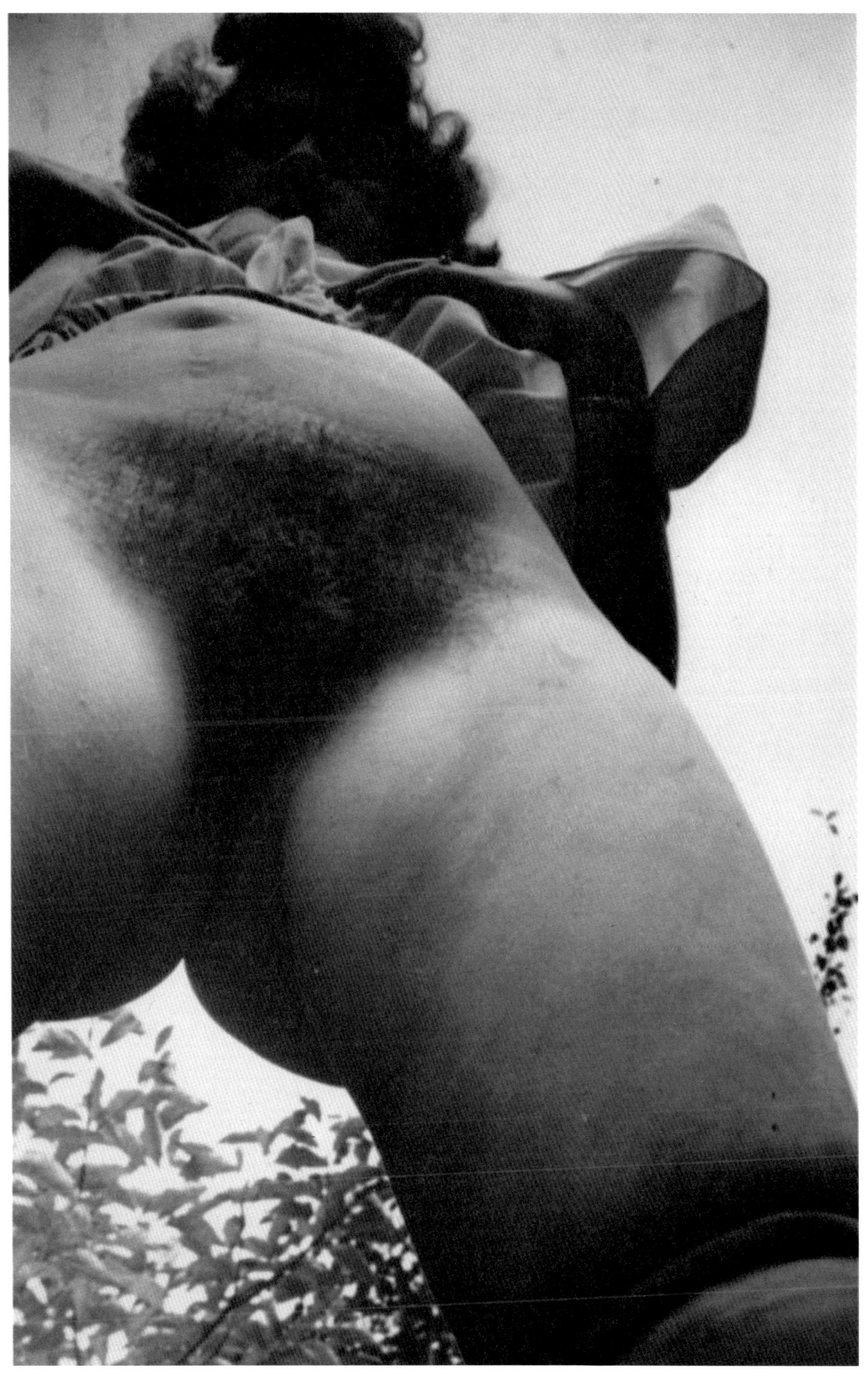

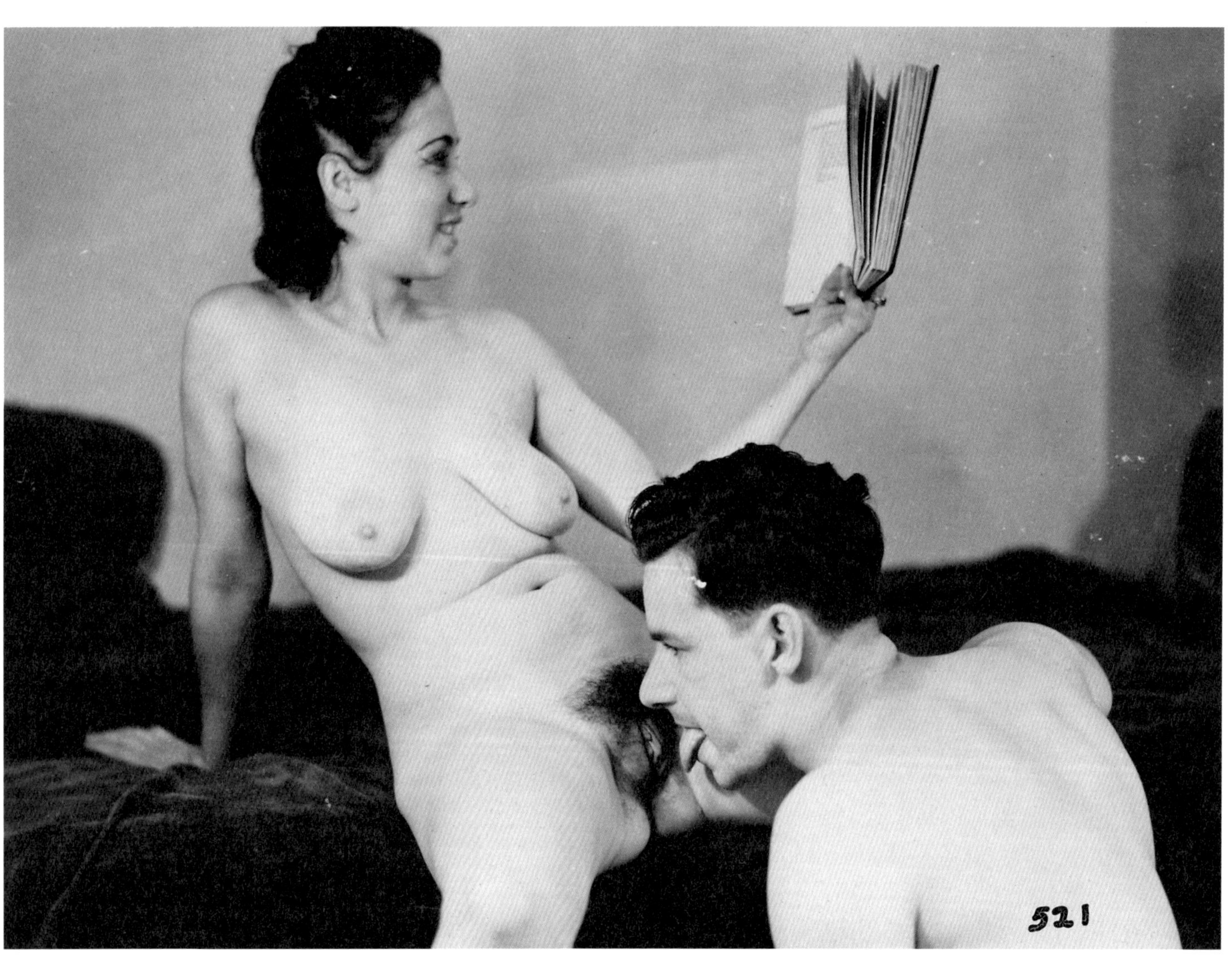

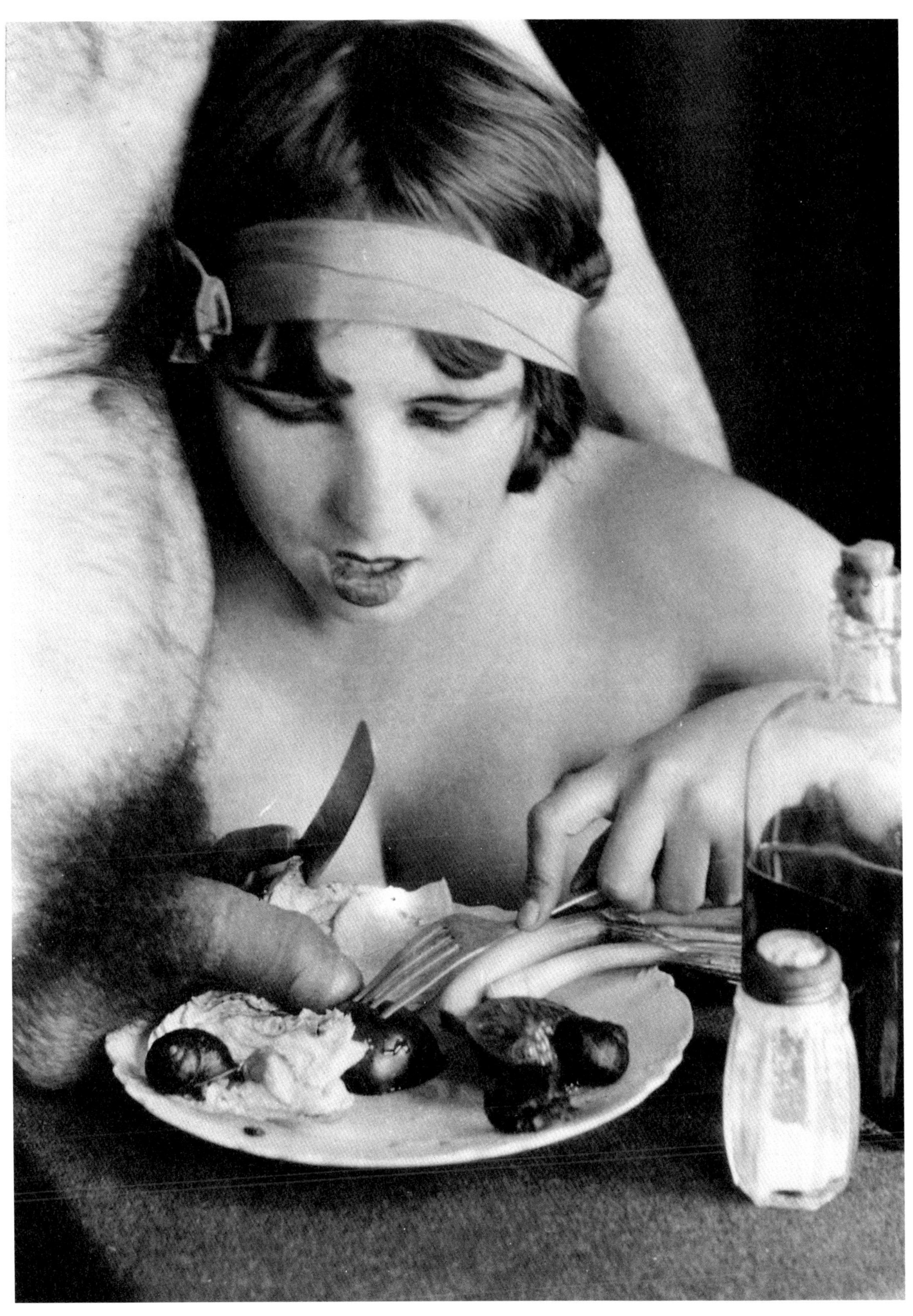

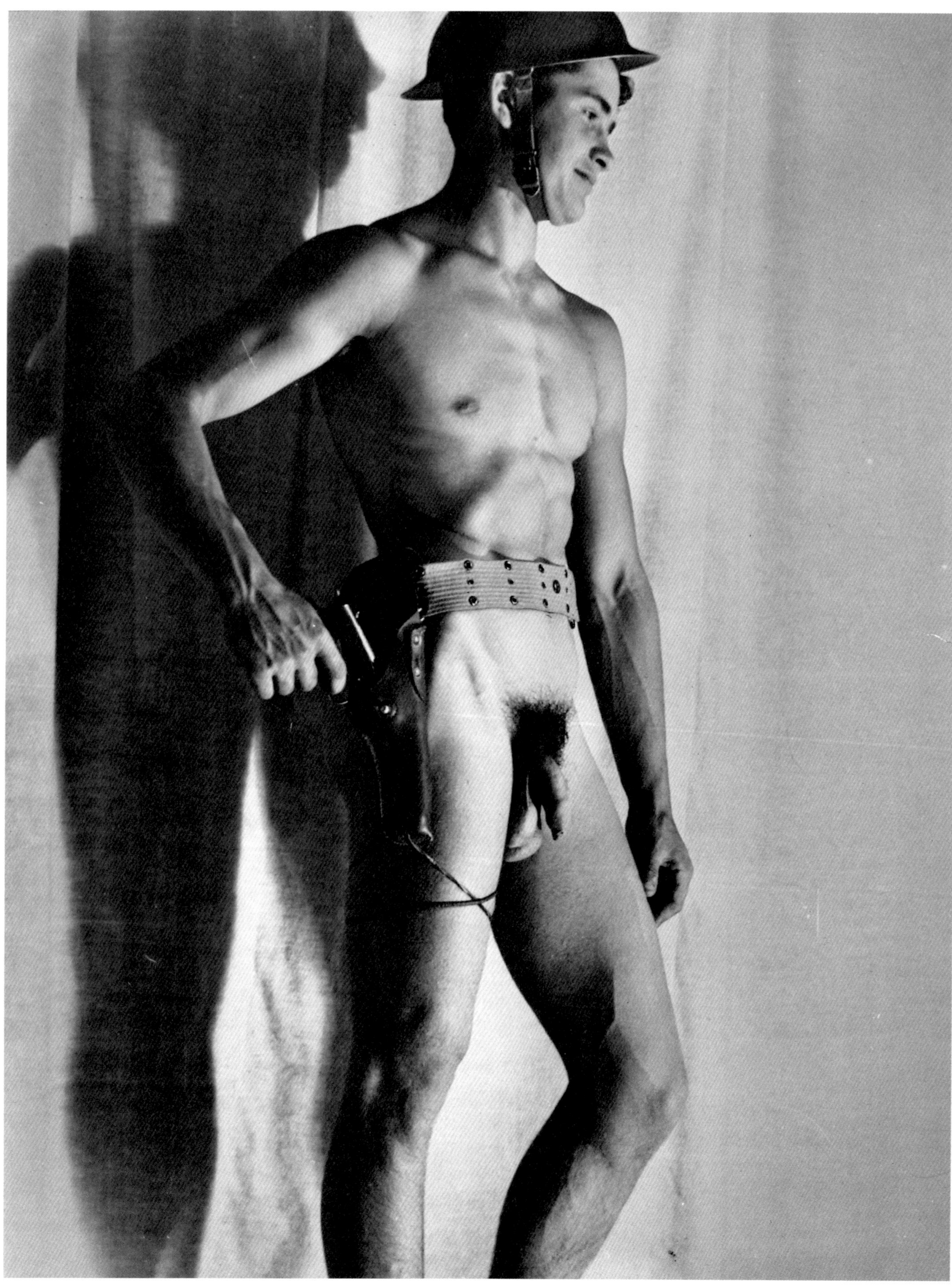

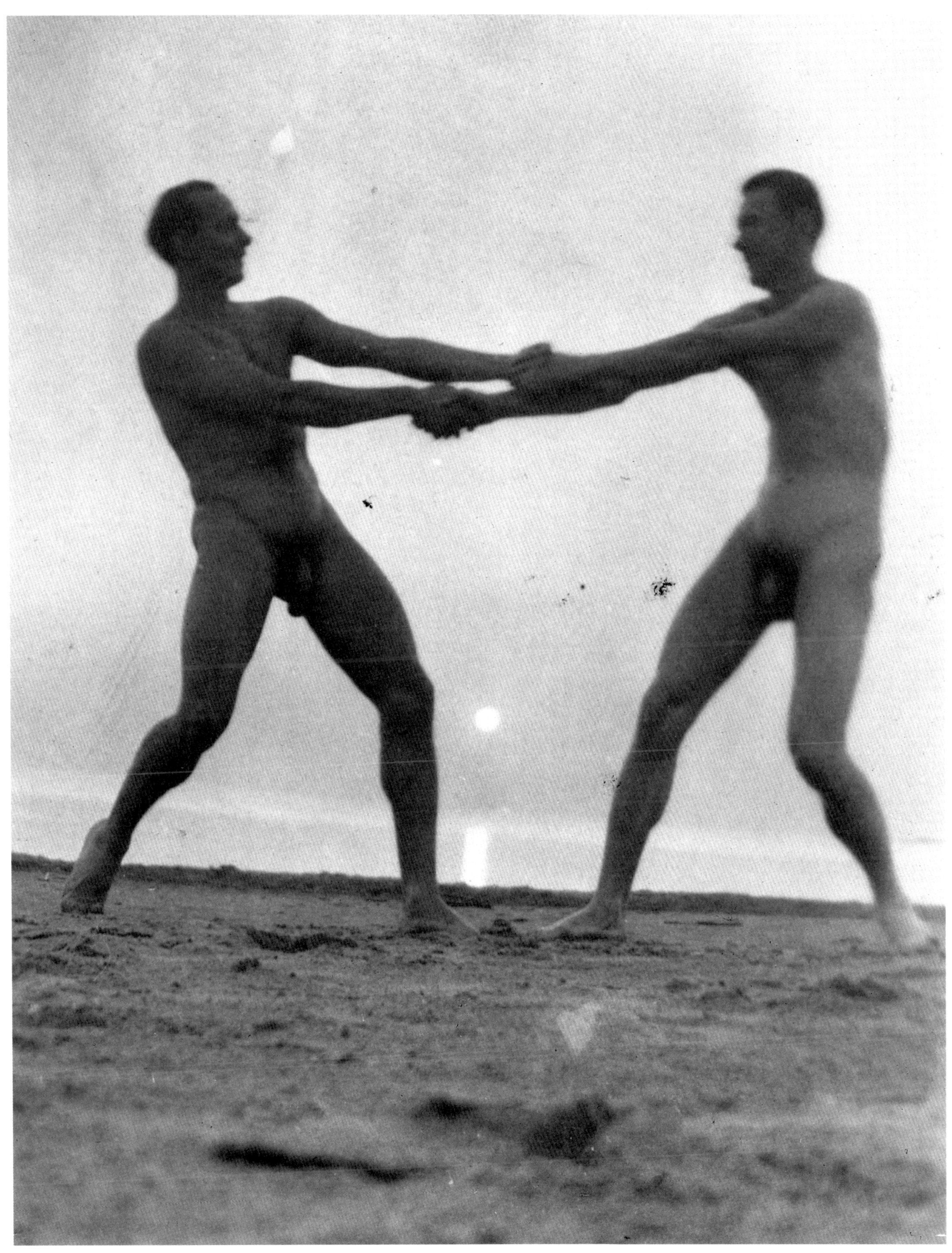

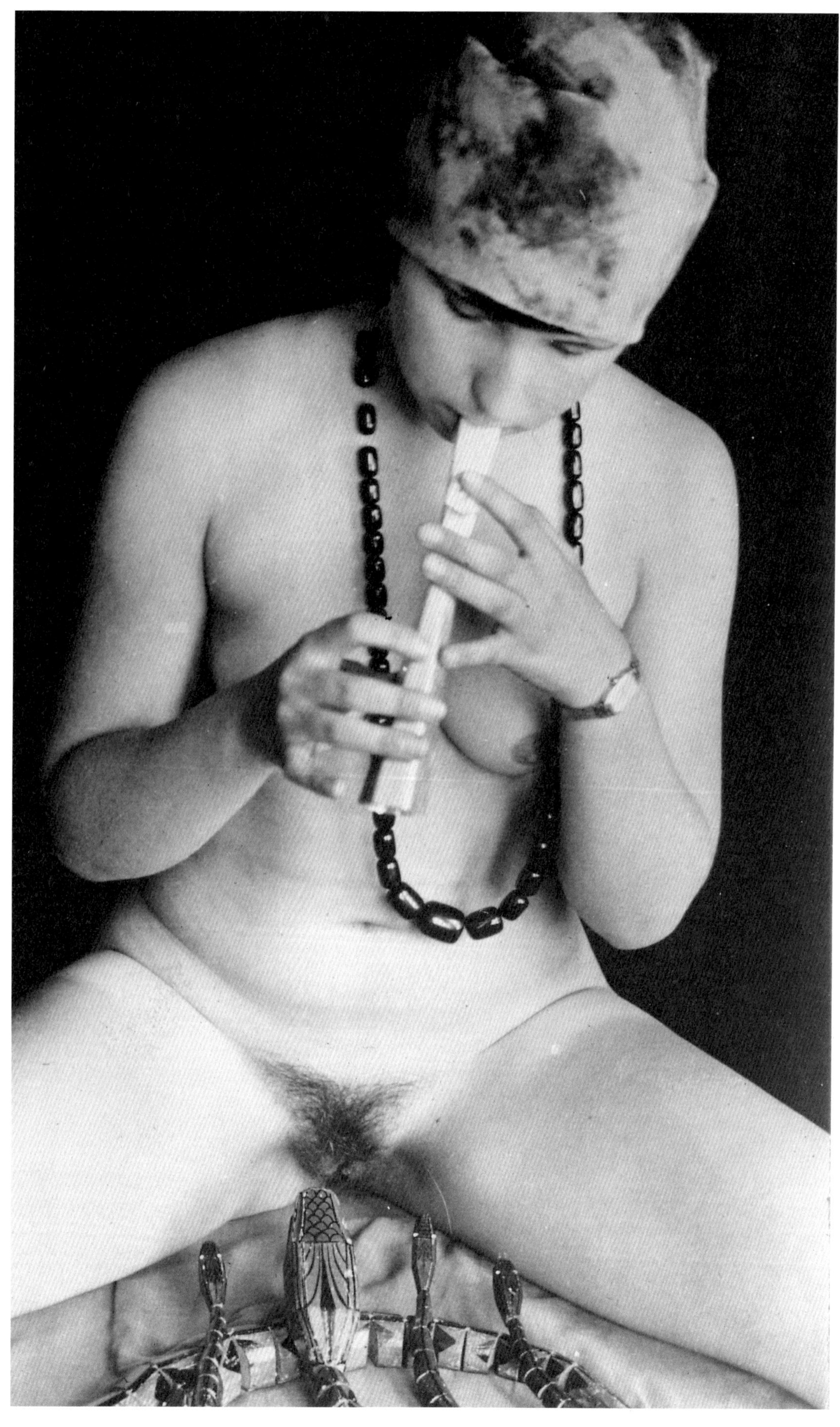

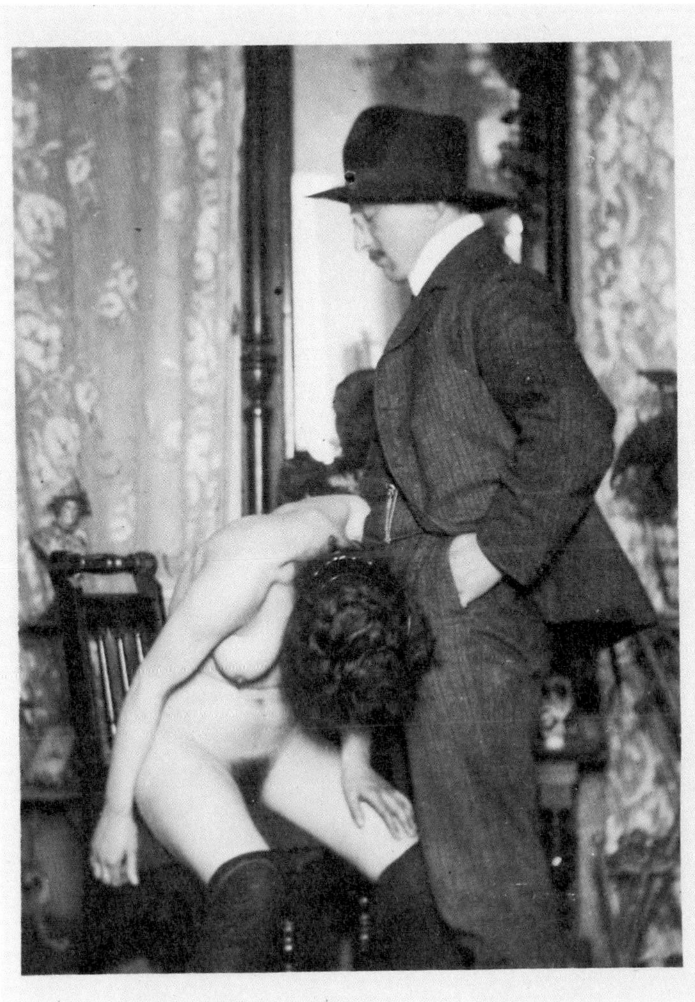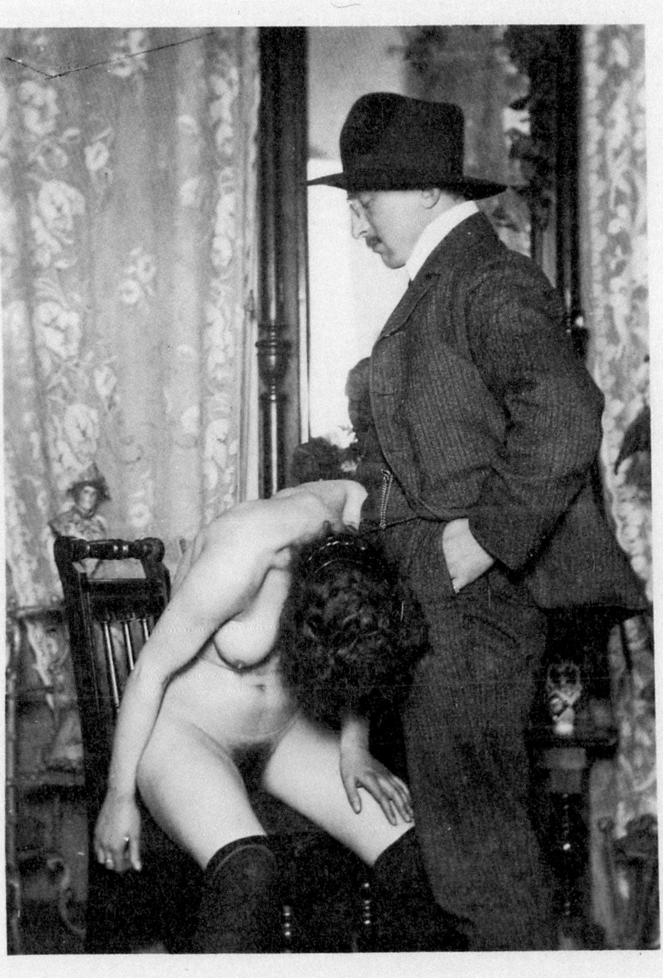

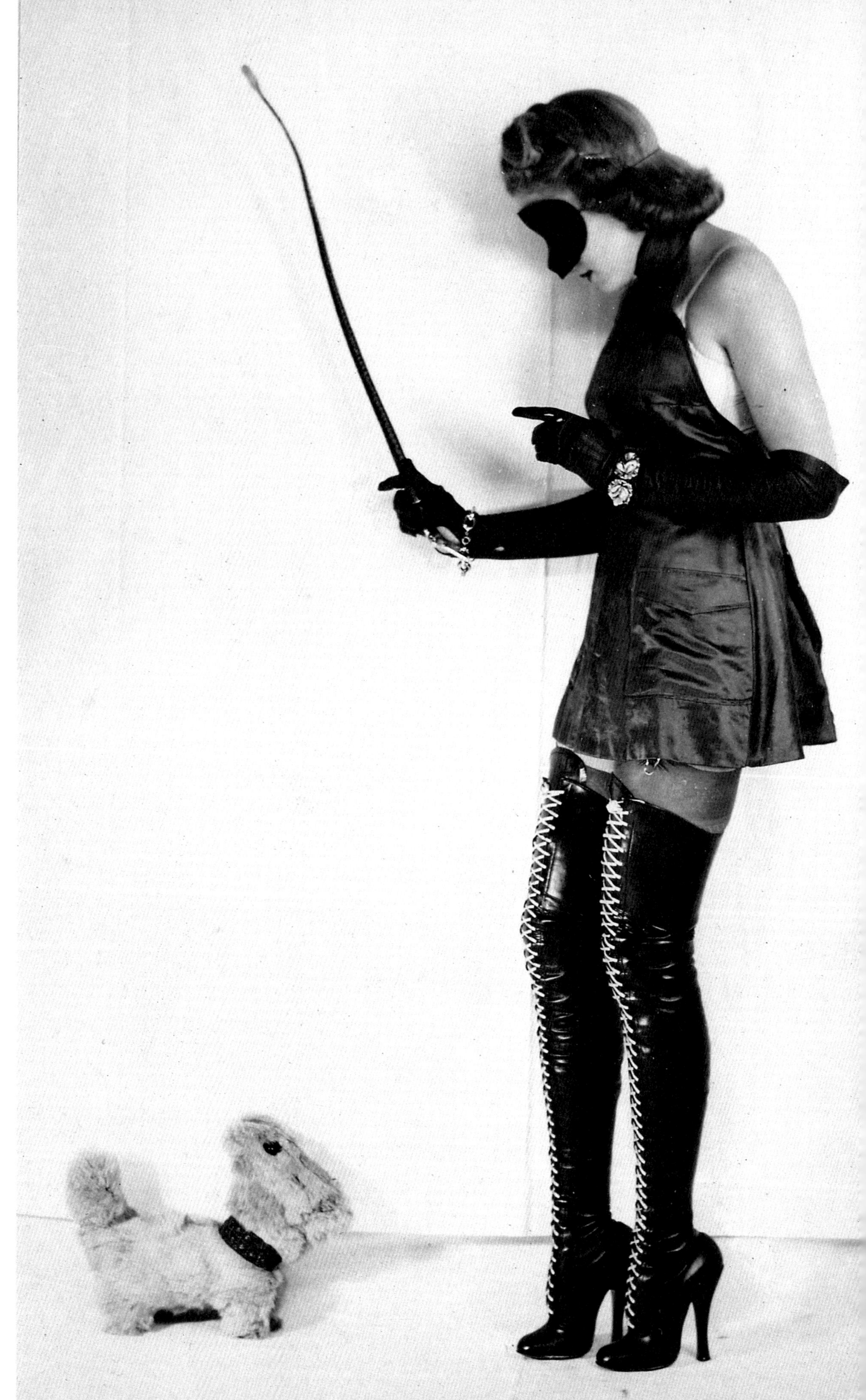

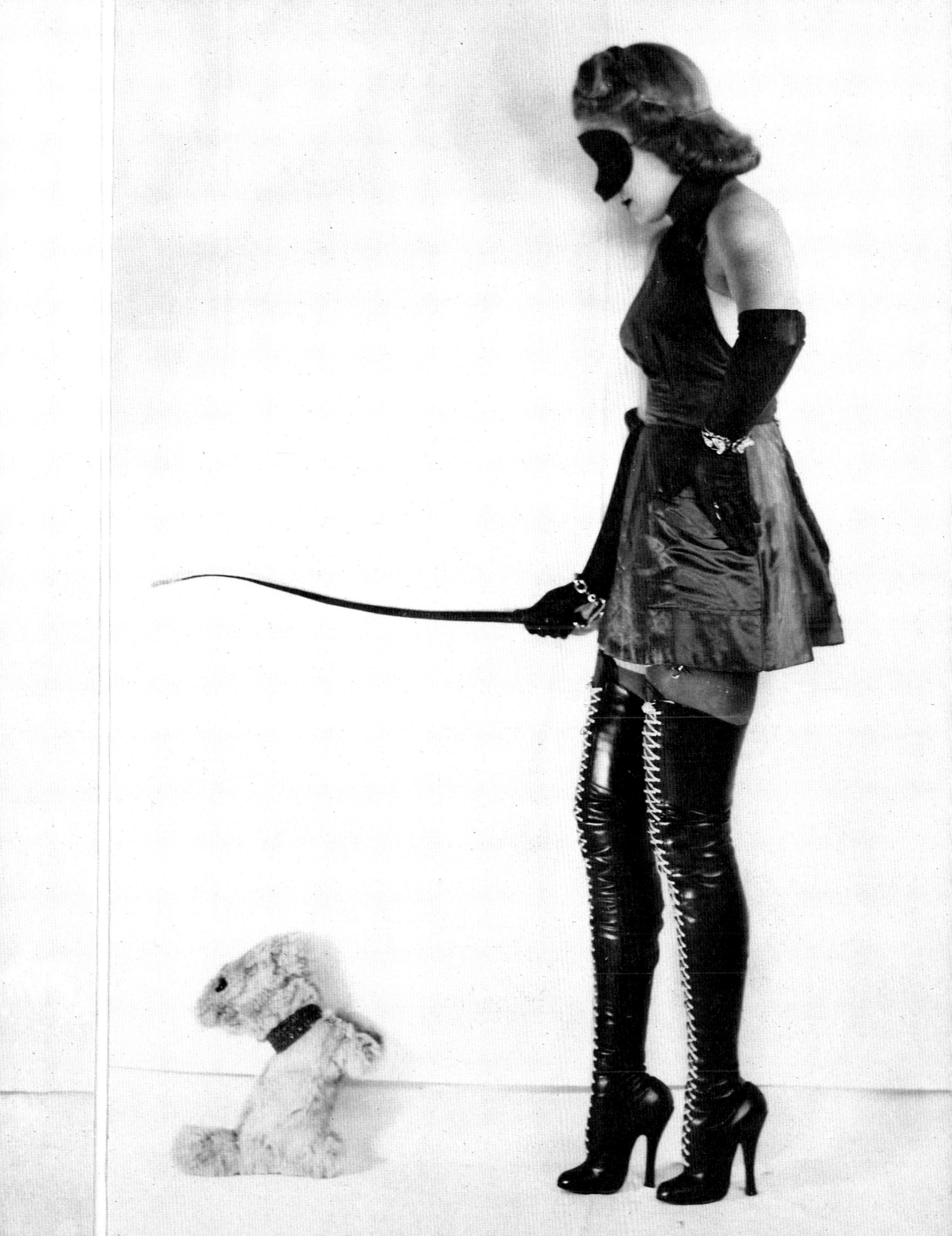

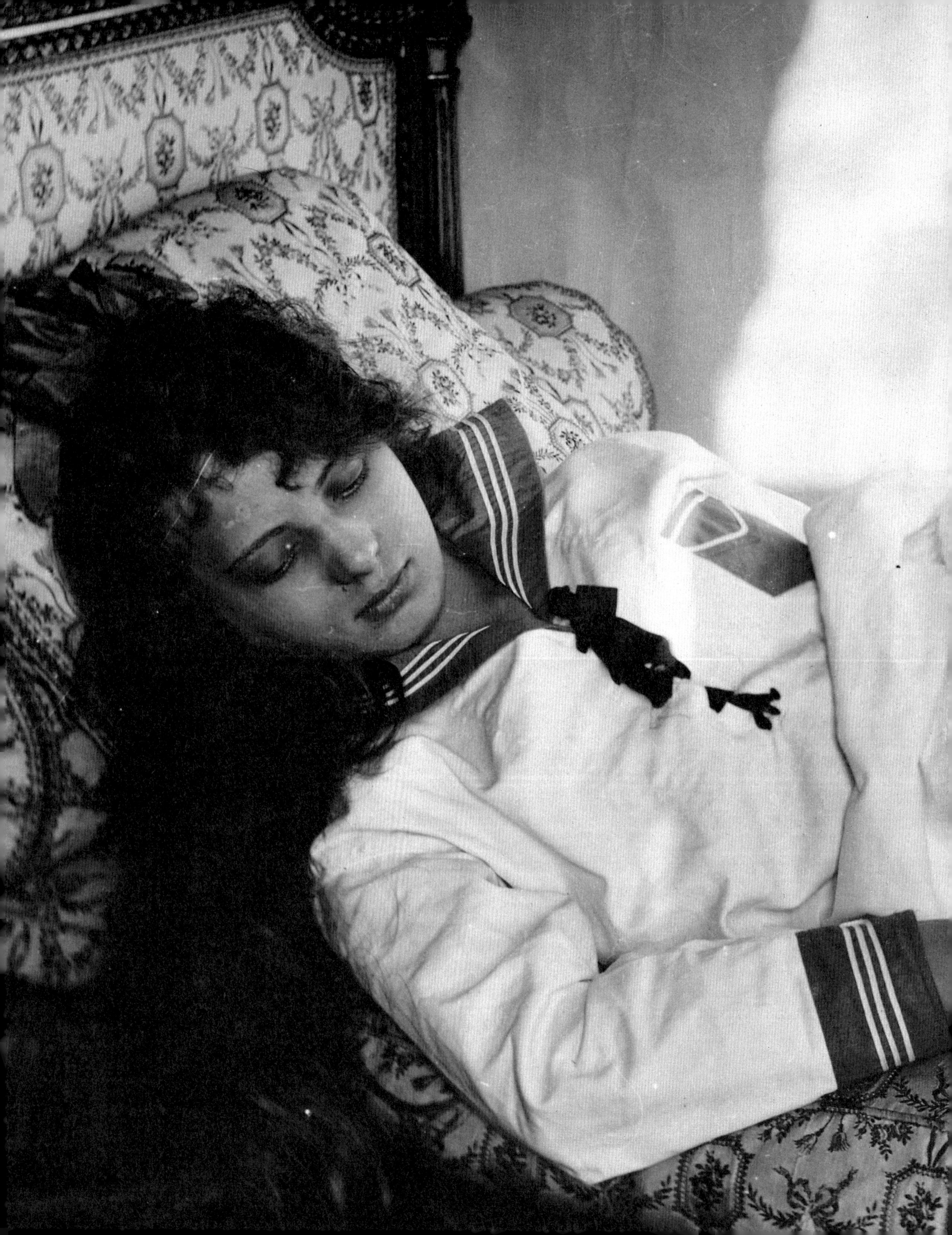

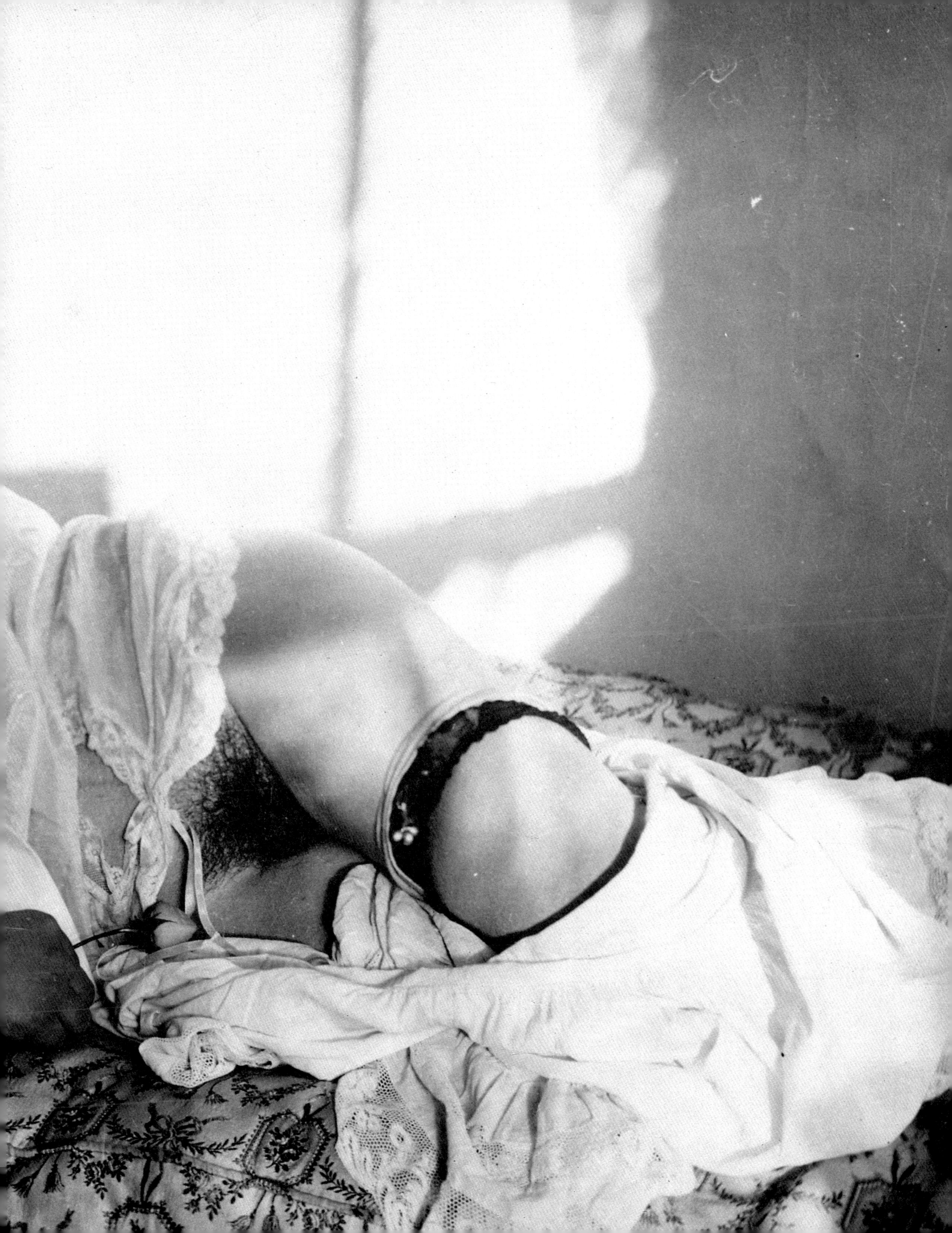

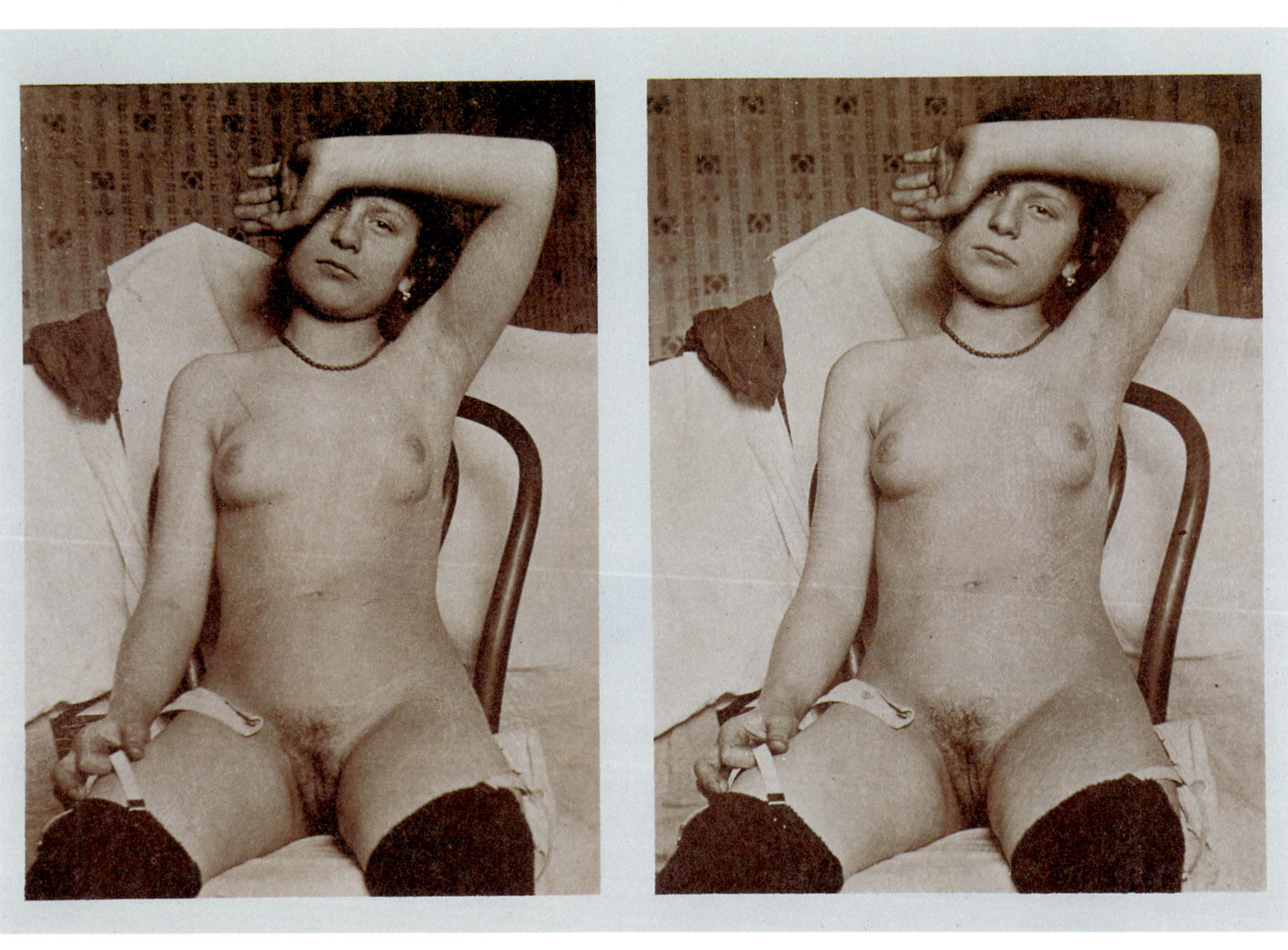

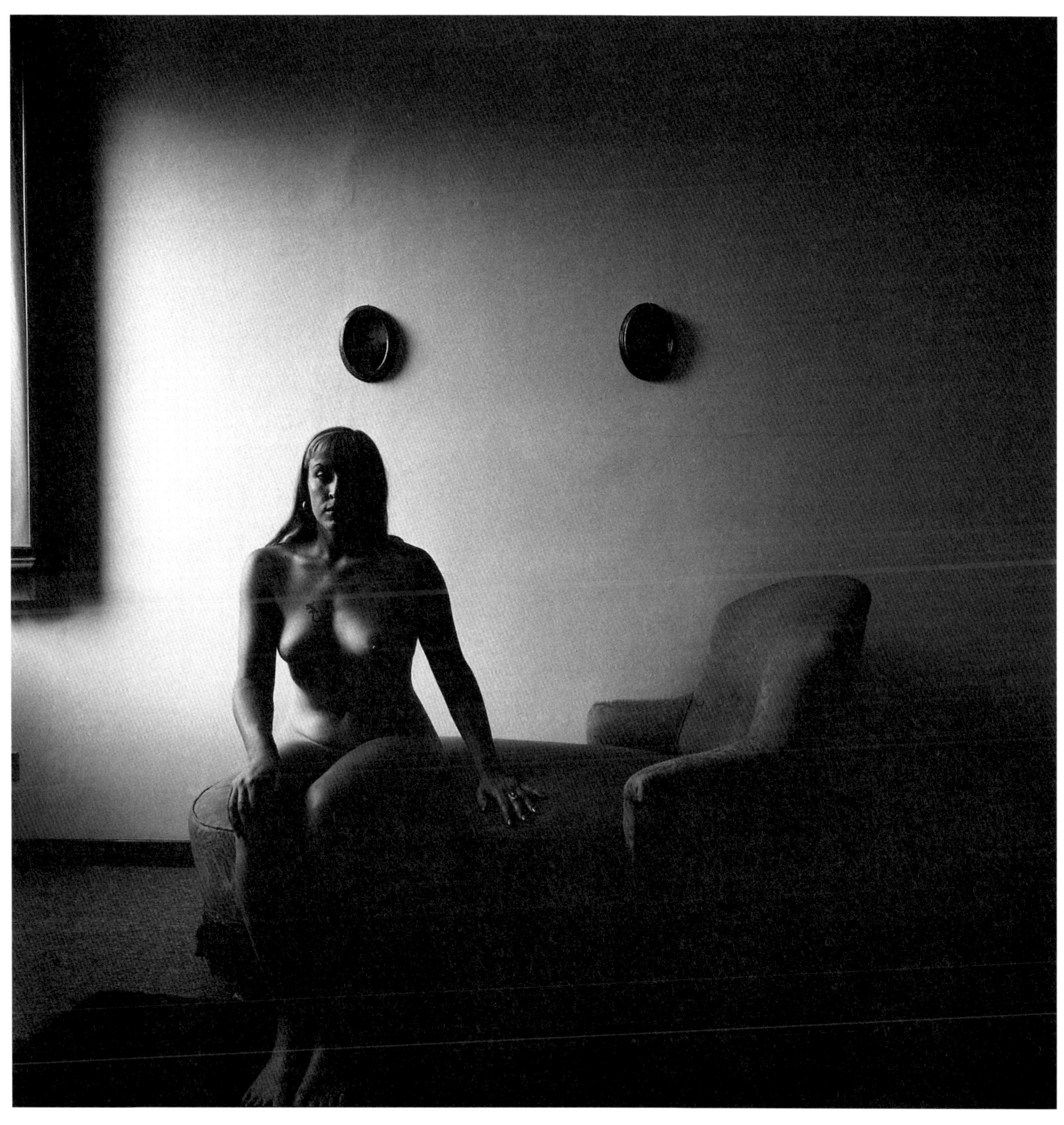

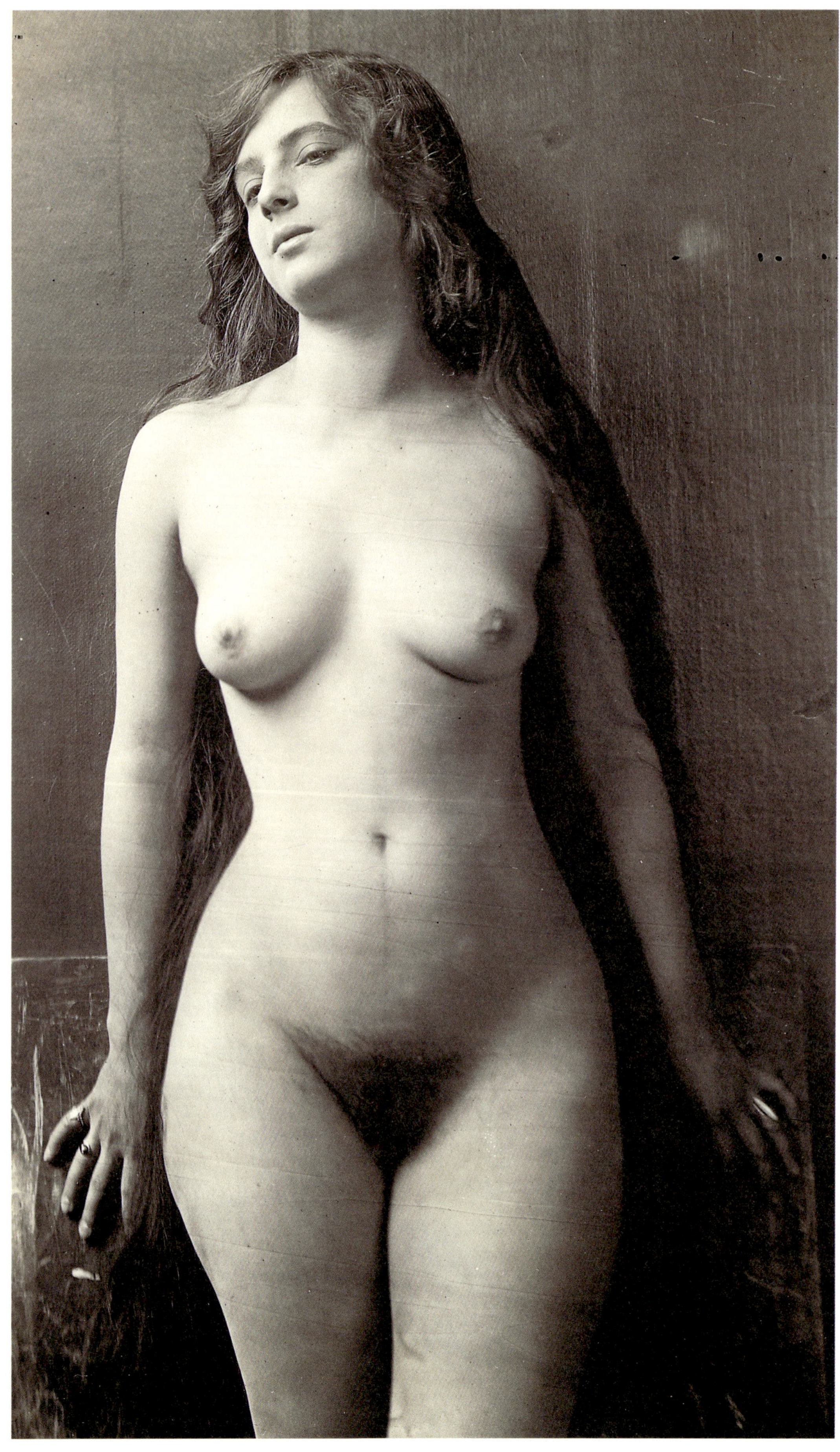

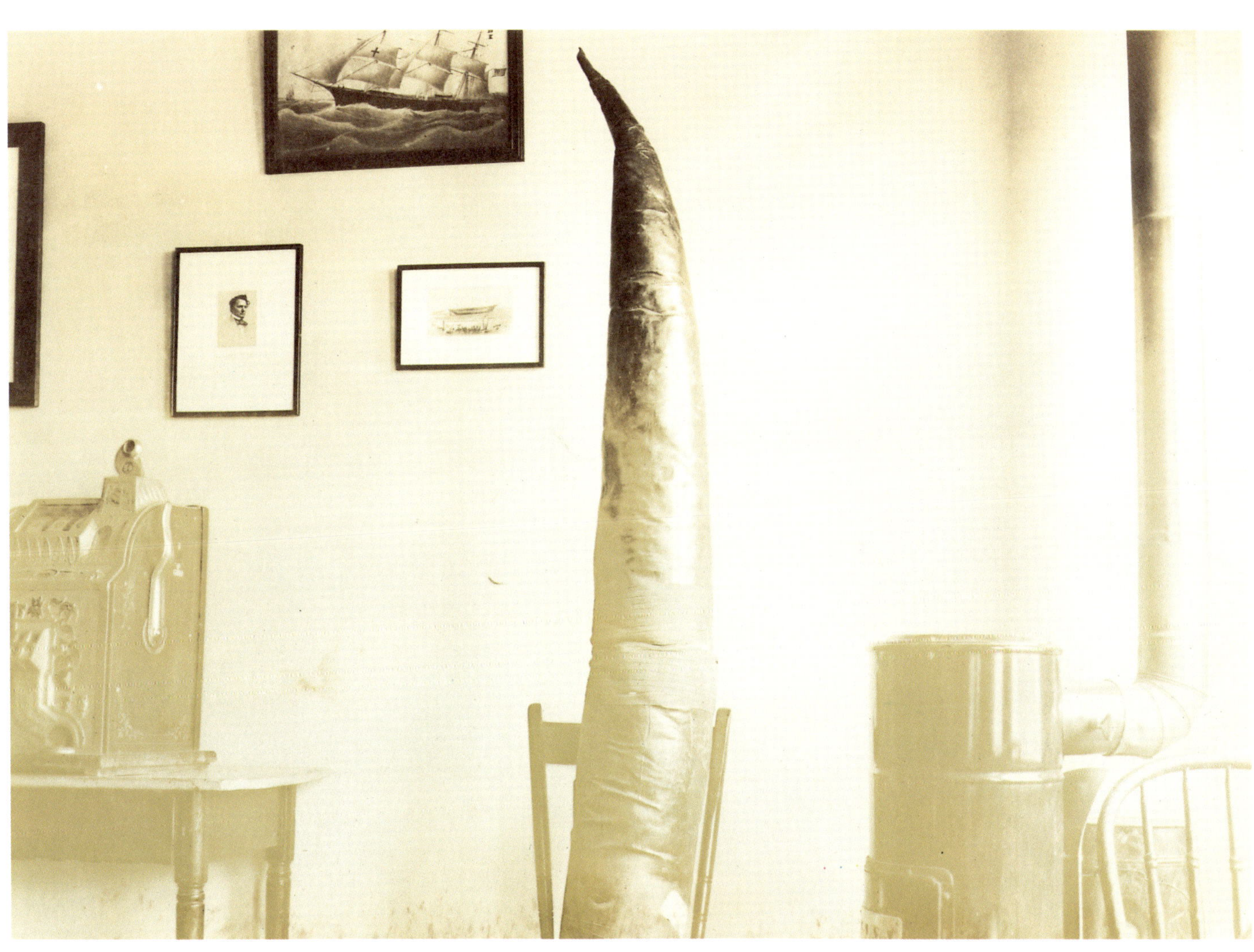

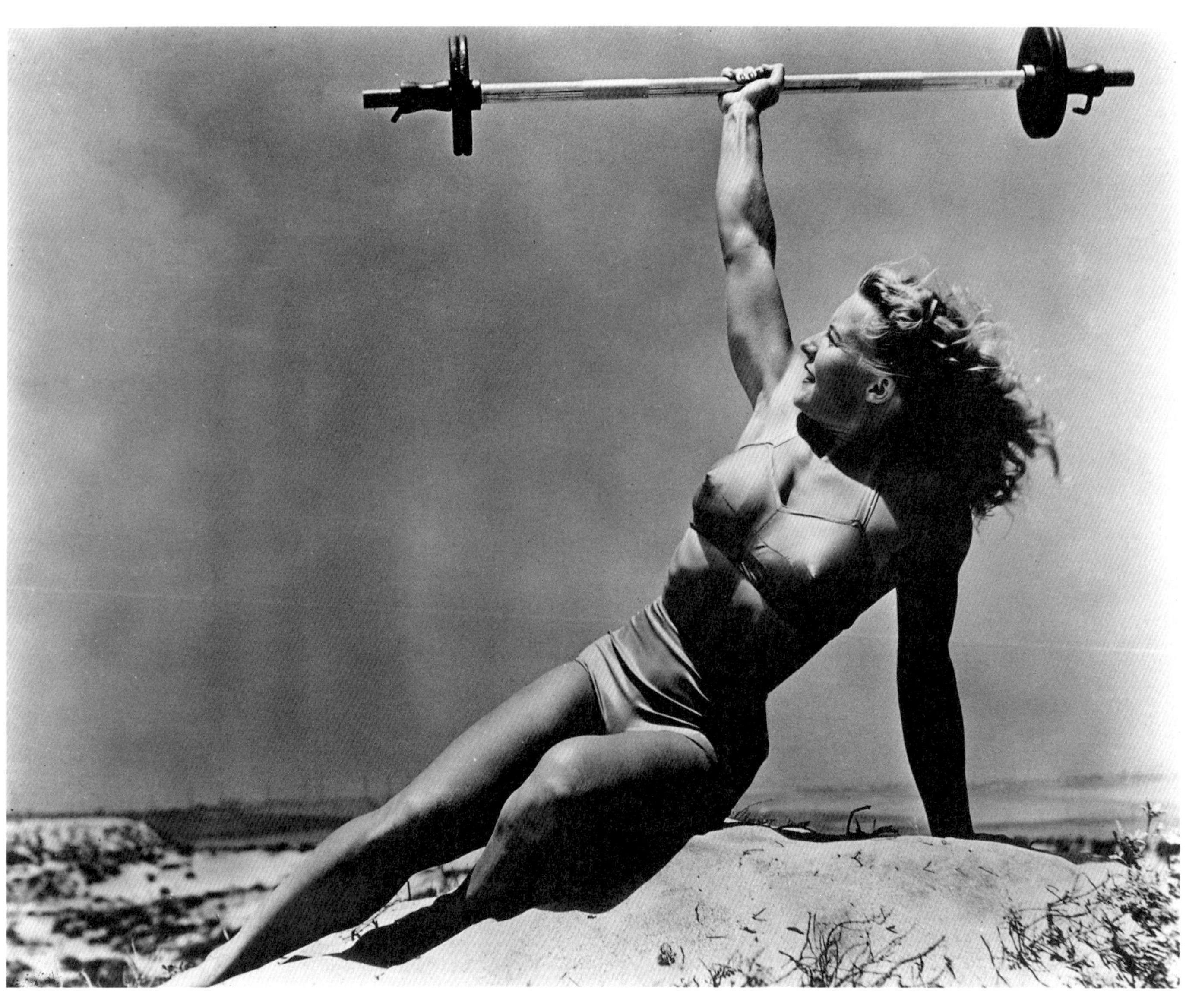

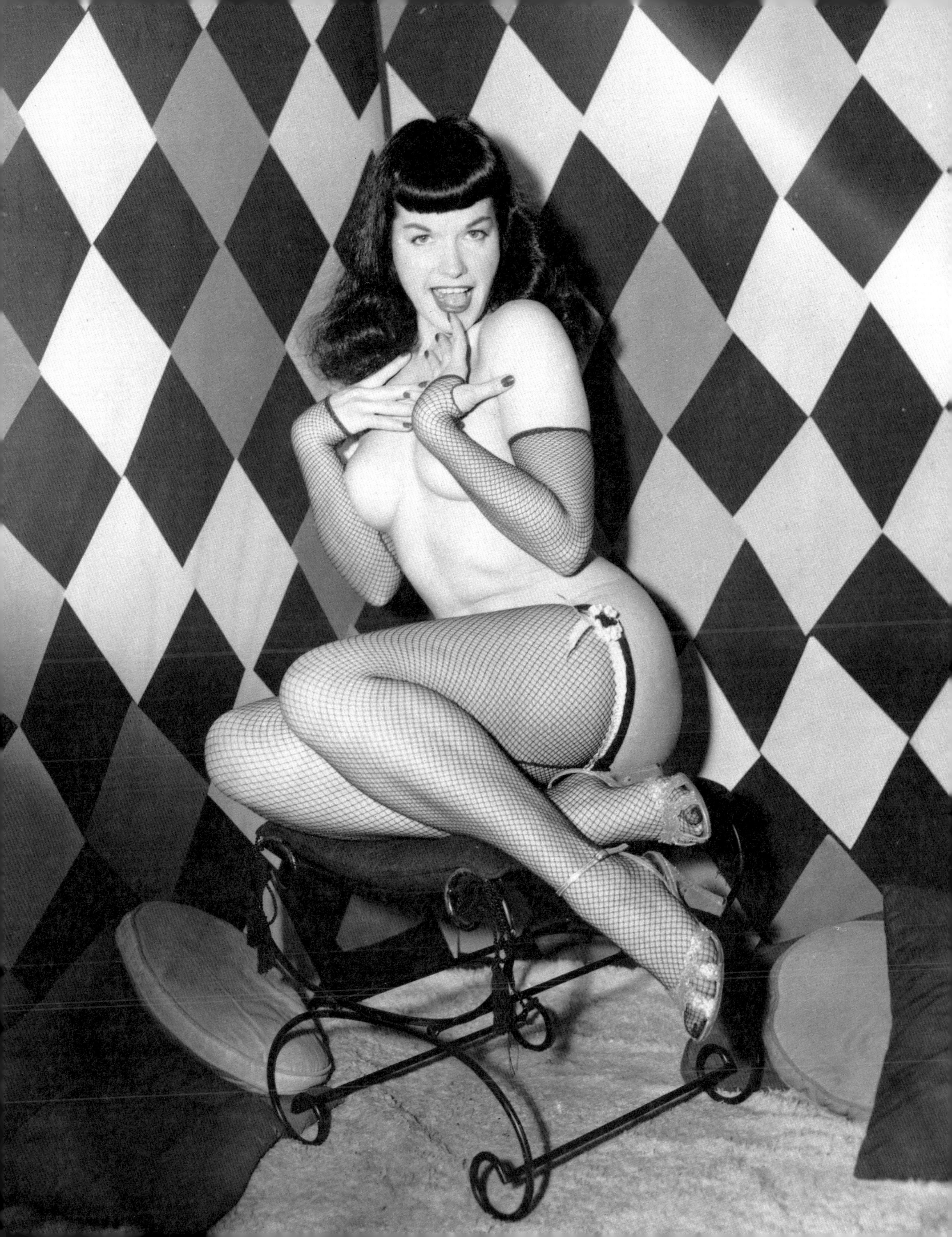

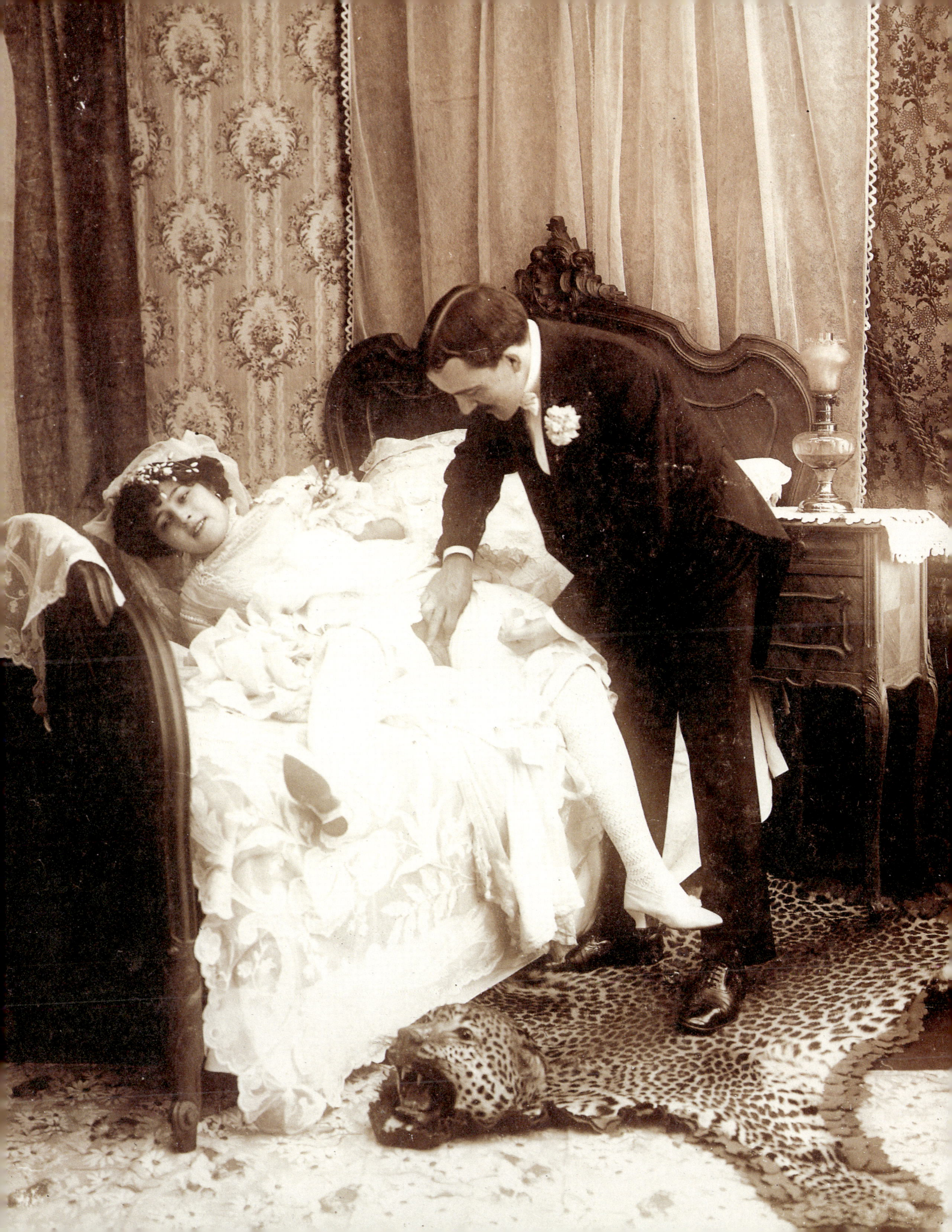

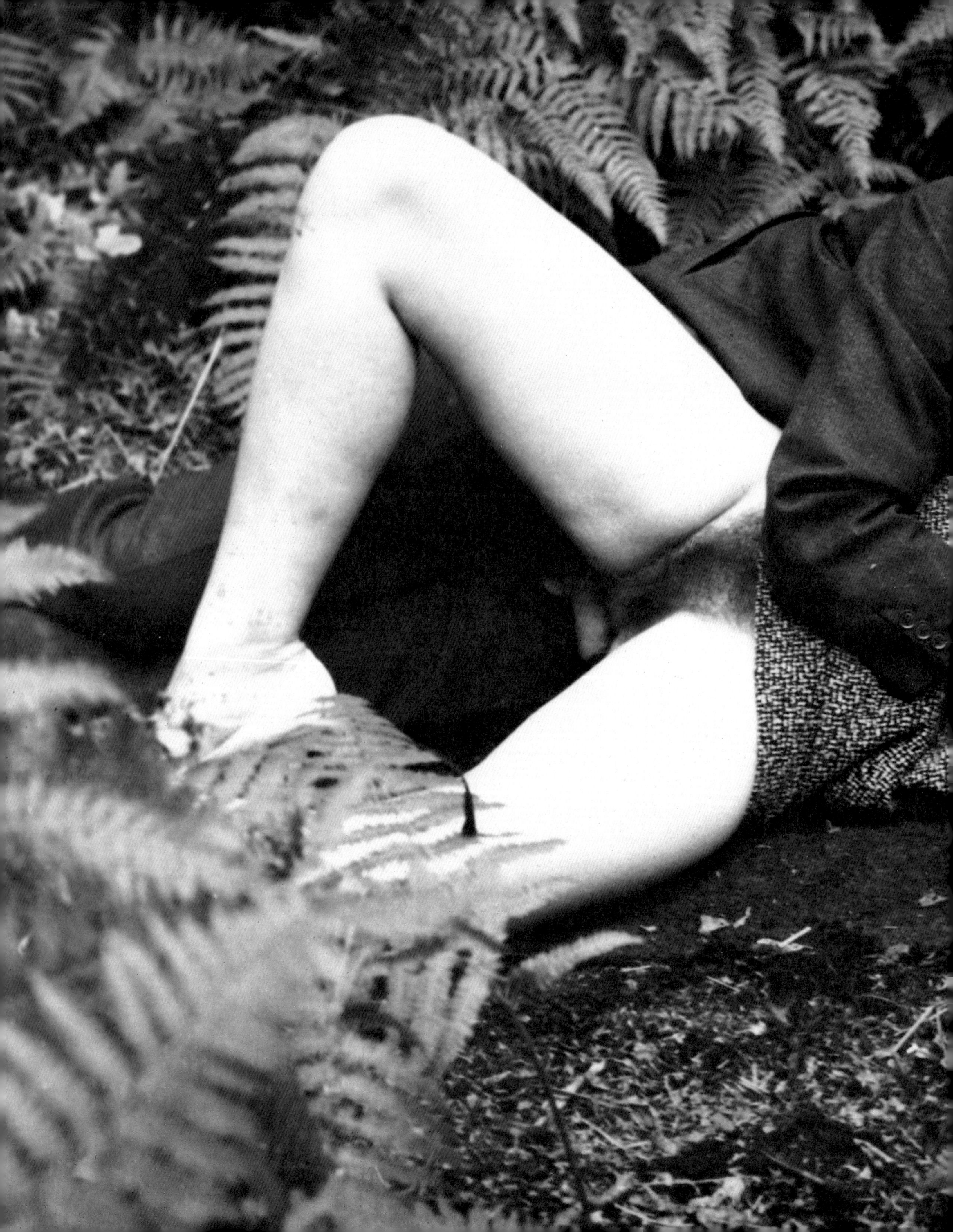

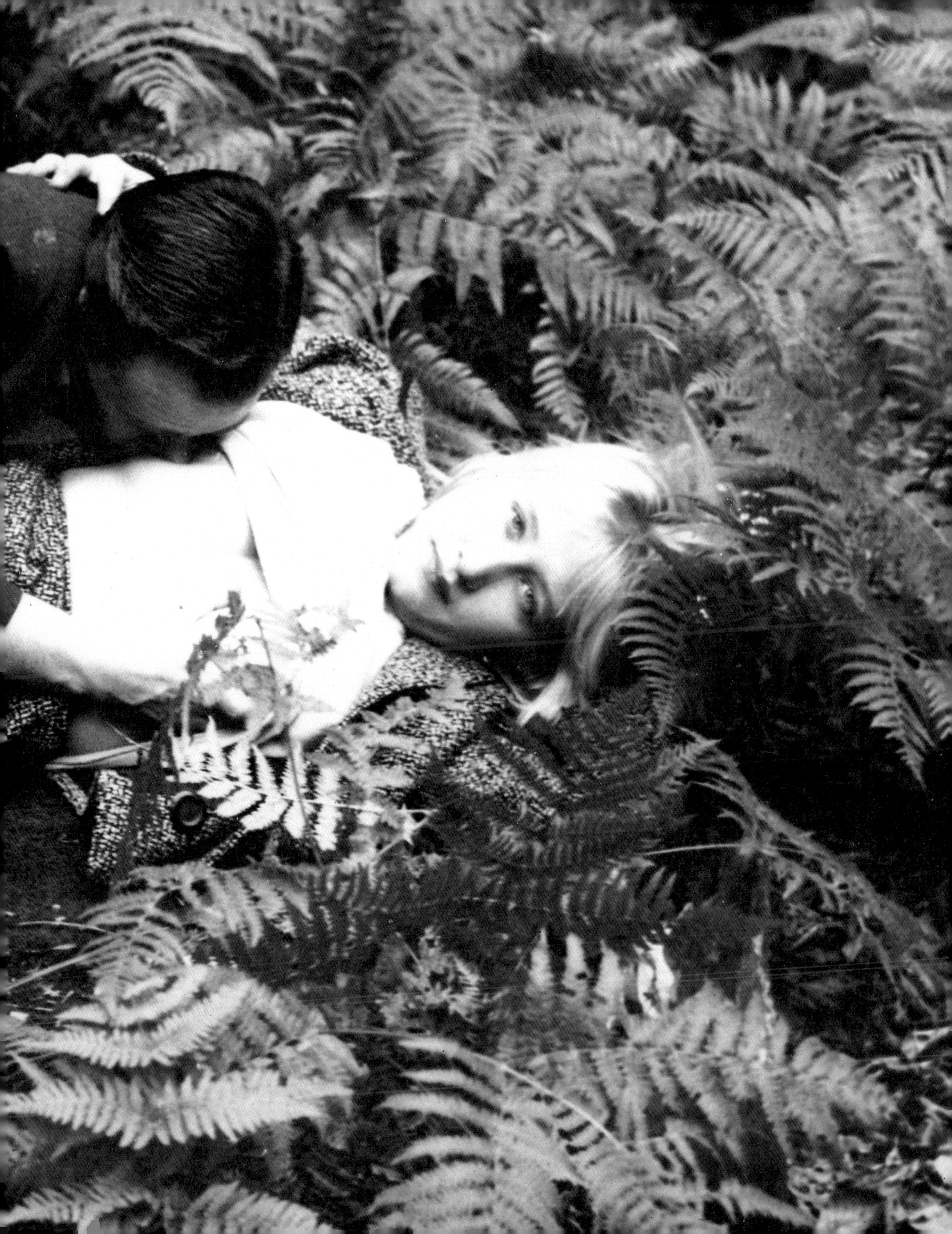

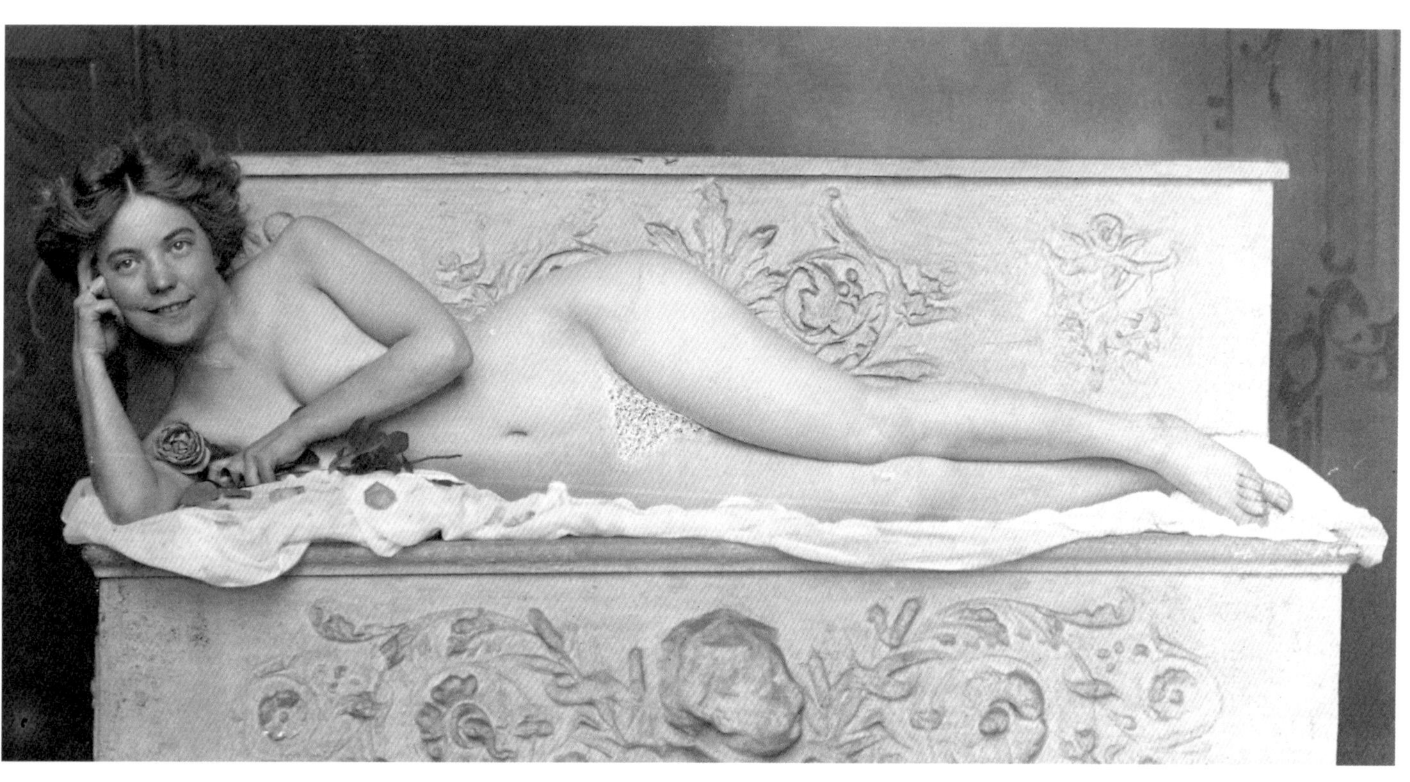

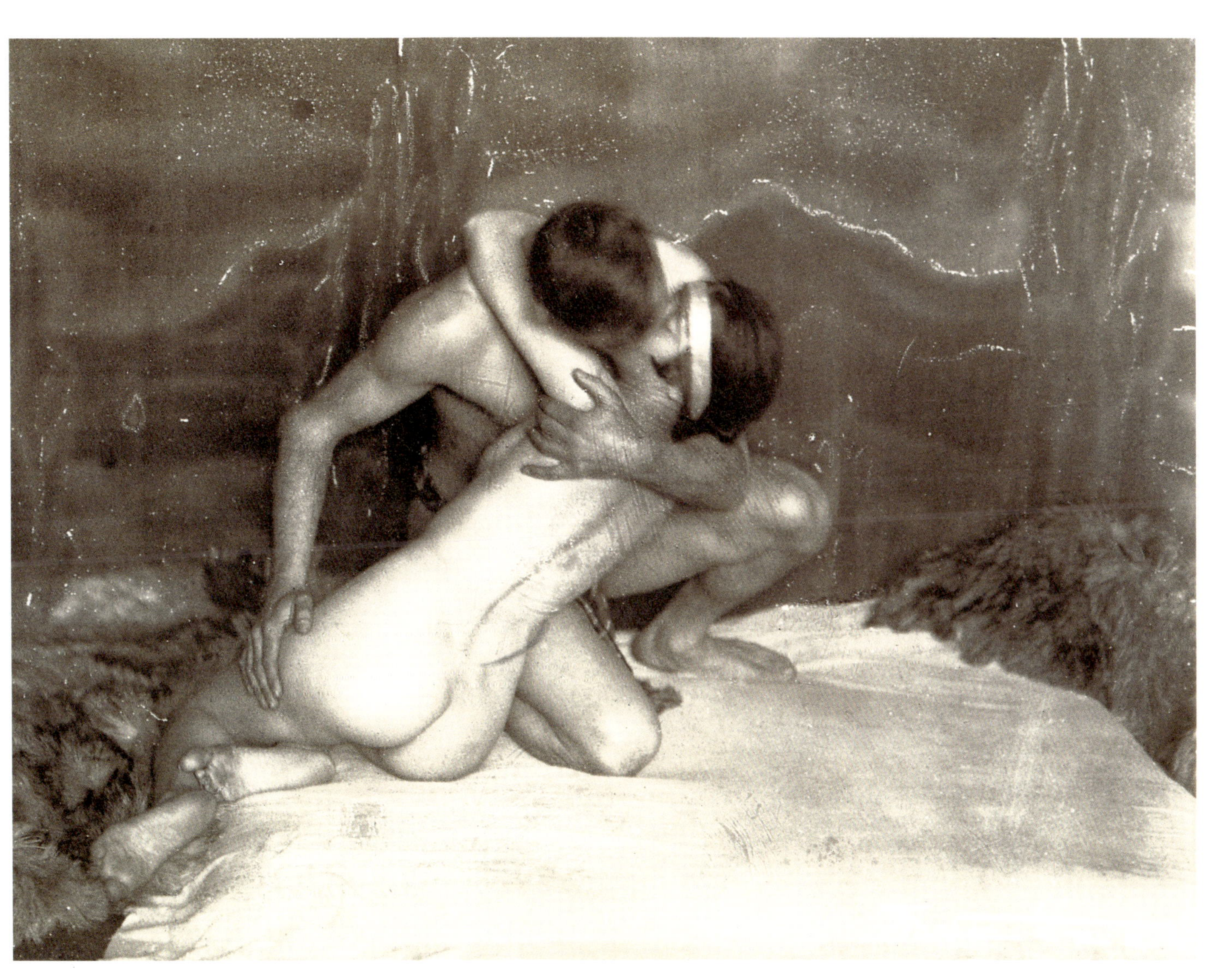

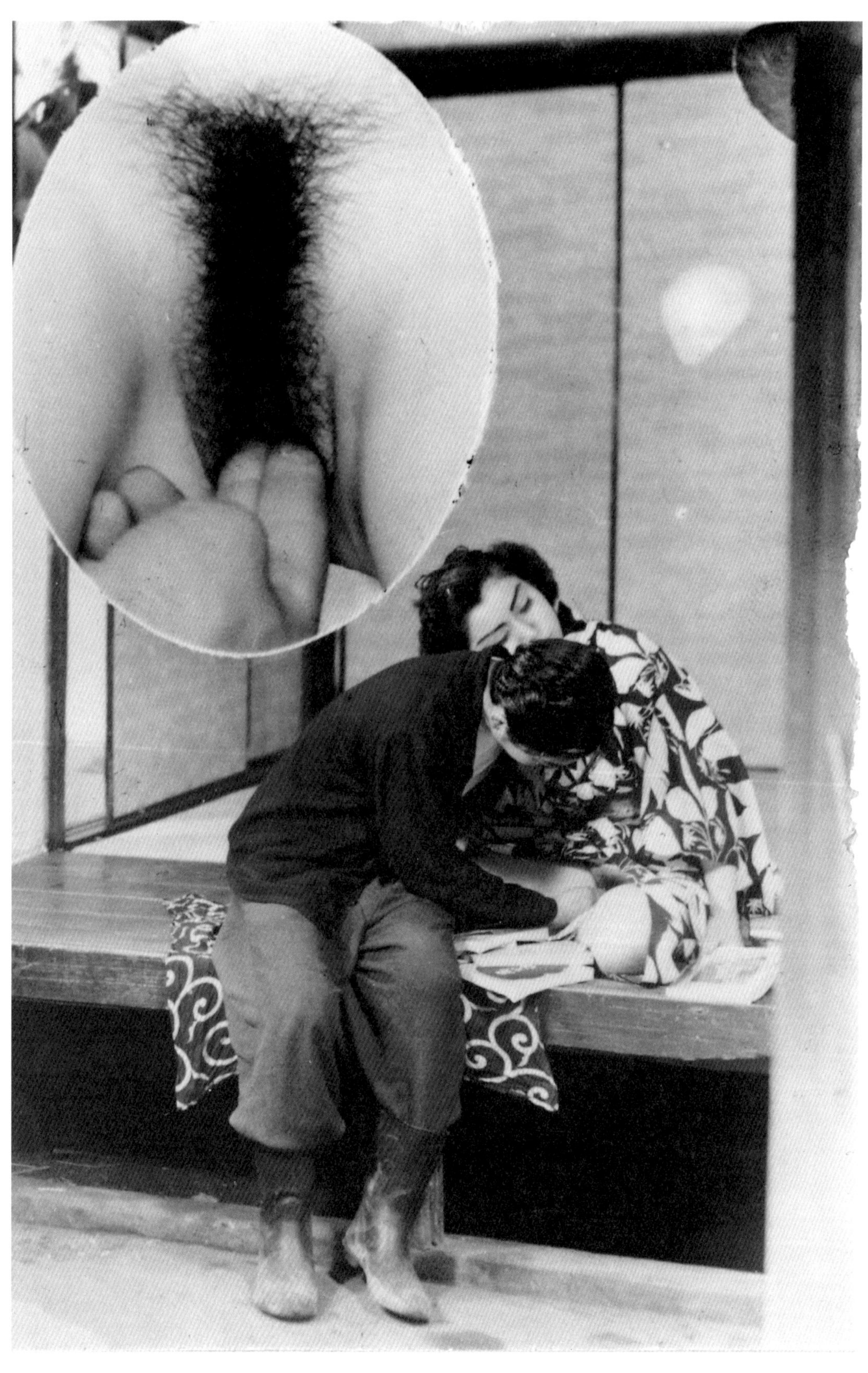

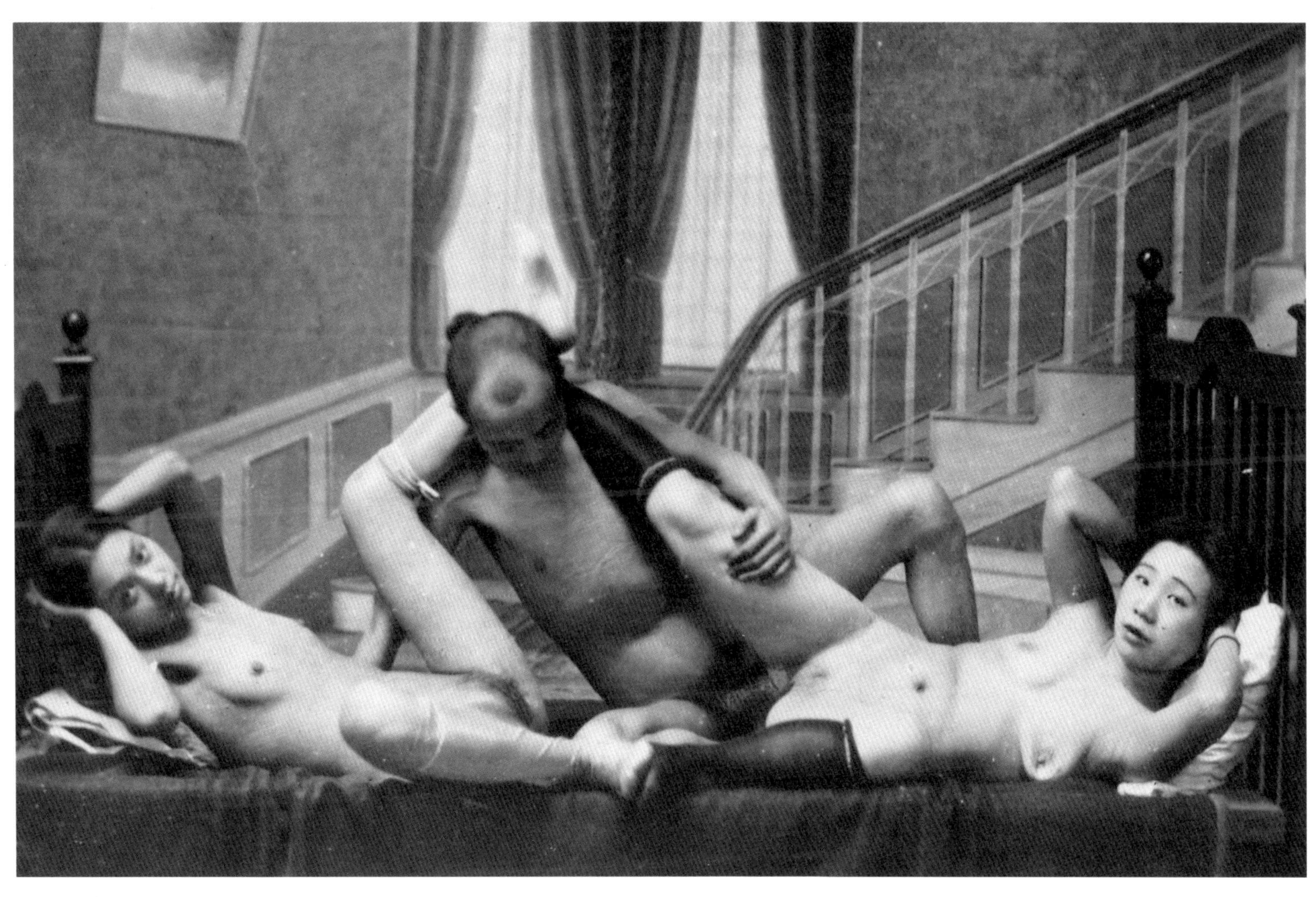

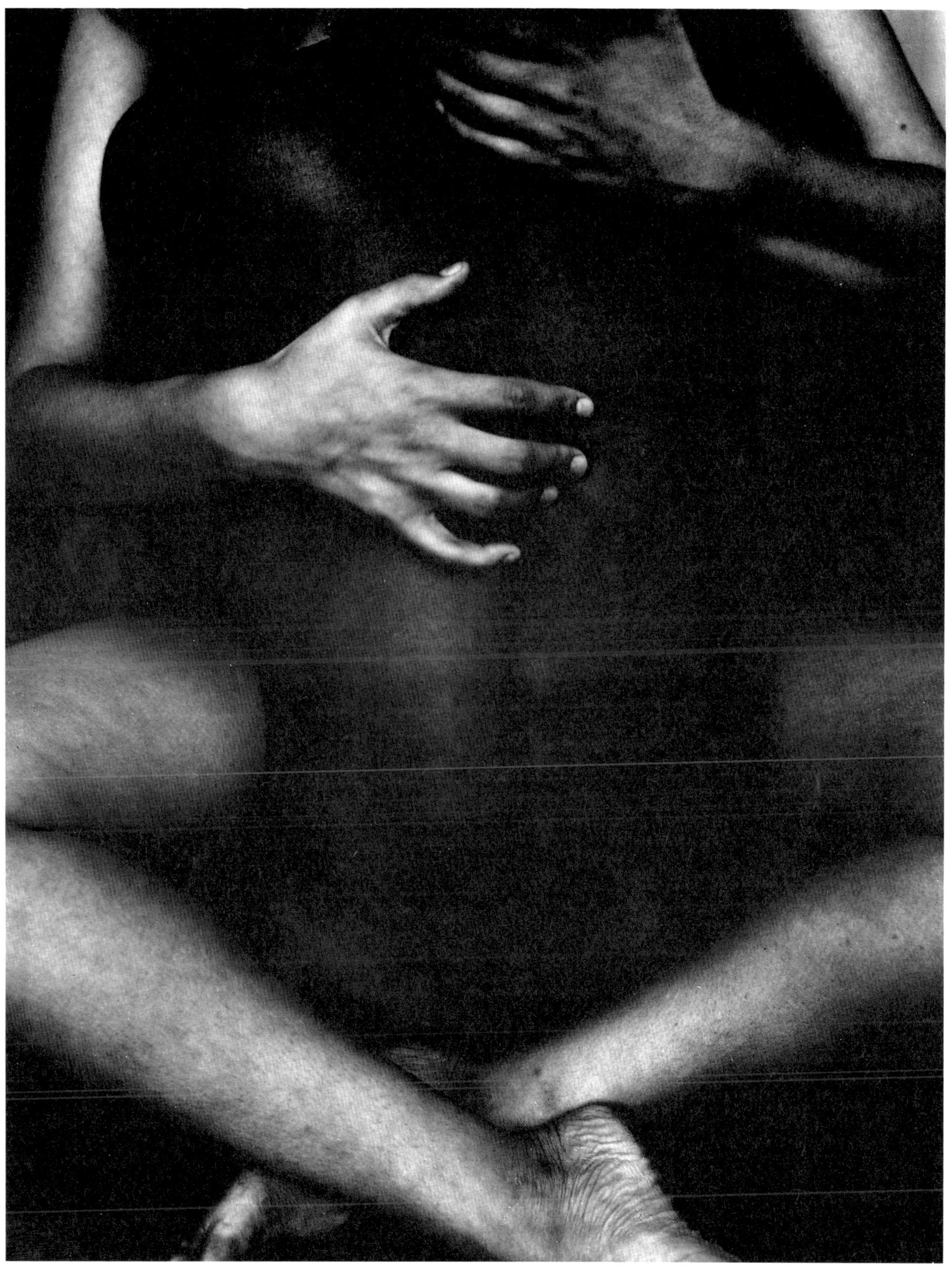

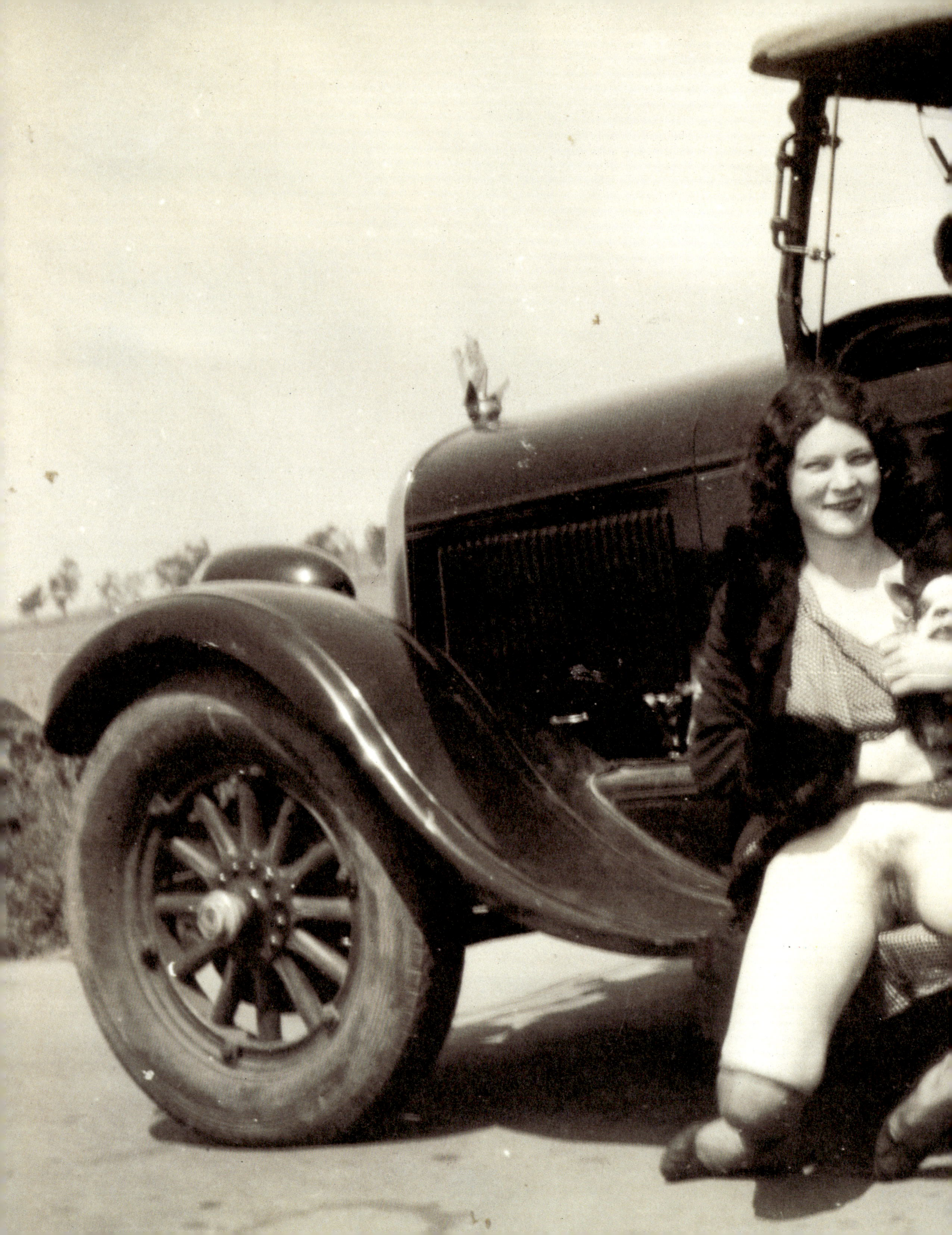

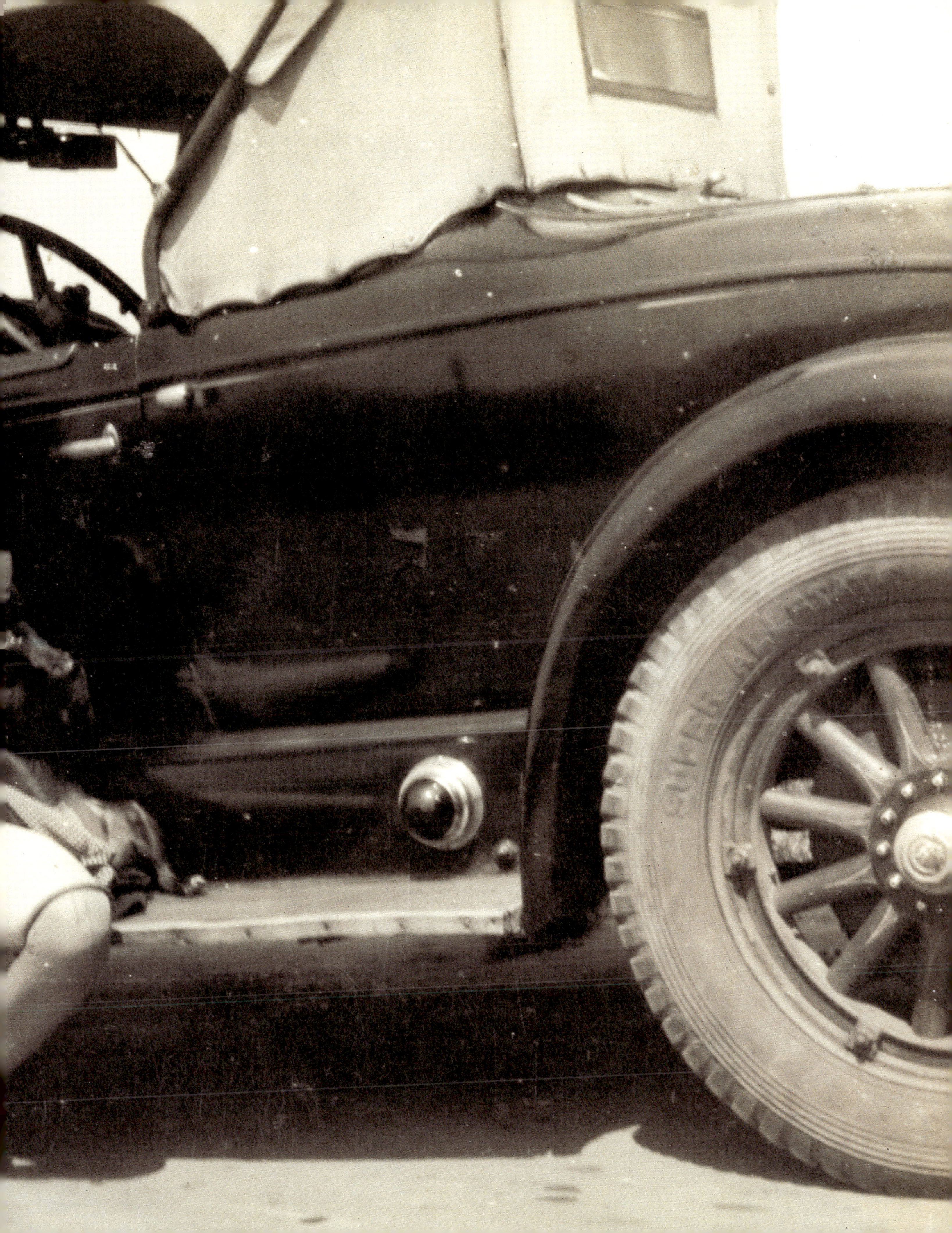

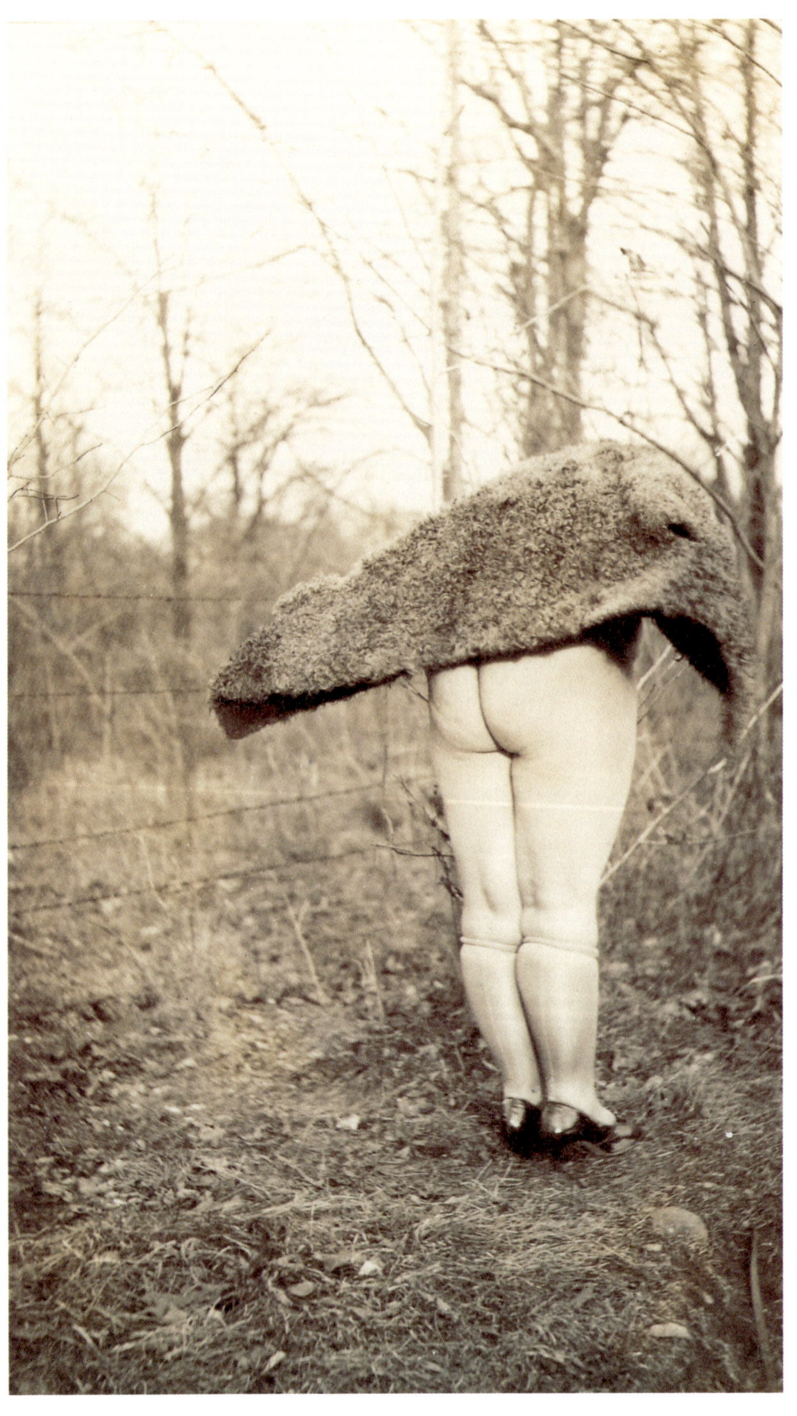

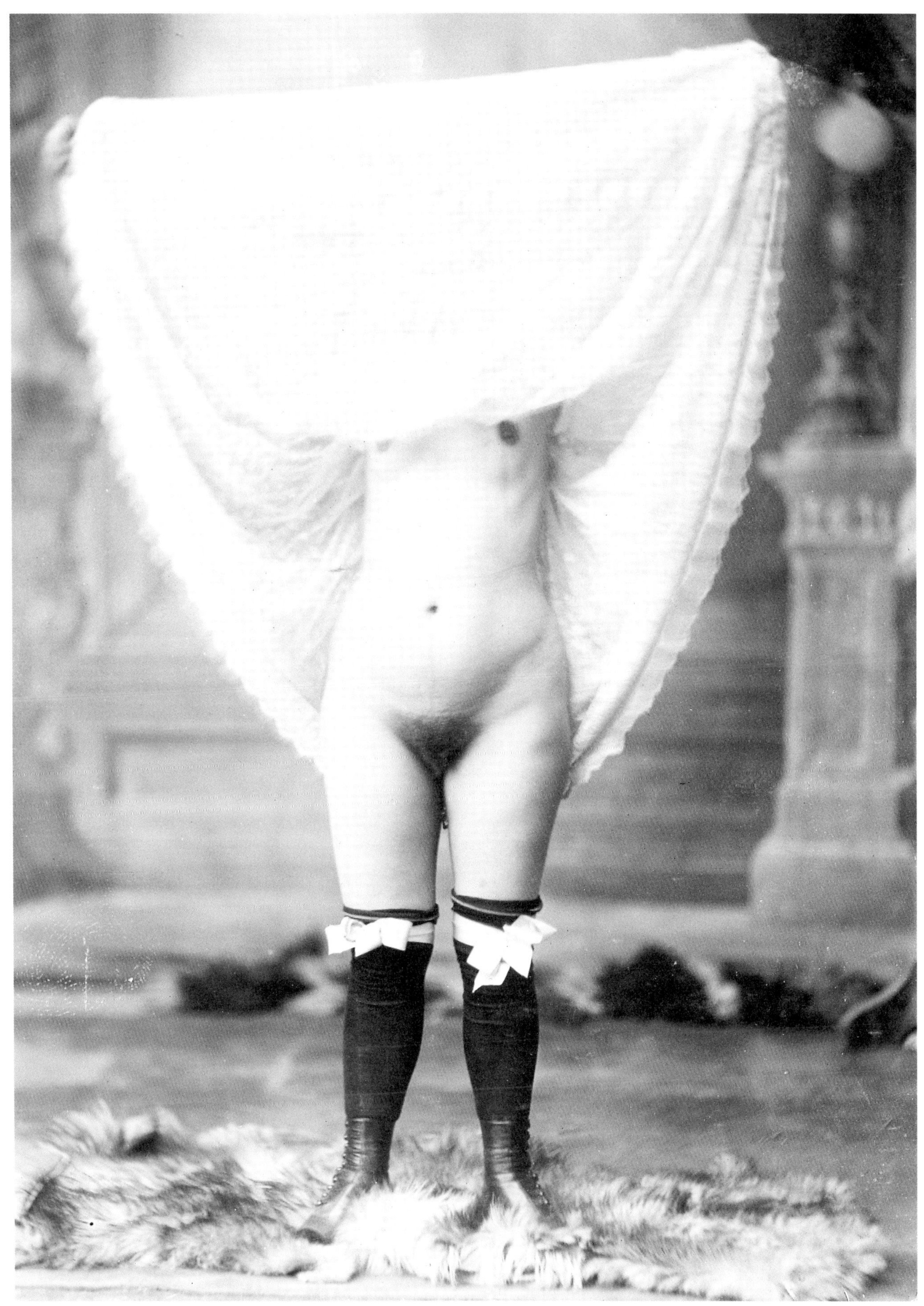

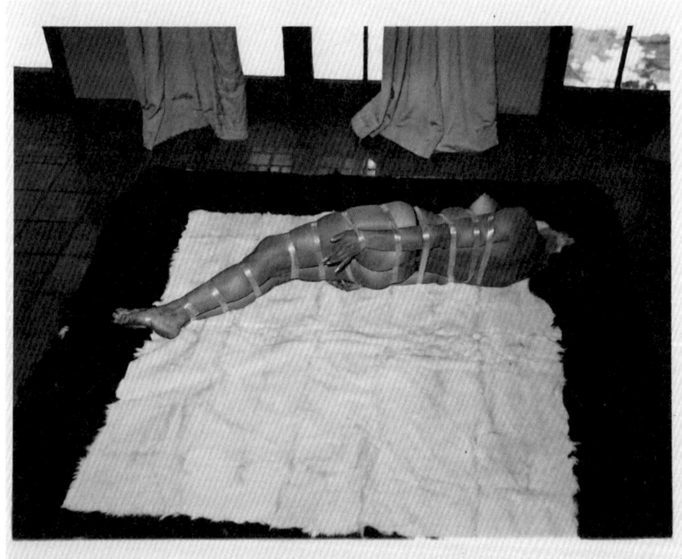
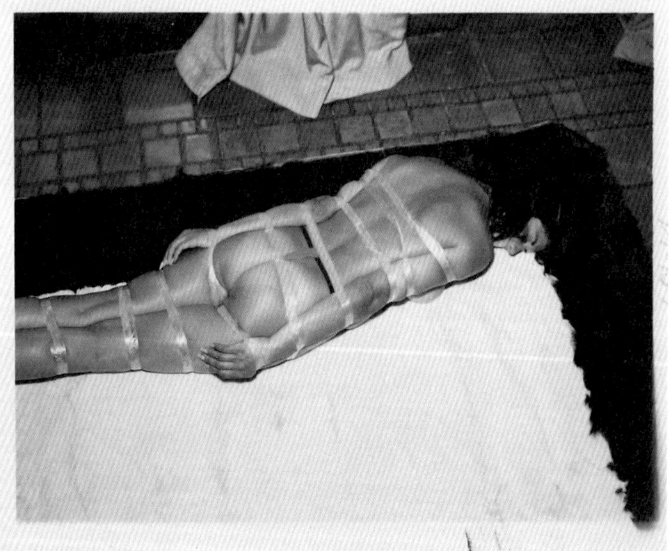

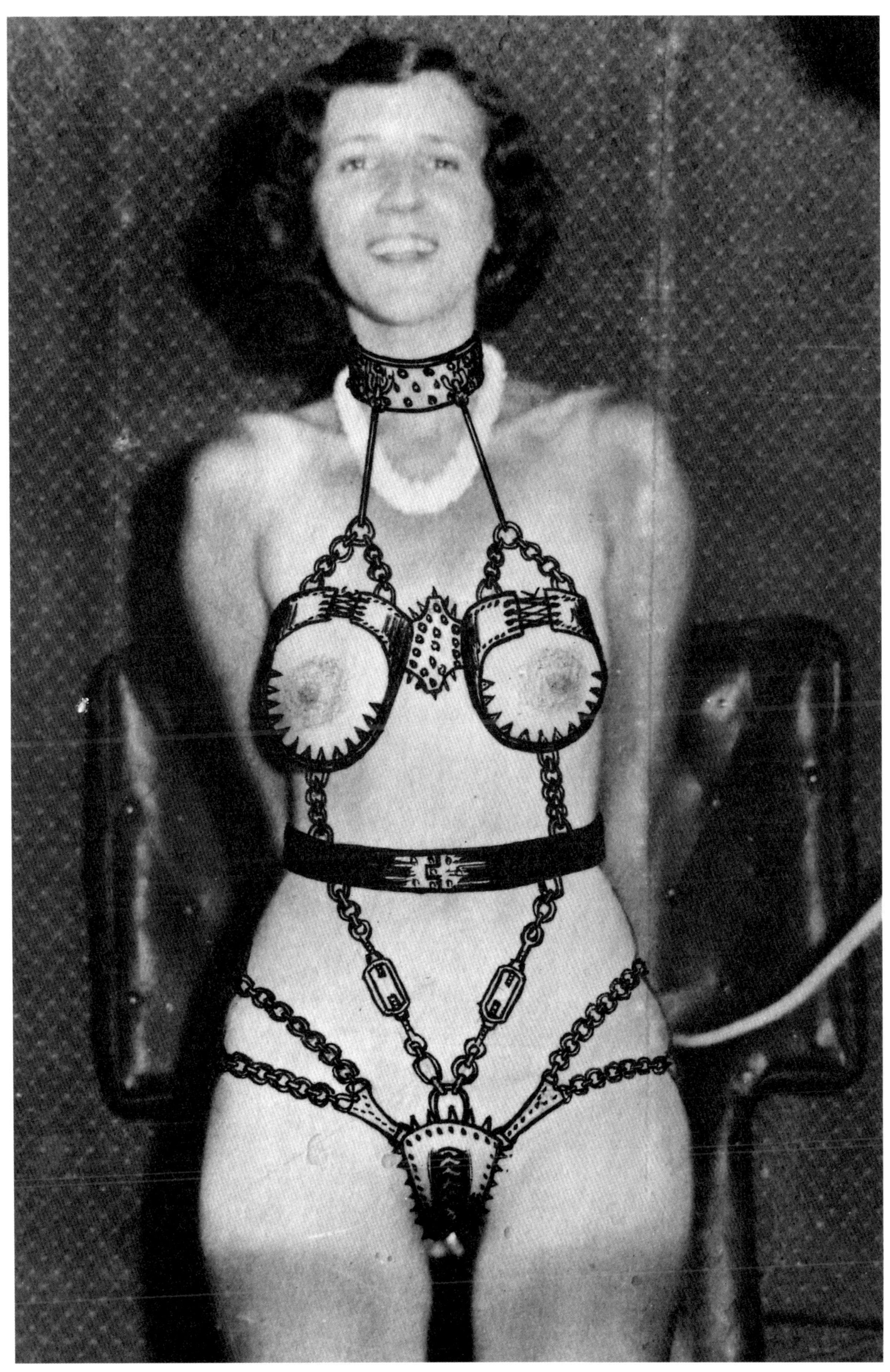

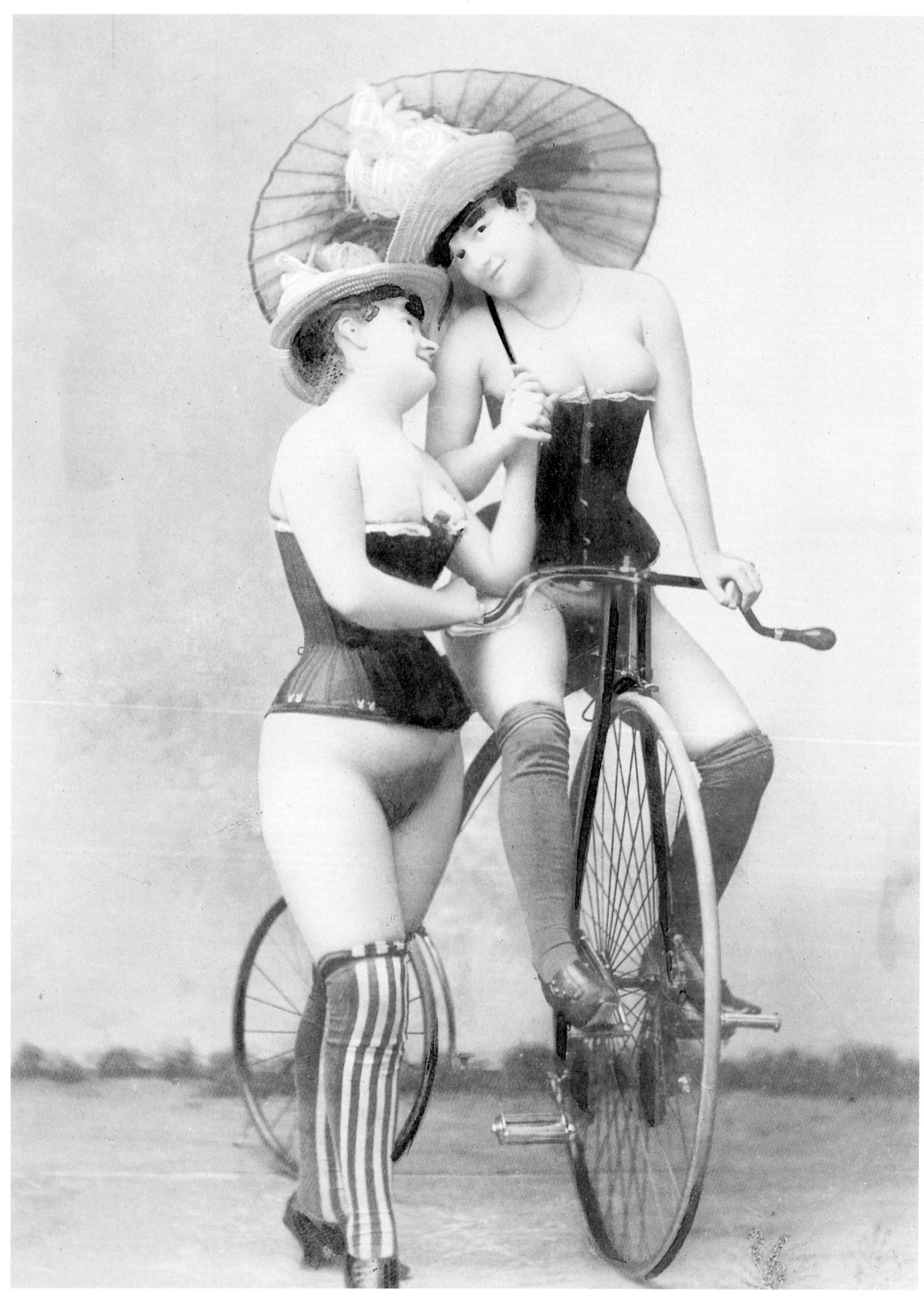

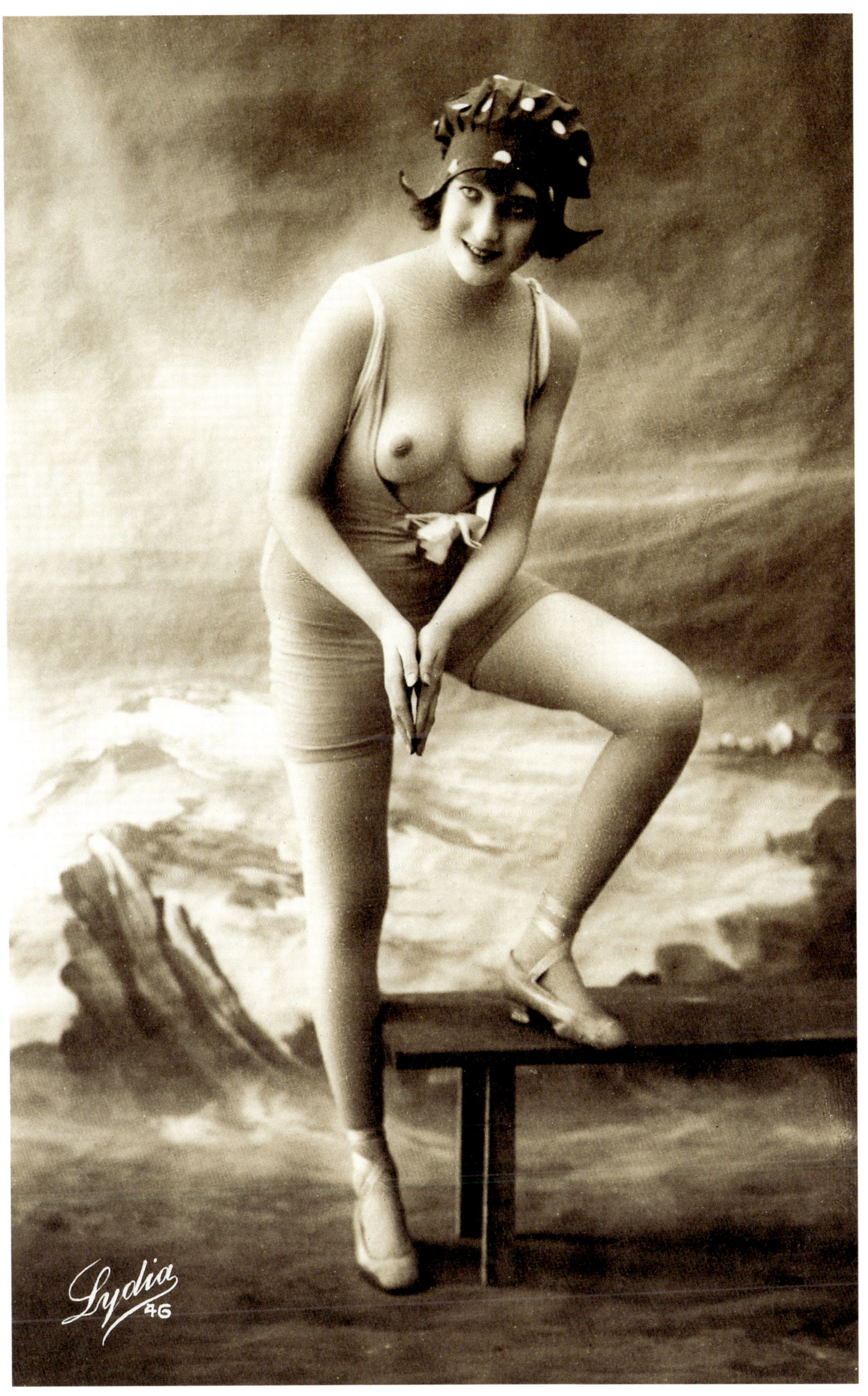
Lydia
46

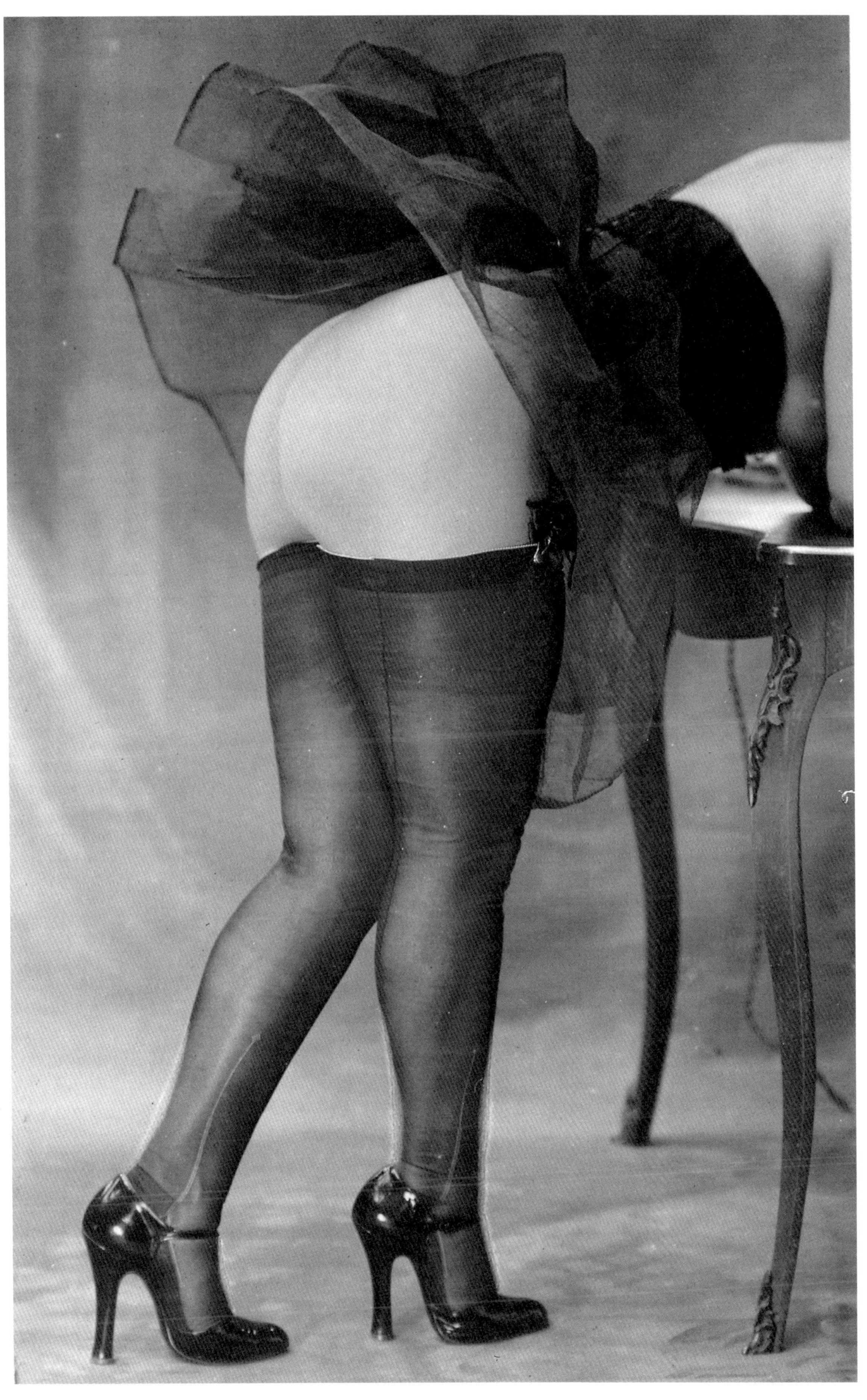

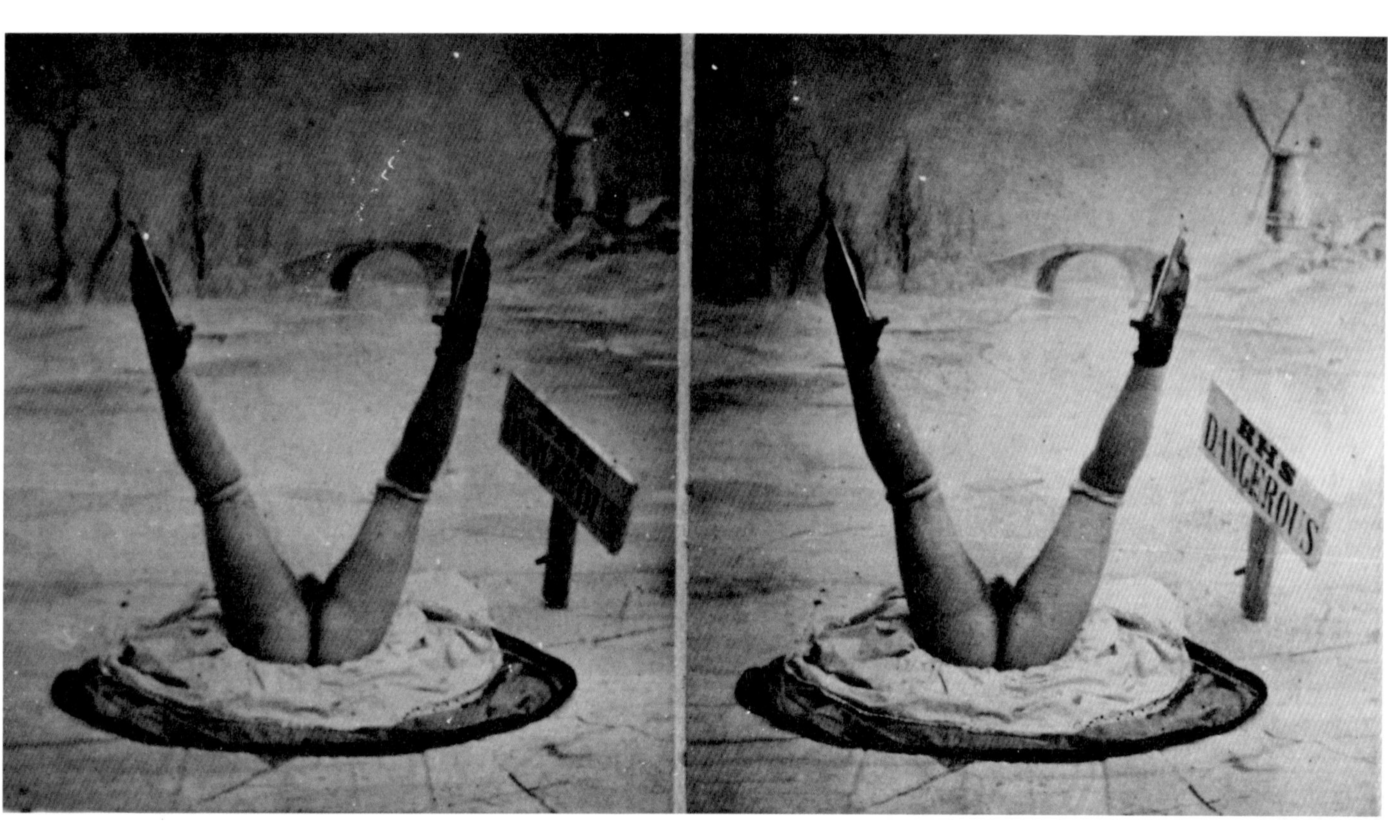
DANGEROUS
DANGEROUS

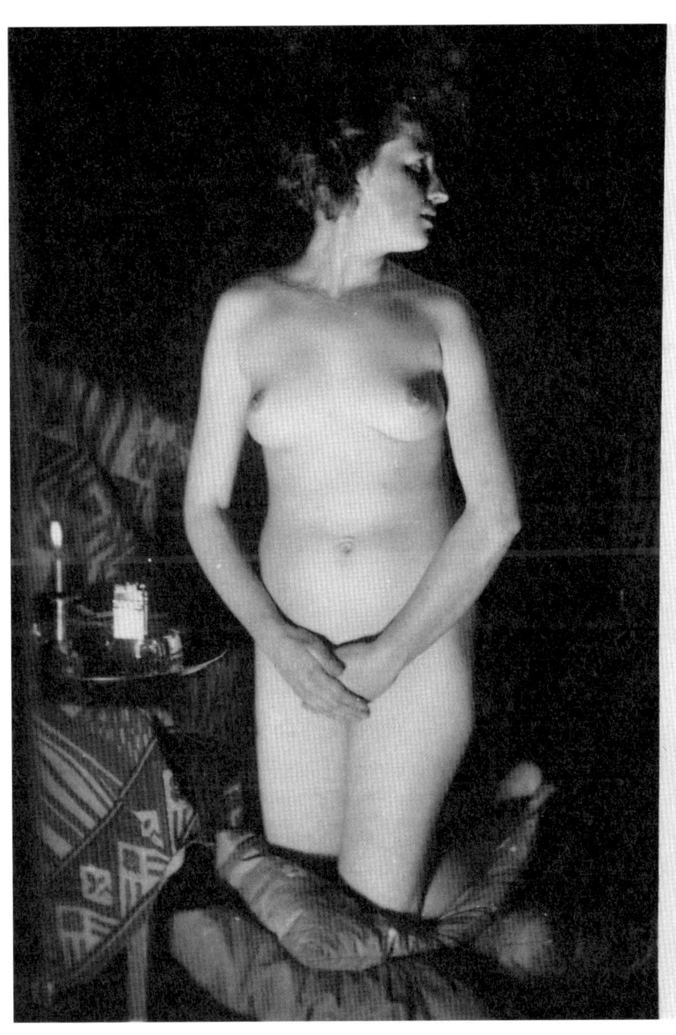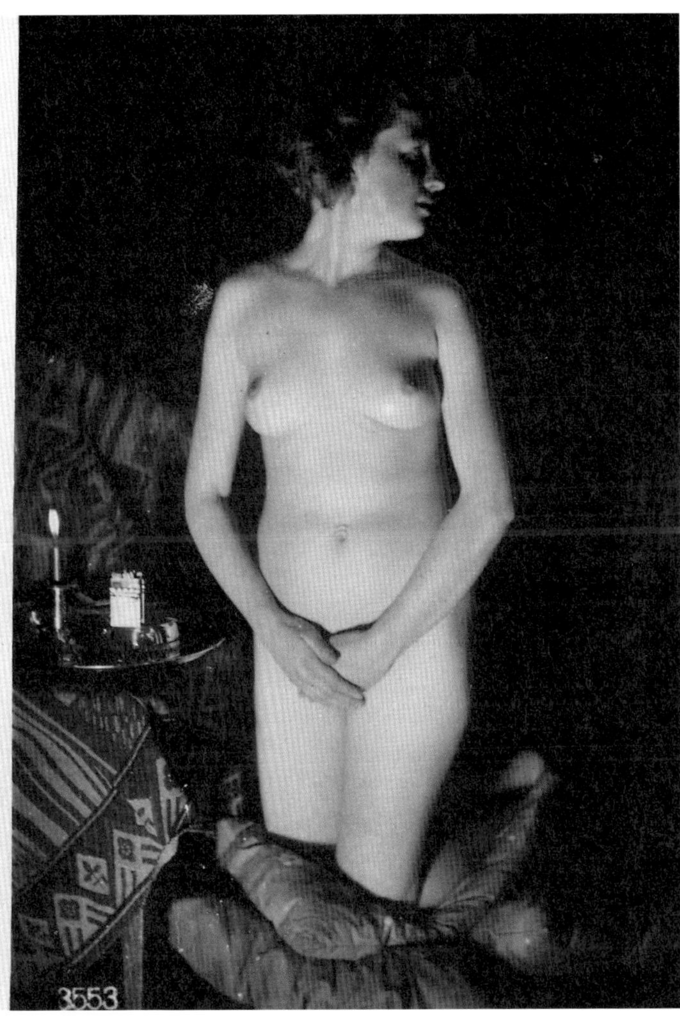

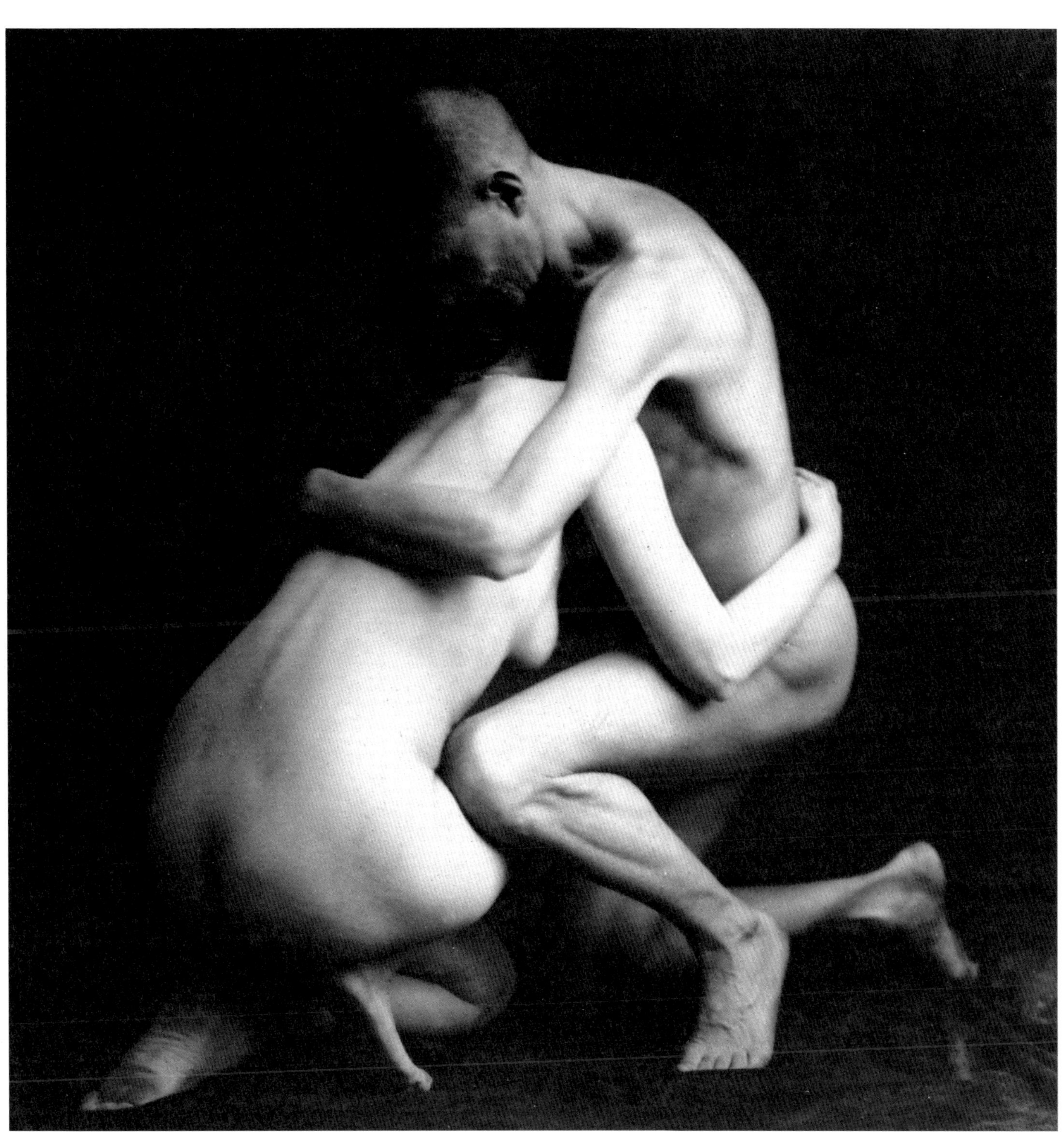

COLLECTING SEX

JENNIFER PEARSON YAMASHIRO

The life and works of Alfred C. Kinsey have attracted much attention from the time that his first colossal study on sexual behavior appeared. Four biographies and numerous analyses of Kinsey's research have since been published.[1] These books and articles written over the past fifty years have contributed to his enduring legacy. However, our memories of the man, both preempted and propelled by his death in 1956, can be attributed to the deep cultural impact made by his two landmark publications, *Sexual Behavior in the Human Male* (1948) and *Sexual Behavior in the Human Female* (1953).[2] Neither the medical press that published the work nor Kinsey himself expected the books to be popular with the general public. Despite the intended scholarly audience and relatively small printings, they became best-sellers. As a result, Kinsey's name surged into American culture in the form of song lyrics, polite conversation, jokes, and even cartoons (figure 1).[3] Some regarded him as a hero and a pathfinder, others as a dangerous influence, and still others as an accomplished entomologist who was not qualified to conduct sex research.[4] Despite the differing interpretations of the man responsible for these groundbreaking scientific queries, there is no denying that the male volume made the name Kinsey synonymous with sex.

The Kinsey Reports forced Americans to acknowledge the schism between their perceptions and their practices in sexual matters. Kinsey's studies offered a "peek" into the sex lives of average citizens, not of glamorous movie stars and sex symbols who had or were rumored to have had unconventional lifestyles. During the 1940s and 1950s, the nation was shocked by the reports' statistics that 37 percent of adult men had had a homosexual experience that resulted in orgasm and almost 50 percent of women had had pre-marital sex. These findings upset the country's dominant patriarchal beliefs that masculine strength was heterosexual and respectable femininity for the single woman meant virginity. Kinsey was not interested in such ideals; he was concerned with Americans' actual sexual practice. He did not scrutinize displays of

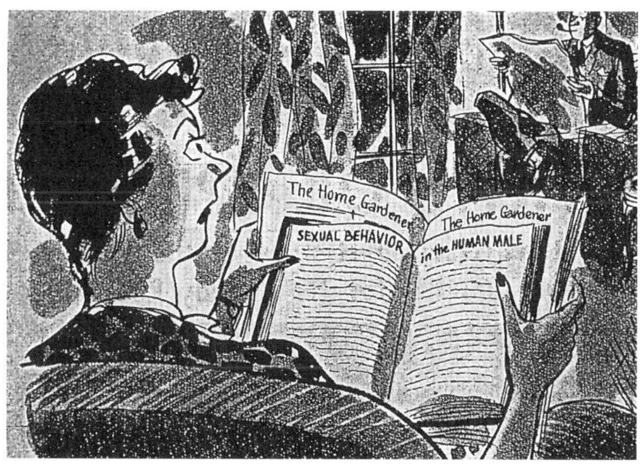

FIGURE 1
Even before Kinsey's volume on male sexuality hit the bookstores, the media generated much interest in this college professor's research. This cartoon appeared in the *New York Times* on January 4, 1948, several months before the release of *Sexual Behavior in the Human Male.*

sexual behavior as they were, for example, enacted in the movies.[5] However, he did rely on a wide array of representations, including visual images, to extend his knowledge and inform his theories.

From even the earliest stages of his sex research, it is clear that Kinsey valued visual representation. He collected and used imagery in a number of ways. Despite considerable speculation, Kinsey and his colleagues had substantial, scholarly reasons for amassing an archive of erotica. The main purpose of this resource was to complement the data on sexual behavior that was obtained through interviews. Kinsey and his research team viewed a variety of materials, including visual imagery, as useful, even scientific data. Kinsey referred to art as data in his response to an antiquarian's lead on available Asian art: "We might be interested in acquiring additional Oriental material. It would depend, however, upon the nature of the material and how much it added to the *stock of data* that are already available from the considerable collection that we now own."[6] Viewing imagery as data was central to his philosophy and collecting art became vital to his research. Interestingly, many of the people with whom he corresponded adapted his use of the word "data" when writing about visual works, calling materials like prints and drawings "data." This obscures the specific objects or media being discussed, but applying the term data to a variety of sexually explicit materials also sweeps them into the respectable world of science. In this domain, the issue of erotica versus pornography is suspended and the sexually explicit items become imbued with an air of propriety and legitimacy.

Photographs appear to have had special value for the research. Compared to many of the other materials Kinsey collected, the time and attention given to the organization of the massive archive of sexually explicit photographs attest to their significance. Recently, the photographs and films that were produced internally have been recognized as more representative of "truth" than images obtained from other sources.[7] However, the painstaking classification of all of the photographs reveals that the collection functions as documentary evidence. The effort Kinsey and his colleagues made to amass such a collection corresponds to the taxonomic methodology upon which he had relied as an entomologist. Kinsey believed that collecting an enormous amount of material (whether the subject was bugs or sex) was fundamental to scientific exploration. About his gall wasp collection he stated in 1936: "At long last I may be able to convince somebody that I have been laying a foundation in all these eighteen years—on which the finished structure may now rise rapidly."[8] Once his collection of wasps was in place, he was poised to write prolifically about his subject. However, his new research topic overwhelmed these plans. It was as a scholar, a scientist, and a taxonomist that Kinsey sought to attain an enormous number of personal histories for his study of sexual behavior.[9] It is probable that, by the same reasoning, he believed an extensive collection of erotica would enhance the solidity and persuasiveness of his conclusions—just as his impressive collection of gall wasps had formed the basis of his expertise in entomology.

At last scholars are beginning to look beyond the events of Kinsey's life to investigate the forces that shaped his vision and his research.[10] However, the importance of his sex-related collection is still often overlooked. Only a few articles have been devoted to the institute's holdings of erotica.[11] Though these articles do focus on the photographic collections, *Peek* presents the widest selection and largest number of photographs from the vast archive to date. This volume introduces the Kinsey Institute's collection of photographs as well as their original scientific function, the reasons and methods for accumulating them, and the size and scope of this rich visual resource today. Just as Kinsey's research projects attempted to look behind closed doors into the private sexual lives of average Americans, *Peek* allows a wider audience to get a glimpse of a selection of photographs from the Kinsey Institute. The images are remarkable for their diversity in representation and in concept. The photographs themselves raise the question, What constitutes an erotic or sexual picture? A substantial number of images in this book, noticeably, do not depict sexual activity at all. Yet they are part of the photography collection at a scientific research institute specializing in the study of sex. One might ask if eroticism is seen in the photograph of a male nude physique (page 46), an awkwardly posed pair with hidden faces and exposed genitals (page 40), an "exotic" hula dancer, or a passionate embrace (page 49). The wide range of the images in the institute's collection suggests that eroticism differs according to the observer. Perhaps a better question is, Can eroticism ever really be visible in a photograph or do photographs merely have the ability to stimulate arousal in some viewers?

IN THE BEGINNING

Before Kinsey joined the emerging field of sex research and published the extraordinary male and female volumes, he had spent nearly twenty years researching gall wasps and teaching biology at the main campus of Indiana University (IU) in Bloomington, Indiana. The transition of his professional and public persona from bug specialist to sex doctor is most often attributed to his role as the lead faculty member in charge of coordinating a new course on marriage. Although Kinsey had advocated for sex education and expressed interest in the variation of sexual practices long before 1938, the marriage course did provide a unique opportunity for him to express factual information as well as his own views on the subject of sex.

Here, Kinsey introduced visual images in one of his first public forums: the classroom. During the years that Kinsey gave the biology lectures in the newly forged, team-taught marriage course at Indiana University, he showed his coed classes slides of sexual intercourse and of male and female genitalia (figure 2).[12] Kinsey's use of

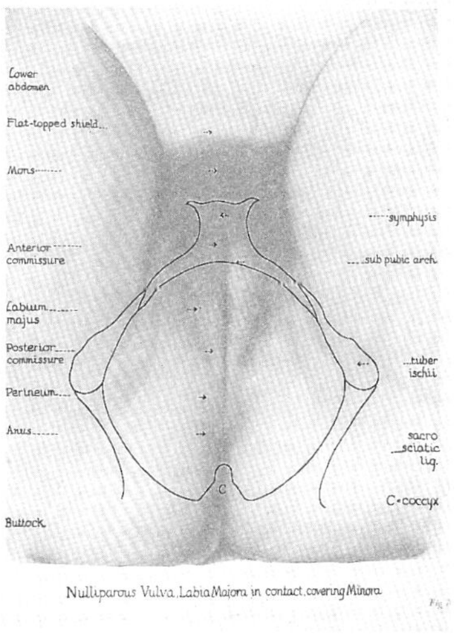

FIGURE 2
Kinsey showed slides to illustrate facts given in his biology lectures for the marriage course. He used Robert Latou Dickinson's *Atlas of Human Sex Anatomy* (1933) as a source for imagery. The vulva, pictured here, may have been shown to Kinsey's class.

images at the preliminary stage of his career in sex confirms that he regarded imagery as essential in his teaching as well as later in his research.

The structure of Indiana University's marriage course and the content of Kinsey's lectures diverged sharply from the focus on morality that was espoused by hygiene courses once taught throughout the nation's universities.[13] In contrast to its predecessor, the interdisciplinary marriage class at IU covered a wide range of topics, including the economic, ethical, and legal aspects of marriage; the sociology of the family; pregnancy, birth, and venereal disease; the biological basis of human sexual response; human reproduction; and sterility.[14] Students wrote glowing evaluations of the course, and particularly of Kinsey's lectures. Nevertheless, there was opposition to the marriage class (from physicians, ministers, administrators, and faculty) and, more specifically, to the illustrations shown to the students[15]—not to mention Kinsey's appeal for students to contribute their histories, made routinely at the conclusion of his lectures. Initially, in spite of complaints from faculty and community members, Herman Wells, then president of Indiana University, did not ask Kinsey to alter his lectures.[16] Kinsey, as coordinator, did make efforts to eliminate or at least minimize potential controversy arising from the course.[17] In the same spirit, he could have withdrawn the graphic visual components from his lectures. The fact that he did not do so as a precaution provides another early example of his belief in the importance of visual images. The purpose of the slides in Kinsey's lectures was to illustrate points about biological facts and functions, which is markedly different from the political, economic, and cultural analyses of pornography that are taking place in college classrooms across the country today. Although the entrance of sexually explicit materials into the hallowed halls of the academy has recently become a hot topic for debate,[18] it is clearly not a new phenomenon.

RAW DATA

Very soon after Kinsey started studying human sexual behavior in the late 1930s, he began collecting a wide variety of supplemental material relating to sexual practice. Kinsey accepted diverse materials from the many people who were willing to make contributions. He separated these intellectually into two groups: recorded data and observed data:

> The recorded data consisted of sexual calendars, correspondence, fiction, and graffiti, as well as "some 16,000 works of art." Observed data referred to studies conducted by gynecologists, obstetricians, urologists, and other clinicians, along with information gathered "from the direct observation of mammalian sexual activities and human sociosexual relationships."[19]

Although his research team underwent rigorous training before taking histories, it is somewhat ironic that the very atmosphere of working on a team might have been what prepared him to trust the accuracy and integrity of recorded and, especially, observed data. Indeed he welcomed observed data from medical doctors (most notably Robert Latou Dickinson) and sexual enthusiasts alike.[20] Information from such sources quickly became part of the institute's records. "Former staff members recall that Kinsey often remarked, 'Our data shows such and such,' when referring to materials that only recently had been subsumed into his own data after being contributed by someone else."[21] At any rate, Kinsey regarded observed and recorded data as information valuable to his research. This attitude, extending to visual arts in general and to photographs in particular, reveals his working definition of data as any record that could shed light on the subject at hand. In order for these materials to be useful, Kinsey relied upon his own scientific objectivity to interpret them—and in the cases of observed data, Kinsey trusted the objectivity of other observers in recording the information.

Without disrupting the immense cultural value of the Kinsey Institute's photographic archive, perhaps it is worth considering the tension between scientific objectivity and voyeurism—albeit Kinsey and his colleagues emphatically denied any relationship between the two existed. Of course, the concept of objectivity is vastly different today—if indeed it still exists at all—than it was forty or fifty years ago. Today, it is widely recognized that all research is imbued with the author's subjectivity. The disclosure or recognition of a point of view does not render automatically the conclusions of a study or analysis false, erroneous, or sloppy, by any means. Often the effect is quite the reverse. Contrary to the contemporary perspective that subjectivity has replaced objectivity, Kinsey believed firmly that facts could be observed, recorded, interpreted, and reported without distortion. The institute's interest in photography and film seems related to the scientific investment in objectivity.

In the classroom, Kinsey used images as illustrations of fact, but in the research they played another role. Although the pages of his lengthy studies are peppered with tables and statistics rather than images, it is clear that he saw depictions as raw data to be interpreted. Art could aid the scientists in several ways. According to the author (probably Kinsey) of an internal institute document, "representations of sexual action...are indispensible [sic] sources of data for any scientific study of sex."[22] This declaration of value is supported by a list of possible contributions. The author states that representations have the capacity to provide information about the creators' and consumers' desires and sexual interests, attitudes about sexuality specific to social classes and entire cultures as well as present-day attitudes and practices, sexual anatomy, and techniques of activity. In the final point, which states that images and literature may provide insight into a variety of problems from the biological, psychological, medical, and social perspectives, a single example of how erotic art may have been useful to the institute's researchers is given.[23] In considering the differences between male and female sexual responses, the research team looked at a number of anatomical studies and scientific laboratory investigations as well as drawings by well-known male and female artists, amateur artists, and mental patients, and graffiti in public rest rooms. This illuminates the range of material that might have been examined, but neither it nor the text of the female volume itself connects particular visual examples to conclusions. However, in a letter to a psychiatrist,

Kinsey discussed his findings on the drawings made by mental patients: "The female material is as totally different from the male material as anything we have said about erotic response of male and female. The male material is, of course, primarily genital and deals with sexual performance in vernacular terms. The female material is primarily social and only incidentally erotic."[24] In most cases, the actual and direct use of specific images in the scientific analyses and investigations by Kinsey and his colleagues remains vague. Nevertheless, this example confirms that Kinsey's interpretation of visual material contributed to and supported his thinking.

Despite a lack of clear examples of exactly how art informed the research, much effort was devoted to transforming the photographs into data. Of the estimated 75,000 photographs at the institute today, the largest component is the Documentary Collection, which contains about 50,000 images ranging in date from the 1880s to 1970.[25] For decades, each photograph in the Documentary Collection was mounted onto an 8x10" piece of card stock and then assigned to a category, which was represented by a code. (This code was an adaptation of the code developed to record, concisely and confidentially, sexual histories.) The category to which it had been allocated was either stamped or printed on the upper left-hand corner of the card stock. As an initial stage in the sorting process, photographs were divided into four basic, though incongruous, groups: special photographic formats (such as stereo cards and cabinet cards), special interests (like anthropology and tattoo), sexual behaviors, and male and female figure photography. There are approximately fifty different major categories, each meticulously defined, stemming from the four main branches. These are arranged alphabetically by code, literally from A (ANL for analinctus) to Z (for zoophilia).

The majority of the photographs in the Documentary Collection depict either male and female figures or various sexual activities. For these, the subjects' state of undress and their positions were given additional attention in order to create further divisions. For instance, the combination print of a nude woman seated on a hillside, gazing at the sky (figure 3) is classified as ♀ FIG XG SIT HND BLW. The first

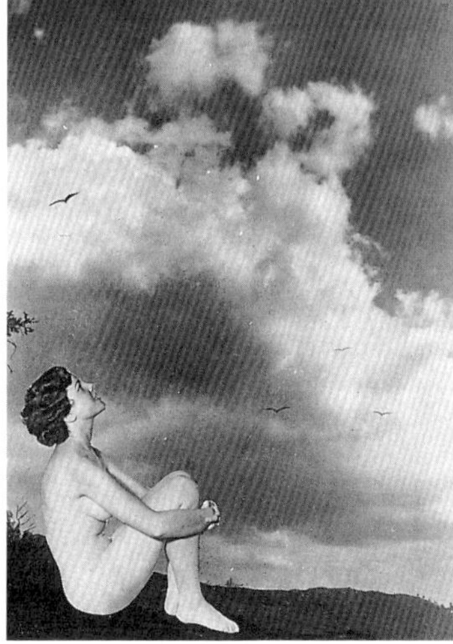

FIGURE 3
This is one of thousands of
female figure photographs in
the Kinsey Institute's collection.

portion of the code is easily decipherable; it signifies the female figure category. The enormity of this category required that it be further divided to be meaningful and navigable. Therefore, the rest of the code indicates the exposure (or, in this case, concealment) of the model's genitalia and her position. XG translates loosely as covered genitals. ♀ FIG XG is defined as "female figure, nude, with genitalia concealed by the pose or by some minimal cover not acceptable on the beach, e.g., a small G-string, a sequin, a wisp of gauze, etc. Or, the pubic hair may be painted out."[26] In this photograph, it is the subject's pose that covers her genitalia, but we can appreciate the care and detail with which other possibilities are considered and listed. The remainder of the classification, SIT HND BLW, indicates the subject's position. The seated position is defined, very specifically, according to the precise measurement of angles (figure 4). Paul Gebhard, responsible for overseeing the classification and organization of the photographs, admitted that while he had a protractor for measuring the positions, he became adept at judging the angles without instruments, depending solely on his eyes.[27] HND BLW designates the position of the model's hands. Comparable to the parameters for determining whether a model was sitting, standing, stooping, squatting, or kneeling, the instructions for judging the hand position are equally thorough: "If either one or both of the hands (which includes up to the wrist) are above a horizontal line drawn at the bottommost visible point of the breasts, then classify the photo 'Hand-Above.' If not, or if it is impossible to discern, then classify 'Hand-Below.' Ignore perspective." Despite the clinical impression left by a majority of the positional definitions, a few of the codes reflect popular culture. The use of "69" provides the most notable example of vernacular sexual terminology entering the coding system. Pages 38–9 were classified as GO 69 HT (genital oral, 69, heterosexual), meaning "genital oral mutual" (fellation and cunnilingus at the same time).

For the sake of confidentiality, very little, if any, information about the photographs' provenance was recorded. The usual details about the history of an image's production, sale, circulation, and ownership are replaced at the institute by this elaborate classification system. Although part of the reason for not recording (or tracing) provenance was to maintain confidentiality of the donor, in many cases this information may have been unknown by the previous owner. At any rate, this organizational system effectively

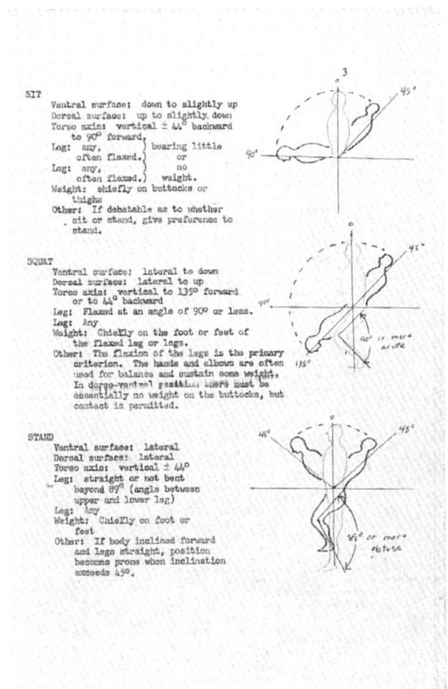

FIGURE 4
At Kinsey's request, Paul Gebhard organized the photography collection. To do so, Gebhard adapted categorical divisions from the sex research and created subdivisions according to the subjects' positions. Here, sitting, standing, and squatting are defined with amusing precision.

removed the photographs from their cultural context and refashioned them as data to be used in a scientific sphere. Still the question remains, If this photograph was seen as evidence of sexual behavior and interests, what exactly did it document? Surely it was not viewed as proof of the human nude in nature. The printing technique alone is enough, in this case, to reveal that manipulation in the darkroom was responsible for the placement of the figure. Rather than such a literal reading, the photograph's value to scientific research as raw data depended on interpretation. Careful and thoughtful analysis could render useful information about the attitudes and fantasies of the artist and the viewers, among other things. And fantasy was an activity significant enough for it to be addressed in Kinsey's standard interview.[28]

PRINCIPLES OF COLLECTING

Despite the evidence that attests to Kinsey's belief in the value of visual images, there is considerable confusion about his reasons for collecting them. Kinsey is often accused of collecting indiscriminately, trying desperately to get a sample of everything. It is not easy to identify a pattern in his collecting that reveals his motivations, particularly because of the scale of Kinsey's collecting endeavors.[29] However, a number of theories have been advanced. A favorite seems to be the simple statement that Kinsey was a collector by nature.[30] Others conjecture that Kinsey was driven to dominate and control everything around him and collecting offered one outlet for this compulsion. In connection with Kinsey's intense curiosity and ambition to cover his research topics thoroughly, he illuminates the purpose of the collection throughout his extensive correspondence. Indeed, he did have a goal, and a strategy. In September 1948, Kinsey wrote enthusiastically to his friend Dr. Sam Bernard Wortis, director of the psychiatric division at New York's Bellevue Hospital, about the expansion and development of the collections. In this letter he identifies at least one of the reasons for collecting supplementary material:

> You will be interested to know that both our library and collections have about tripled since you were here. Outright donations are beginning to come in, and we have had a splendid donation of the major portion of the time of two older outstanding artists. Consequently, our art collections are beginning to build up with a number of original things, including very ancient and Oriental things. With this increased material, we are beginning to get an insight into some of the physiologic aspects of diverse cultures, which distinctly helps in our consideration of our own *American behavior*.[31]

During the late 1940s, Kinsey was interested in Asian erotica, especially Japanese works. Apparently, he felt that the difference between it and U.S. erotica could contribute greatly to the elucidation of what distinguished American interests. Yet, a few years later, Kinsey also stated that his global investigation of human sexual activity was to "contribute to our understanding of the origon [sic] and social significance of sexual behavior."[32] Kinsey's interest in origins extended also to erotic representations and writings: "Dr. Sickman of the Kansas City Museum has been here in Bloomington the last two days…. He is helping us push back our data on the erotic material in China in the early centuries. This early material is important because it shows the origin of so many later things."[33] Thus, his academic pursuit was blended with a sense of pride and delight in having been able to attain some "very ancient things." Of course finding the source and following the proliferation of sexual behaviors in representation and in practice was not Kinsey's primary objective. Nevertheless, his interest in origins reveals a conceptual connection to contemporary studies in other fields. Anthropological research was moving in this direction during the mid-twentieth century, focusing on the outward movement of cultural artifacts from a single point of origin.[34]

Paul Gebhard, one of Kinsey's core research team members and the subsequent director of the Institute for Sex Research, shed light on another reason for collecting supplementary material, simultaneously providing an explanation for the accumulation of an extensive collection of sadomasochistic imagery. In his sworn statement for *U.S. v. 31 Photographs*, the federal court case that protected the institute's right to import erotica from abroad, Gebhard proclaimed that erotic representation contributed an important dimension to institute studies. Erotica supplemented the case histories with interests and activities, such as sadomasochism, that were not widely documented in the interviews.[35] It is worth noting that the Documentary Collection contains almost as many sadomasochistic photographs as female figure photographs. Arguably, this does not represent an accurate statistical relationship between the production and circulation of S&M photographs compared to that of, say, pinup girls.[36] The proportions of the collection were affected by Kinsey's research interests, the materials' availability on the market, and the individuals who donated materials. In addition to collecting in order to supplement the histories, identify national sexual characteristics, and investigate the intellectual pursuit of origins, Kinsey collected erotica in order to contribute to his general knowledge about sex. In his first book, a high school biology textbook, Kinsey remarked the following about the rewards of collecting: "It shows how complete a work you can accomplish, in what good order you can arrange the specimens, with what surpassing wisdom you can exhibit them, with what authority you can speak on your subject."[37] The last portion of his statement reverberates with significance. Considering that he leapt from entomology into human behavioral research, being able to speak with authority in the field of sex was vital for Kinsey.

AMASSING THE COLLECTION

As Kinsey's research branched beyond the Bloomington campus of IU and into the homosexual underground of Chicago, his access to an assortment of supporting materials also expanded. Some of the young men he met on Rush Street in Chicago had a number of items that piqued Kinsey's interest: a sexual diary, love letters, "revealing" letters written by a priest, and a collection of erotic photographs.[38] Photographs had the dual advantage of being both accessible and affordable. As a result, Kinsey employed the medium in various ways: they were both collected and generated by the institute. It was in 1938 that Kinsey first began to acquire photographs of a sexual nature. These were diverse in the subjects they depicted, ranging from dancers (figure 5) to genitalia (figure 6) to female figures. He followed a lead given to him in 1939 by one of his male subjects from Chicago for art model photographs. Within a few years, Kinsey's search for this type of imagery led him to Al Urban, an artist well known for his physical culture photographs. In the 1940s and 1950s, Kinsey acquired thousands of male physique photographs by popular photographers such as Al Urban, Lon of New York, and Bruce of Los Angeles, as well as recognized studios like the Western Photo Guild and the Athletic Model Guild. He even managed to acquire two commercial, but unusual, portfolios of photographs featuring the female bodybuilder Pudgy Stockton (page 134). Almost as fascinating as the photographs of Pudgy is the front cover of the portfolio that broadcasts the measurements of her physique (figure 7).

Kinsey collected widely and he relied on his professional contacts to kindle the growth of the collections. In his letters, he frequently asked the recipient to let him know about any relevant material and how he might obtain it. He had direct contact with a number of artists, collectors, booksellers, art dealers, and museum professionals; he also asked for assistance in expanding the collections from physicians, psychologists, counselors, prison wardens, servicemen, academic colleagues, and public relations professionals—in short, virtually anyone with whom he was in contact. These friends of the research informed Kinsey about materials available for acquisition, sometimes offering their opinions about quality and value. Through this grapevine network, his contacts eventually became international. To Kinsey many of these individuals were often more than just passing acquaintances. He customarily kept up correspondence for years, discussing many different subjects over the course of time. One letter from Al Urban comes to mind. Four years after Kinsey first wrote to Urban, the photographer contacted him, proposing that Kinsey write an anatomy textbook to be illustrated with his own photographs:

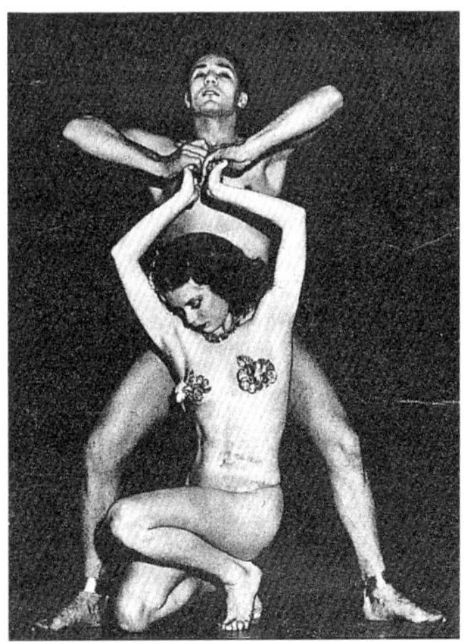

FIGURES 5 AND 6
Dancer Tito Valdez and his female partner caused a sensation on the New York stage with their "love dance" and scanty costumes. This photograph of the dancers and a close-up of male genitalia were among the first photographs to be acquired by Alfred Kinsey in 1938 to complement his studies on human sexual behavior.

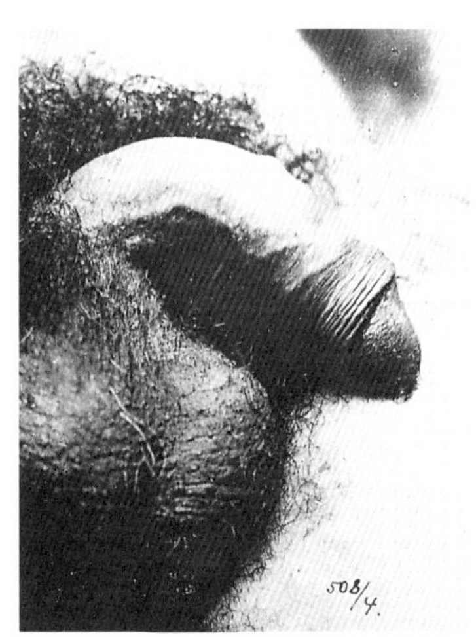

Recently, there have been several requests by doctors who have purchased nudes from me that I publish a book on anatomy for the medical profession, the medicos stating that most of the models featured in these medical books were fat, etc. I thought of you, that if you could write the text, I can easily supply the finest in photography having access to the best built men in America—right here on the West Coast.[39]

Kinsey turned down the photographer's offer and even managed to politely complain about the high prices of Urban's pictures, despite the special discount he received.

Many friends of the research made valuable contributions to the development of the collection over the years. Connections with several federal and state institutions proved to be very profitable, chiefly in terms of volume. Kinsey even imagined that the Federal Bureau of Investigation would support his research project by sending confiscated materials to him in Bloomington. In 1945, Kinsey wrote to his friend Wortis: "If we can get cooperation through police sources and through the FBI in building up our collections of materials, that would be especially valuable."[40] It was a bold move on Kinsey's part even to suggest this, given the politics of the McCarthy era.[41] Although the FBI did not cooperate in this manner, fifteen police departments across the country, some in major metropolitan areas and others in small towns, did send confiscations to the Institute for Sex Research. Several examples of police donations are reproduced in *Peek*. The two collages, one of buttocks (page 64), the other of penises (page 65), were given to the institute by police departments. The amateur photograph of a naked woman barbecuing (page 111) and the more seamless studio image of a woman basking in the gentle spray of a shower (page 35) also came to Bloomington as gifts from police. Such donations dwindled as police confiscations themselves dissipated. By the end of the 1960s, when such gifts ceased altogether, police departments had donated over 10,000 photographs. Soon after embarking on the new research path of sexual behavior, Kinsey apparently became interested in sexual offenses and planned to analyze this occurrence in greater depth in the future.

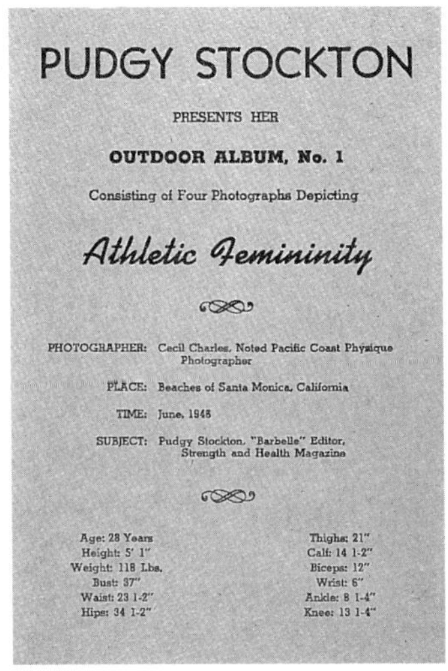

FIGURE 7

The impressive female bodybuilder Pudgy Stockton was active during the mid-1940s. Her physical dimensions, listed on the cover of the portfolio, are a far cry from a "pudgy" build!

The volume *Sex Offenders* was not published until 1965; however, Kinsey, Pomeroy, and Gebhard did a substantial amount of research in prisons before 1956.[42] Contacts that they developed while conducting this research led to the cooperation of over a dozen U.S. prison facilities. Over the years, a number of wardens sent hundreds of photographs from prisons and even more drawings produced by inmates. Images collected and made by prisoners constitute a unique set of work by amateurs at the Kinsey Institute. In addition to drawing freehand from imagination, inmates made erotica by tracing and augmenting commercial images. The prison works range from homemade comic books to modified girlie playing cards (figure 8). They are of interest for the fantasies that they depict, but also for representing the sorts of materials that were considered contraband in correctional institutions during that era. Another institutional affiliation that yielded rich contributions to the collections was the post office. Support from postal authorities is somewhat ironic in light of the trouble Kinsey had receiving shipments of materials he had ordered through the mail. During the 1940s, he frequently complained about the post office in his letters. In 1947, Kinsey wrote to an American military officer in Japan, advising him to avoid sending materials through the post office, if possible: "The post office is most difficult and I urge you to send everything in the future by express, if you find any possible way of doing so. Then nobody except the Customs can open it and I think that will be satisfactory to us. The post office is more difficult to control because any clerk down the line can cause trouble."[43] He later discovered that "any clerk down the line" in the Customs Bureau could cause trouble for him too.

Presumably Kinsey was able to acquire thousands of photographs because they were readily available. Unfortunately, much of the history regarding the circulation and sale of erotic materials is hazy. However, the number of duplicates sent to the Institute for Sex Research from different dealers and donors supports the assumption that erotic imagery was ubiquitous, in one small way. For example, five different sources, all from different cities located across the United States, sent the same amateurish photograph of three women engaged in sexual activity (figure 9). The fact that the same image came into the possession of at least five of Kinsey's supporters suggests that it was popular and/or easily obtainable even though it

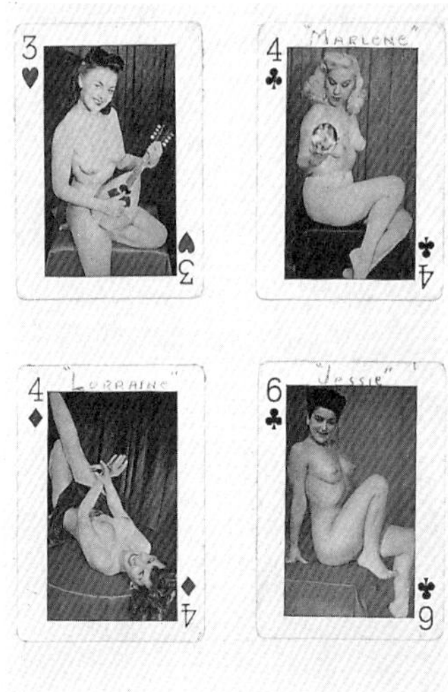

FIGURE 8
A prison inmate named some
of the models pictured in this
set of playing cards.

was probably not made by a professional photographer or intended for bulk production. We expect that some photographs, like those made of burlesque performers and stars would have been mass-produced and commercially available. However, it is enlightening to find that some of the amateur images were distributed widely as well. While the historical aspect of circulation through duplicates is intriguing to contemporary scholars, acquiring duplicates was one of Kinsey's pet peeves. So to avoid overlap, duplicates were identified and recorded as carefully as possible. Of course the size of the photographic collection alone thwarted even the most diligent efforts to steer clear of repetition altogether. Hence, it is possible to find duplicates (usually assigned to different categories) in the Documentary Collection.

Besides collecting photographs from external sources, the institute also made them. Prior to 1949 when a permanent staff photographer was hired, Paul Gebhard, who joined the staff in 1946, made photographs internally. Once Kinsey hired William Dellenback, however, it was possible for photographic projects to multiply. In addition to making photographic copies of original artwork that the institute could not afford to acquire, Dellenback photographed objects from the institute's collection as well as those in other public and private collections. He made, for example, hundreds of 8x10" black and white photographs of Moche pottery vessels (that he shot in Peru during the summer of 1954) and color transparencies of the extensive collection of Japanese erotic prints at the Boston Museum of Fine Arts. Having photographic copies of unobtainable originals was a good alternative to having nothing. Although Kinsey was often interested in acquiring ancient and original objects and images for his collection, at times his budget and other constraints did not allow him to do so. Kinsey wrote to a commercial bookseller located in Kyoto, Japan, in 1950: "We are also interested in the various erotic objects which you describe in the last paragraph of your letter. We have a fair collection of these already but could very well make additions to our list. We cannot afford to get objects that have high value because of their age or their special interest to art collectors. We have to be satisfied with photographs of such items."[44] When he could not acquire original prints and paintings, photographs sufficed.

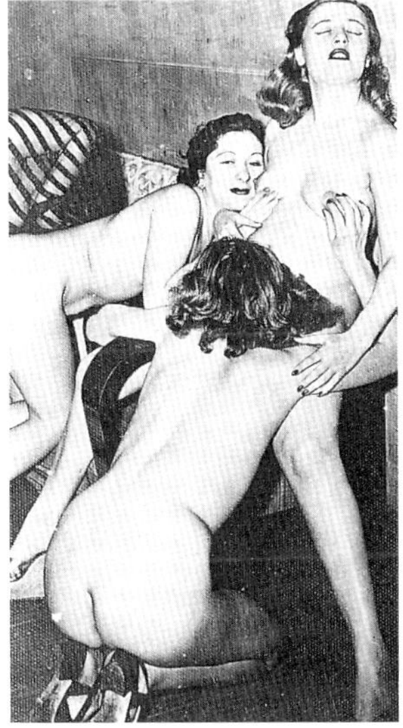

FIGURE 9
Five different copies of this photograph were sent to the Institute for Sex Research between 1953 and 1972. Two came from individuals in Maryland and the others were sent by people living in California, Indiana, and Washington, D.C.

Over the decades, Dellenback also produced a pictorial history of the institute by making portraits of staff and visitors. Not only did he record the progress and development of the research program, he also made photographs for specific institute projects. In the documentary mode, Dellenback made approximately 200 still photographs to complement a study on the variation of genitalia and female breasts. Examining and photographing anatomical differences was the preliminary step toward observing sexual behavior firsthand. The latter was accomplished, in part, through film. Dellenback recorded the sexual behavior of higher mammals, including chimpanzees, cattle, hogs, and, occasionally, humans. When the opportunities arose, Dellenback filmed human sexual activity in Bloomington as well as other locations. Empiricism was the purpose of the filming, as Pomeroy explains:

> It must be understood that, while they [the films] anticipated in some respects what Masters and Johnson were to do later, our films were in no way comparable to what the Saint Louis scientists were able to accomplish. Ours was an extremely small sampling: twenty homosexual couples, ten heterosexual couples and about twenty-five males and females engaged in masturbation.... [T]he observations were useful only in the way they were intended—that is, for the first time to provide us with firsthand knowledge of what actually occurred in a wide range of sexual behavior.[45]

The films, like the photographs, were valuable data.

A PROGRESSIVE ARCHIVE

The heyday of collecting for Alfred Kinsey was short-lived, lasting roughly from 1948 through 1950. After the publication and commercial success of the male volume, Kinsey had the resources and the network to collect valuable and rare erotica. His international contacts enabled him to acquire materials from a wide variety of cultures and time periods. However, Kinsey's collecting was hindered on occasion by two factors: budget constraints and the United States Customs Bureau. It should be noted that Kinsey invoked limited funds on occasion as a device to ward off pesky dealers. However, the problem with Customs more seriously hindered his ability to collect materials than insufficient funds.[46] It also caused more of a disturbance to his research than annoying and persistent dealers did. Officers in Indianapolis and New York had begun seizing and detaining shipments to the Institute for Sex Research by the end of the 1940s. Kinsey's attorneys encouraged him to continue to order materials from overseas, though budgetary constraints began to slow the institute's acquisition of art by early 1951.[47] In 1952 Kinsey decided to stop purchasing material from abroad since the constant seizures made by Customs failed to initiate a decision or forfeiture proceedings and prevented him from receiving the materials he had purchased.[48] The case was finally settled in 1957, over a year after Kinsey's death, when a federal judge ruled in the institute's favor. Thanks to Kinsey's persistence, Herman Wells's support, and the legal decision, it was possible to build the archive of sexually explicit materials at a conservative midwestern university during the height of the Cold War. By 1956, the year of his death, Kinsey had amassed an estimated 20,000 photographs.[49]

Kinsey's interest in the erotic elements in art, especially photography, seemed to embrace two concepts of documentary. In the most straightforward sense, photographs offered evidence, inasmuch as any form of representation can, that activities like cunnilingus and group sex actually occurred. It is possible that of all the externally produced photographs, the amateur images may have had the most direct relationship to practice. Arguably, these images offered a glimpse into the average person's sexual experience, sharing the aim of Kinsey's scientific project. However, according to the function of visual imagery as raw data at the institute, photographs also gave insights into issues of arousal and desire as well as class and cultural differences. On the one hand, it seems that Kinsey believed that eroticism could be seen and documented in photographs. Yet the photographs were not naively or simply understood as transparent media, a window on reality. Kinsey valued these images not only for their function as records, but also for their ability to convey, stimulate, and reveal desires.

Kinsey's vision laid a progressive foundation for collecting compelling materials diverse in subject matter and media. Unlike the holdings in most visual repositories, especially those in fine art museums, Kinsey collected imagery regardless of aesthetic value. In fact, he once remarked: "The values do not depend on the authorship of the material, nor upon its intrinsic worth as art, but upon the fact that the material has wide public distribution. In fact, French postcards and cheap Japanese prints may be more significant in a scientific study of sex than the world's finest art."[50] Kinsey's assessment was probably based on the understanding that the primary audience for fine art was an elite group and, as a result, too narrow to consider in isolation. For a brief period, from 1949 to 1951, however, Kinsey became intensely interested in the fine arts and made an effort to obtain the histories of established artists and writers and to study their acclaimed masterpieces. In January 1950, Kinsey wrote to Tennessee Williams:

> As you may know, we are making an extensive study of the erotic element
> in the arts. This covers painting, music, writing, the stage, etc. One of
> the plays we have studied in some detail has been your "Streetcar." We
> have been fortunate enough to obtain histories from a high proportion
> of the actors and two of the companies which have put on the play
> "Streetcar," and it has made it possible to correlate their acting with
> their sexual backgrounds.[51]

Kinsey discussed creativity and their works with a wide array of artists, including actors, writers, and visual artists.[52] While the correspondence reveals some of Kinsey's ideas regarding the arts, his thoughts are not complete. He had planned to write a volume on erotic expression in the arts. We can only lament the fact that he ran out of time before he was able to do so. Nevertheless, his use of imagery, commitment to collecting, and interest in diverse visual representation are tributes to his rich legacy.

Today, the visual holdings encompass a massive and unique collection of photographs, films, and art. In addition to the Documentary Collection and Dellenback's archive of photographs, the institute has several hundred amateur albums (pages 58–9), over 1,500 turn-of-the-century postcards (page 153), close to six hundred photographs by George Platt Lynes (pages 25, 30–1) as well as a large collection of his 8x10″ vintage negatives, and nearly three hundred photographs by Wilhelm von Gloeden (pages 92–3). The photography collection also includes numerous reproductions of original images not housed in the institute's collection. The film collection is similarly extensive, including films made internally and thousands of other films and videos. Among these is a particularly rich cache of stag films. Sexy posters and lobby cards, advertising both mainstream films and blue movies, complement the film collection (figure 10).

The collection currently consists of over 7,000 two-dimensional and three-dimensional works of art from ancient to modern times. Perhaps motivated by Kinsey's interest in origins, the institute has a number of ancient artifacts including an Egyptian terra-cotta of a couple in coitus that dates from 3200 B.C., Moche pottery vessels, the world's only surviving copy of a sixteenth-century illustrated volume of Chinese erotic poetry (*Su Wo Pien*), and Roman frescoes and figurines. The art collection, like the photography collection, also contains work by celebrated masters such as Rembrandt, Marcantonio Raimondi, Pablo Picasso, Henri Matisse, Marc Chagall, Pavel Tchelitchew, and Lenore Fini as well as work by amateurs. The amateur work ranges from graffiti to images made by prisoners and children. The art collection also has a number of items that are perhaps better described as ephemera. Examples of these include decks of playing cards; novelty bar accessories like phallic swizzle sticks and a set of "Busty" coasters; girlie

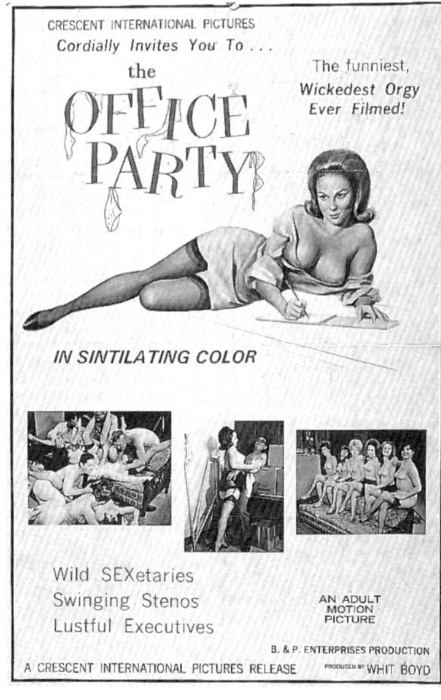

FIGURE 10
During the Second World War, when women started entering the workforce in great numbers, the office became another landscape for erotic representation.

ashtrays, flasks, and inkwells; and, my personal favorite, a collection of "fancy" latex condoms. Many of the pieces in the visual collection are connected in some way to items in the library and archives, which contain manuscripts, diaries, ephemera, books, journals, and other materials.[53]

The collection, well preserved at the research center that bears Kinsey's name, has supported the institute's initiatives and mission in a number of ways since its incorporation in 1947. The diversity of materials and the range of makers are unique among collections and valuable for current researchers. The collection continues to flourish in this manner. Coins, T-shirts, and hats bearing sexual jokes and innuendoes; glass-plate copy negatives of nineteenth-century photographs; delicate porcelain Japanese sake cups; snapshots of participants, clad in swimwear, at a beach event called Hispandex; hundreds of Polaroids of prostitutes from the 1970s and 1980s; and several sexualized spoofs on the wildly popular Beanie Babies are among the gifts recently given to the institute. These fascinating cultural artifacts are balanced by fine art contributions. A few exceptional examples of fine art photographs are reproduced as plates in *Peek*. In the last decade, the institute has received gifts of work created by accomplished professional artists, including Joel-Peter Witkin (figure 11), Mariette Pathy Allen, Pierre et Gilles, Akio Takamori, and George Lange. Emerging artists like Laura Abel, Heather Firth, Laurie Long, and Kiriko Shirobayashi, among others, have also been generous in donating their work to the institute. The collections have grown in a pattern that reflects Kinsey's original intention, gaining strength through diversity.

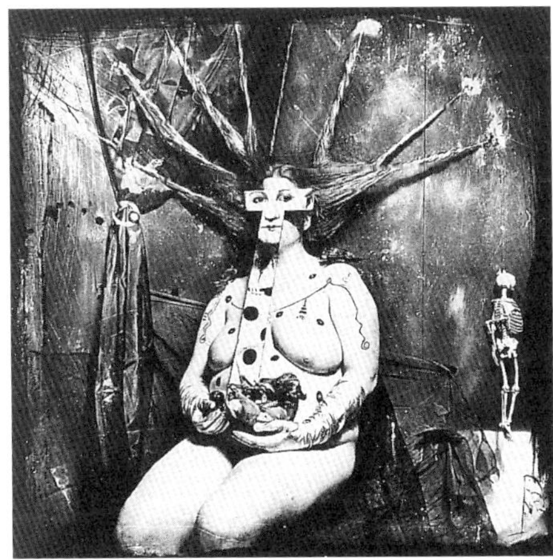

FIGURE 11
Celebrated photographer Joel-Peter Witkin generously donated his 1984 *Portrait of Nan* to the Kinsey Institute's permanent collection in 1990.

NOTES

In order to maintain the confidentiality of individuals who donated materials to the collections, initials will be used in the notes instead of names. For the sake of brevity, Kinsey's initials, ACK, will be used for citing his correspondence.

1 Although the books and articles on Kinsey's research and its impact are too numerous to name here, the four biographies are: Cornelia V. Christenson, *Kinsey: A Biography* (Bloomington, IN: Indiana University Press, 1971); Wardell B. Pomeroy, *Dr. Kinsey and the Institute for Sex Research* (New York: Harper & Row, 1972); James H. Jones, *Alfred C. Kinsey: A Public/Private Life* (New York: W. W. Norton & Co., 1997); and Jonathan Gathorne-Hardy, *Alfred C. Kinsey: Sex the Measure of All Things: A Biography* (London: Chatto & Windus, 1998).

2 Alfred C. Kinsey, Wardell Pomeroy, and Clyde Martin, *Sexual Behavior in the Human Male* (Philadelphia: Saunders, 1948) and Alfred C. Kinsey, Wardell Pomeroy, Clyde Martin, and Paul Gebhard, *Sexual Behavior in the Human Female* (Philadelphia: Saunders, 1953).

3 Many of the cartoons that appeared did not seem to trouble Kinsey. However, at least one comic strip did, causing him to consider legal action, which does not appear to have taken place. In a letter to his lawyer, Kinsey expressed his distress over a character called Dr. Pinsey (see ACK to Pilpel, September 13, 1952, ACK correspondence, Kinsey Institute Archive [hereafter KIA]): "I enclose some copies of a comic strip that has been running through a whole stream of newspapers throughout the country for the last month or twl [sic]. A number of my friends including our legal member on our staff…feel that it can do us a great deal of damage and that it is so obviously associated with us that we have grounds for complaint and might consider some way of forcing them to stop this strip. It began in a mild way but by now Dr. 'Pinsey' is making sexual advances to those from whome [sic] he is obtaining scientific information. This might very well color the reactions of a considerable segment of the public to our total research, and it is of course, a total perversion of any fact connected with the research."

4 All of the biographers include sections or chapters about the reactions to the publication of the research. Of course, Kinsey's studies were controversial upon publication and some aspects of the reports remain, to a slim minority, controversial even today. For more information about past and present controversies regarding the male and female volumes as well as particular aspects of Kinsey's research, please visit the Kinsey Institute's website http://www.indiana.edu/~kinsey

5 David Allyn, "Private Acts/Public Policy: Alfred Kinsey, the American Law Institute, and the Privatization of American Sexual Morality," *Journal of American Studies* 30 (1996): 405–28. See especially pages 414–15.

6 ACK to RS, January 26, 1951 (ACK correspondence, KIA). RS was an antiquary from Baltimore who corresponded with Kinsey from 1947 until 1953. Emphasis is mine.

7 Paul Gebhard, interview with the author, January 19, 1998. A full transcript of the interview is at the Kinsey Library.

8 ACK to Ralph Voris, July 8, 1936 (ACK correspondence, KIA).

9 Kinsey's ambition was to obtain 100,000 sexual histories. Together, he and institute researchers recorded close to 18,000 histories. Although the final figure is short of the goal, it is impressive nonetheless, and Kinsey's study remains the most comprehensive of its kind to date.

10 Judith Allen is currently doing exciting new research in this direction. Her book, *Kinsey's Women: Sexed Bodies, Heterosexuality, and Abortion, 1920–1960*, is forthcoming.

11 Former Kinsey Institute curator James Crump is the author of two articles and I am the author of the others. Please see James Crump, "The Kinsey Institute Archive: A Taxonomy of Erotic Photography," *History of Photography* 18:1 (1994): 1–12; James Crump, "Archiving Sexuality: The Photographic Collection of the Kinsey Institute," *Harms Way: Lust & Madness, Murder & Mayhem*, ed. Joel-Peter Witkin, 2nd ed. (Santa Fe, NM: Twin Palms Publishers, 1994); Jennifer Pearson Yamashiro, "In the Realm of the Sciences: The Kinsey Institute's 31 Photographs," in James Elias et al., *Porn 101: Eroticism, Pornography, and the First Amendment* (New York: Prometheus, 1999): 32–52; and Jennifer Pearson Yamashiro, *Sex in the Field* (doctoral dissertation, forthcoming). Please note that due to significant copy-editing errors in the book *Porn 101*, a clean copy of the article "In the Realm of the Sciences" is available upon request from the Kinsey Institute Library, Morrison Hall 313, Indiana University, Bloomington, IN 47405. Copies of the thirty-one photographs are also available for scholarly study from the Kinsey Institute Library.

In his first article, Crump considers Kinsey's taxonomic approach to collecting photographs in relation to Kinsey's desire to understand eroticism through the study of representation and expression. He concludes that Kinsey was ahead of his time, but unable to pursue the avenue of eroticism in the arts because of his untimely death. Crump's second article considers the institute's photographic archive in relation to the emergence of other archives dealing with sexuality and focuses on Kinsey's understanding of photographs as documents and his interest in diversity. My first article discusses the institute's federal obscenity case that enabled Kinsey to legally amass the archival collections and offers a cultural analysis of the thirty-one photographs that became the focus of the court case. My doctoral dissertation expands on the court case and thirty-one photographs. In the dissertation, I also consider more fully the significance and use of the collections, the theoretical issues that arise from the classification scheme, as well as the content and themes of a selection of the images.

12 Kinsey's second lecture was on the reproductive anatomy. In addition to a frank discussion of the sex organs and their functions, Kinsey showed slides of genitalia and coitus (Gathorne-Hardy, 126). In 1948, Kinsey identified Robert Latou Dickinson's *Atlas of*

Human Sex Anatomy as the source of the slides (Jones, 831, footnote 18). From Dickinson's book, I have selected an image that coincides with one of the topics of Kinsey's lectures. It is possible (though not confirmed) that he showed this image of the vulva to his students.

13 Jones, 321. Please see Jones's biography for a concise explanation of the social hygiene movement and the resulting courses on American college campuses.

14 Ibid., 322–36. Jones provides a full discussion of the development and teaching of the marriage course.

15 Gathorne-Hardy, 123–32. Dr. Thurman Rice, a professor at the IU medical school in Indianapolis, used to give the lecture on sex that had formerly been incorporated into the curriculum through the hygiene course. Rice offered to share the material he had collected on sex education over the years, and Kinsey slighted him by replying that he did not need it. Later, Rice attended one of Kinsey's biology lectures and was outraged by the slides shown in the class because he found them to be arousing.

16 In May 1940, however, pressure from critics reached a climax. As a result, President Wells gave Kinsey a choice. He could either continue teaching the marriage course if he altered some sections of his lectures and disbanded the practice of private "conferences" (essentially interviews conducted to obtain histories for his research), or give up teaching the marriage course and continue with his sex research. In September 1940, Kinsey responded to Wells. He chose the research. After Kinsey received several prestigious national grants, the university gave him a course reduction in 1942 to further support his research program. In 1945 Kinsey was appointed a research professor. This released him from teaching responsibilities altogether.

17 He asked only tenured faculty to give lectures for the marriage class. He also established the practice of having the team of faculty (including himself) deliver lectures for one another before presenting the material to the class.

18 For a discussion of expanding university curricula dealing with pornography, please see James Atlas, "The Loose Canon," *The New Yorker* (March 29, 1999): 60–65. For a specific example of a legal situation that arose out of one English professor's assignment to define pornography, see Stephen F. Rhode, "A Study in Free Expression," *Los Angeles Daily Journal* (September 6, 1996): 6.

19 Paul Robinson, *The Modernization of Sex: Havelock Ellis, Alfred Kinsey, William Masters, and Virginia Johnson* (New York: Harper & Row, 1976), 99–100.

20 The Kinsey Institute once housed all of Dickinson's papers. Although some important pieces of Dickinson's archive are at the institute, much of it is now at the Countway Library of Medicine at Harvard. In addition to the Dickinson material, the Kinsey Institute has important manuscript collections central to twentieth-century sexology, including some of the papers of Havelock Ellis, Harry Benjamin, and John Money.

21 Jones, 509.

22 "Significance of Erotic Art and Literature in Scientific Studies," unpublished memorandum (Customs case file 1953-1956, KIA). This document bears no date or initials that identify the author. However, the position in the writing and the location of the document makes it probable that Kinsey wrote the memo.

23 Ibid., 3.

24 ACK to Sam Bernard Wortis, January 10, 1947 (ACK correspondence, KIA).

25 On February 3, 1997, the institute's current director John Bancroft, former director Paul Gebhard, and I met to discuss naming the bulk of the Kinsey Institute's photography collection. The name Documentary Collection was agreed upon with the understanding that the term "documentary" did not preclude the possibility of aesthetic merit in individual photographs, but rather referred to the original, scientific motive for collecting the material.

26 These definitions, typed onto the same 8x10″ cardstock used to mount photographs, are housed at the beginning of each major category in the Documentary Collection.

27 Paul Gebhard, interview with the author, January 19, 1998 (Kinsey Institute Library).

28 For a list of the questions that refer to sexual behavior and fantasy, please see *The Kinsey Interview Kit*, compiled and edited by Joan Scherer Brewer (Bloomington, IN: The Kinsey Institute, 1985), 89–90. *The Kinsey Interview Kit* is available through the Kinsey Institute Library.

29 Please see "Collecting Nature, Archiving Erotica" in *Sex in the Field* (chapter two of my dissertation) for a fuller discussion of these and other theories regarding Kinsey as a collector.

30 Two recent examples of characterizing Kinsey as a "collector by nature" are in the Kinsey Institute's 50th anniversary exhibition catalog. Please see John Bancroft, "Foreword," in *The Art of Desire: Erotic Treasures from the Kinsey Institute* (Bloomington, IN: The Kinsey Institute, 1997), 5; and Jennifer Pearson Yamashiro, "History of the Kinsey Institute Collections," *The Art of Desire*, 9. I regret that I too fell back on this phrase of convenience, since viewing his enthusiasm or drive to collect as part of his personality pitches it as "natural." Calling Kinsey a collector by nature reduces his involvement with this activity to a characteristic, trait, or instinct that does not need to be questioned or considered in greater depth. This simple phrase effectively precludes the need to search for Kinsey's motivations, strategies, and priorities in amassing his collections. On the contrary, his practice of collecting and aspects of his collection are virtually untapped resources of information.

31 ACK to Sam Bernard Wortis, September 16, 1948 (ACK correspondence, KIA). Emphasis is mine.

32 ACK to P. D. Perkins, October 4, 1951 (ACK correspondence, KIA). P. D. Perkins was a commercial bookseller and art dealer with an office located in Japan. This quotation was excerpted from a form letter Kinsey wrote for Perkins to use in the event that the customs office in Japan questioned the exportation of any of the material directed to Kinsey.

33 ACK to Sherman Lee, January 15, 1949 (ACK correspondence, KIA). Sherman Lee, an expert in Chinese art and the assistant director at the Seattle Art Museum, was one of Kinsey's contacts in the professional art world.

34 Franz Boas is usually recognized as the "father of historical particularism." This movement examines the origin and subsequent diffusion of objects and practices throughout cultures. I am grateful to my colleague Thomas Albright for bringing this parallel trend in anthropological research to my attention.

35 Paul H. Gebhard, affidavit in support of the Claimant's motion for summary judgment in *U.S. v. 31 Photographs*, 11. Gebhard's statement reflects the importance of collecting material to supplement the interviews: "[W]hile there is an extensive literature of sadomasochistic orientation, ranging from books like those libeled in this case to popular contemporary writers and 'comic-books,' very few individuals have been found with histories of overt sadism or masochism. A study of sado-masochistic literature may provide insight into this situation, where the interest is widespread but appears seldom to materialize as overt behavior."

36 Although the Documentary Collection does not give an accurate ratio of content to production and circulation, it does seem fairly representative of the range of erotic photographs that were being made from the end of the nineteenth century through the mid-twentieth century.

37 Alfred C. Kinsey, *An Introduction to Biology* (Philadelphia: J. B. Lippencott, 1926), 40.

38 Jones, 374.

39 Al Urban to ACK, March 29, 1948 (ACK correspondence, KIA).

40 ACK to Sam Bernard Wortis, April 2, 1945 (ACK correspondence, KIA).

41 Kinsey's research also contradicted J. Edgar Hoover's 1950 statement about the escalation of sex crimes. See Pomeroy, 207–208, for more details about the differences between the FBI's reports and Kinsey's findings. For a comprehensive summary of Kinsey's interactions with the FBI, please see Jones, 631–34.

42 Paul H. Gebhard, John H. Gagnon, Wardell B. Pomeroy, and Cornelia V. Christenson, *Sex Offenders: An Analysis of Types* (New York: Harper & Row, 1965). See Pomeroy, 200–224, for an overview of Kinsey's work in prisons.

43 ACK to RT, July 19, 1947. RT was an officer in the United States Air Force. While serving in Japan during World War II, the lieutenant ardently collected erotica for Kinsey. Although this was before the institute had greater means at its disposal (that came with the royalties from the male volume), Kinsey advanced RT money so that he could collect at Kinsey's expense.

44 ACK to P. D. Perkins, September 18, 1950 (ACK correspondence, KIA).

45 Pomeroy, 177. Pomeroy devotes a chapter to the issue of direct observation and filming. Please see Pomeroy, 172–187.

46 For fuller accounts of the court case see Kenneth R. Stevens, "*United States v. 31 Photographs*: Dr. Alfred C. Kinsey and Obscenity Law," *Indiana Magazine of History* 71:4 (1975): 229–318 and my essay "In the Realm of the Sciences."

47 See ACK to P. D. Perkins, September 18, 1950, and ACK to RS, January 26, 1951 (ACK correspondence, KIA).

48 See ACK to P. D. Perkins, February 11, 1952 (ACK correspondence, KIA). "I certainly appreciate your continued interest in our research and hope that the things you have sent will come through. I am discouraged, however, that nearly everything you have sent through during the past two years is stored up (some of it broken) in the Customs House in New York City. Consequently, I think it is wise to stop all purchases of all foreign material until we get our court case through."

49 The 17,000 photographs, now part of the Documentary Collection, that came to the institute in 1956 or before, together with the photographs made by Dellenback, George Platt Lynes, and Wilhelm von Gloeden, total approximately 20,000.

50 "Significance of Erotic Art and Literature in Scientific Studies" (memo).

51 ACK to Williams, January 14, 1950 (ACK correspondence, KIA).

52 Please see Pomeroy, 188–99, for an overview of Kinsey's involvement with the arts and his contacts with artists.

53 The collection staff is currently engaged in a large-scale project to reintegrate the collections on an intellectual level. The intended result is that the collections be easier to access across media and more conducive to subject-oriented research.

Frontispiece. Untitled, mid-20th century, gelatin silver, h: 6 1/2″ w: 4 1/2″, KI-DC: 12434.

8. Charles Guyette?, Untitled, c. 1940, gelatin silver, h: 3 3/16″ w: 2 1/8″, KI-DC: 65897.

20. Untitled, c. 1915, gold-toned printing out paper, h: 6 1/2″ w: 4 1/2″, KI-DC: 39253.

21. Untitled, c. 1905, gelatin silver, h: 7 3/4″ w: 6″, KI-DC: 63801.

22. Charles Guyette?, Untitled, nd [pre-1959], h: 3 1/4″ w: 5″, KI-DC: 49956.

23. Untitled postcard, nd, gelatin silver, h: 3 3/8″ w: 5 1/4″, KI-PC: 1049.

24. Untitled, c. 1940, gelatin silver, h: 3 7/8″ w: 3 1/2″, KI-DC: 16714.

25. George Platt Lynes, Untitled, 1940, h: 7 1/2″ w: 9 1/4″, KI-GPL: 47. © Copyright the Estate of George Platt Lynes.

27. Untitled, c. 1925, gelatin silver, h: 5 15/16″ w: 3 15/16″, KI-DC: 41411.

28. Untitled, c. 1940, gelatin silver, h: 6 1/8″ w: 4 5/16″, KI-DC: 20054.

29. Untitled, early 20th century, gelatin silver, h: 3 1/2″ w: 5 3/8″, KI-DC: 13414.

30–1. George Platt Lynes, nd [pre-1954], gelatin silver, h: 3 1/4″ w: 5″, KI-DC: 30437. © Copyright the Estate of George Platt Lynes.

32. Untitled, mid-20th century [pre-1961], gelatin silver, h: 4 1/4″ w: 2 5/8″, KI-DC: 34452.

33. Untitled, c. 1900, gelatin silver, h: 5 9/16″ w: 4 1/2″, KI-DC: 2843.

34. Untitled, c. 1930s or 1940s [pre-1946], gelatin silver, h: 4 1/4″ w: 3 1/4″, KI-DC: 11414.

35. Untitled, nd [pre-1961], gelatin silver, h: 5 5/8″ w: 3 7/8″, KI-DC: 27659.

36. John Alexander Scott Coutts?, aka John Willie, Untitled, 1939, h: 5 1/2″ w: 2 3/4″, KI-DC: 46323.

37. Untitled, c. 1940, gelatin silver, h: 3 1/4″ w: 4 5/8″, KI-DC: 66204.

38–9. Untitled, c. 1925, gelatin silver, h: 4 5/8″ w: 6 1/4″, KI-DC: 36610.

40. Untitled, c. 1925, gelatin silver, h: 5 11/16″ w: 3 15/16″, KI-DC: 35383.

41. Untitled, c. 1895, gelatin silver, h: 5 7/8″ w: 3 7/8″, KI-DC: 8309.

42–3. Untitled, mid-20th century, gelatin silver, h: 11″ w: 8 1/2″, KI-AA: 29.

44. Bill Paul, *John*, 1997, Polaroid, h: 3 3/4″ w: 2 7/8″, 97.7.3.

45. Untitled, mid-20th century, gelatin silver, h: 7″ w: 4 7/8″, KI-DC: 32101.

46. Untitled, c. 1950s, gelatin silver, h: 4 1/2″ w: 6 5/8″, KI-DC: 30201.

47. Untitled, c. 1950, gelatin silver, h: 3 3/8″ w: 4 1/2″, KI-DC: 52944.

48. Untitled, nd [pre-1961], gelatin silver, h: 3 7/8″ w: 2 13/16″, KI-DC: 27648.

49. Untitled, c. 1955, gelatin silver, h: 4 3/8″ w: 3 1/16″, KI-DC: 56961.

51. Untitled, c. 1945, gelatin silver, h: 5 3/8″ w: 2 7/8″, KI-DC: 8344.

53. Untitled postcard, nd, gelatin silver, h: 5 1/8″ w: 3 3/8″, KI-PC: 1262.

54. Untitled, early to mid-20th century, gelatin silver, h: 3 3/8″ w: 2 3/16″, KI-DC: 28364.

55. Untitled, 1955, gelatin silver, h: 4 1/4″ w 3 1/4″ (size of single image; two images the same size), KI-DC: 15158.

56. Untitled, c. 1970, type-c print, h: 4 3/4″ w: 3 5/8″, KI-DC: 71357.

57. Untitled, c. 1965, Polaroid, h: 2 5/8″ w: 3 1/2″, KI-DC: 57051.

58–9. Untitled, 1936, gelatin silver, h: 8 1/2″ w: 7″, KI-AA: 87.

60. Untitled, c. 1950s, gelatin silver, h: 4 1/4″ w: 3 3/16″, KI-DC: 69725.

61. Untitled, c. 1950s, gelatin silver, dimensions n.a., KI-DC: 55707.

63. Untitled, c. 1890s, gold-toned printing out paper KI-DC: 7571.

64. Untitled, nd [pre-1961], gelatin silver/collage, h: 8 1/2″ w: 5″, KI-DC: 51709.

65. Untitled, nd [pre-1961], gelatin silver/collage, h: 8 1/2″ w: 5″, KI-DC: 30902.

67. Untitled, nd [pre-1947], gelatin silver, h: 8 1/2″ w: 6 1/2″, KI-DC: 50237.

68–9. Untitled, nd [pre-1949], gelatin silver, h: 7 5/8″ w: 9 11/16″, KI-DC: 47311.

70. Untitled, nd, gelatin silver, h: 10″ w: 8″, KI-DC: 30897.

71. Western Photography Guild, Untitled, nd [pre-1950], gelatin silver, h: 10″ w: 8″, KI-DC: 53804.

72–3. Untitled, postcard, nd, gelatin silver, h: 5 3/8″ w: 3 1/2″ KI-PC: 173.

75. Untitled, 1950, gelatin silver, h: 7 1/4″ w: 6 1/8″, KI-DC: 68619.

76. Untitled, c. 1965, gelatin silver, h: 4 1/8″ w: 3 1/4″, KI-DC: 40551.

77. Untitled, c. 1925, gelatin silver, h: 3 7/8″ w: 5 15/16″, KI-DC: 37516.

78. Untitled, nd [pre-1955], gelatin silver, h: 6 3/4″ w: 4 3/4″, KI-DC: 55327.

79. Sheckell, Untitled, c. 1940, gelatin silver, h: 4 9/16″ w: 6 1/2″, KI-DC: 24668.

81. Untitled, c. 1915, gelatin silver, h: 4″ w: 3″, KI-DC: 129.

82–3. Untitled, 1959–1960, type-c and type-r, h: 14″ w: 11 1/2″ (full page), KI-AA: 217 (this amateur album is devoted to a celebration of transvestism).

84. Charles Guyette?, c. 1940, Untitled, gelatin silver, h: 3 3/8″ w: 2 1/16″, KI-DC: 69267.

85. Untitled, nd [pre-1946], hand-colored gelatin silver, h: 6 1/4″ w: 4 1/4″, KI-DC: 55310.

86. Untitled, nd [pre-1959], hand-colored gelatin silver, h: 4 1/8″ w: 2 5/8″, KI-DC: 51265.

87. M. Koch and O. Rieth, *Der Act*, nd, gravure, h: 10″ w: 8″, KI-DC: 54822.

89. John Alexander Scott Coutts, aka John Willie, Untitled, 1936, h: 9 1/2″ w: 6 1/4″, KI-DC: 46012. Courtesy J. B. Rund, Belier Press, Inc.

91. Untitled, c. 1935, gelatin silver, h: 5 3/8″ w: 3 1/2″, KI-DC: 63606.

92. Wilhelm von Gloeden, Untitled, c. 1905, h: 8″ w: 6 1/4″, KI-VG: 234.

93. Wilhelm von Gloeden, Untitled, c. 1905, h: 8 3/8″ w: 6 3/8″, KI-VG: 258.

94. Untitled, c. 1945, gelatin silver, h: 5 1/4″ w: 3 1/4″, KI-DC: 1935.

95. Untitled, c. 1895, albumen, h: 4 7/8″ w: 3″, KI-DC: 33502.

96–7. Paul Burk, *Man Jerking Off*, 1997, gelatin silver, h: 11 3/4″ w: 9 1/4″, 99.7.4.

98. Jon Yamashiro, Untitled, 1991, gelatin silver, h: 9″ w: 6 7/8″, 97.3.1. © Copyright 1999 by Jon Yamashiro. All rights reserved.

99. Leeanne Schmidt, Untitled, c. 1993, gelatin silver, h: 20″ w: 16″, 99.6.1. Courtesy Gallery 292, New York.

100. Untitled, nd [pre-1961], gelatin silver, h: 5″ w: 2 1/2″, KI-DC: 11415.

101.Untitled, nd [pre-1961], gelatin silver, h: 6″ w: 2 1/2″.

102. Untitled, c. 1935, gelatin silver, h: 3 3/16″ w: 2 1/4″, KI-DC: 17678.

103. Untitled, c. 1965, gelatin silver, h: 2″ w: 2 3/4″, KI-DC: 59836.

104–5. Sam Wang, *Reclining Figure on Fallen Beech*, 1991, cyanotype, h: 13″ w: 21″, 99.4.2.

107. Untitled, c. 1900, gelatin silver, h: 4 5/8″ w: 2 13/16″, KI-DC: 8351.

109. Untitled, c. 1955, gelatin silver cutout, h: 4 1/2″ w: 2″, KI-DC: 13128.

108. Untitled, nd [pre-1947], gelatin silver cutout, h: 4″ w: 1 1/2″, KI-DC: 31596.

110. Untitled, c. mid-20th century [pre-1953], gelatin silver, h: 6 1/4″ w: 4 3/8″, KI-DC: 56415.

111. Untitled, 1957, gelatin silver, h: 4 3/8″ w: 3 3/8″, KI-DC: 22991.

113. Undated collage.

114. Untitled, nd [pre-1947], hand-colored gelatin silver, h: 3 9/16″ w: 2 13/16″, KI-DC: 58541.

115. Untitled, 1910, hand-colored gelatin silver, h: 5 3/4″ w: 3 5/8″, KI-DC: 44216.

116. Untitled, c. 1960, gelatin silver, h: 2 3/4″ w: 3 3/4″, KI-DC: 19663.

117. Untitled, nd [pre-1958], gelatin silver, h: 3 7/8″ w: 5 7/8″, KI-DC: 28910.

119. Untitled, 1949, gelatin silver, h: 6 1/4″ w: 4″, KI-DC: 16243.

120. Untitled, c. 1940, gelatin silver, h: 3 3/8″ w: 4 5/8″, KI-DC: 33371.

121. Untitled, c. 1920, gelatin silver, h: 5 3/4″ w: 4 1/8″, KI-DC: 44723.

122. Untitled, c. 1950, gelatin silver, h: 9 1/4″ w: 7 1/4″, KI-DC: 45041.

123. Untitled, c. 1930, gelatin silver, h: 3 3/8″ w: 2 1/8″, KI-DC: 55765.

124. Untitled, nd [pre-1958], gelatin silver, h: 5 1/4″ w: 3 1/4″, KI-DC: 20646.

125. Untitled stereo card, c. 1910, gelatin silver, h: 2 11/16″ w: 4 1/16″ (size of both images printed on one piece of paper), KI-DC: 67522.

126–7. Alexander Scott Coutts?, aka John Willie, Untitled, 1944, h: 5 7/8″ w: 3 15/16″ (image on left), h: 5 15/16″ w: 3 3/4″ (image on right), KI-DC: 46104.

128–9. Untitled, early 20th century, gelatin silver, h: 3 1/2″ w: 5 1/2″, KI-DC: 15356.

130. Untitled stereo card, c. 1910, gelatin silver, h: 2 9/16″ w: 4 1/8″ (size of both images printed on one piece of paper), KI-DC: 67531.

131. Stan Strembicki, Untitled, 1998, gelatin silver, h: 14 3/4″ w: 14 3/4″, 99.15.1.

132. Untitled, 1917, gelatin silver, h: 7 3/4″ w: 4 1/4″, KI-DC: 22506.

133. Dried whale penis, Whaling Museum, New London, CT, 1937, gelatin silver, h: 4 1/2″ w: 6 1/8″, KI-DC: 938.

134. Cecil Charles, *Pudgy Stockton*, 1946, h: 8″ w: 10″.

135. Untitled [Betty Page], nd, gelatin silver, h: 4 3/8″ w: 3 7/16″, KI-DC: 26645

137. Untitled, c. 1900, gelatin silver, h: 6 3/4″ w: 4 3/4″, KI-DC: 59020.

138–9. Untitled, c. 1960, gelatin silver, h: 3 1/2″ w: 5 1/2″, KI-DC: 58533.

140. Untitled, early 20th century, gelatin silver, h: 2 5/8″ w: 5 3/8″, KI-DC: 26056.

141. Untitled, c. 1920s or 1930s, gelatin silver, h: 3 15/16″ w: 5 1/4″, KI-DC: 5662.

142. Untitled, c. 1950, gelatin silver, h: 4 1/8″ w: 2 3/4″, KI-DC: 1319.

143. Untitled, 1918, gelatin silver, h: 2 15/16″ w: 4 /14″, KI-DC: 1038.

145. Judy Dater, Untitled, 1964, gelatin silver, h: 9 1/2″ w: 7 3/8″, unnumbered. © Copyright Judy Dater, 1964.

146–7. Untitled, c. 1923, gelatin silver, h: 2 5/16″ w: 3 11/16″, KI-DC: 15646.

148. Untitled, 1923, gelatin silver, h: 5 1/2″ w: 3 1/4″, KI-DC: 12168.

149. Untitled, c. 1890s, gelatin silver, h: 5 3/8″ w: 3 13/16″, KI-DC: 16102.

150. John Alexander Scott Coutts, aka John Willie, Untitled, c. 1955, h: 3 1/2″ w: 4 5/8″, KI-DC: 60614. Courtesy J. B. Rund, Belier Press, Inc.

151. Charles Guyette?, c. 1940, Untitled, gelatin silver and ink, h: 5″ w: 3 1/2″, KI-DC: 63505.

152. Untitled, c. 1880, hand-colored albumen and ink, h: 5 1/4″ w: 3 7/8″, KI-DC: 19900.

153. Untitled postcard, nd, gelatin silver, h: 5 3/8″ w: 3 1/2″, KI-PC: 1166.

155. Untitled, 1929, gelatin silver, h: 5 3/8″ w: 3 7/16″, KI-DC: 47733.

156. Untitled stereo card, c. 1900, gelatin silver, h: 3 1/16″ w: 5 1/2″ (size of both images printed on one piece of paper), KI-DC: 67641.

157. Untitled stereo card, c. 1925, gelatin silver, h: 2 7/8″ w: 4 1/8″ (size of both images printed on one piece of paper), KI-DC: 67624.

159. Untitled, c. 1930s or 1940s [pre-1949], gelatin silver, h: 6 1/8″ w: 6 1/8″, KI-DC: 5670.

ACKNOWLEDGMENTS

The Kinsey Institute has one of the largest and richest collections of erotica in the world. In addition to the size and scope of the institute's holdings, the value of the collection is enhanced by its history and diversity. This publication celebrates the vast photographic archive, one of the collection's greatest strengths. Without the unmitigated backing of the institute's current director, John Bancroft, it would not have been possible to produce a book featuring this stunning group of photographs. I am grateful for Dr. Bancroft's support of this project and of my other related research projects on the institute's photography collection. Sarah Burns, Janet Kennedy, Patrick McNaughton, Eugene Kleinbauer, James Eli Adams, Claude Cookman, Cheryl Younger, Alan Harris, and Judith Allen have also been incredibly supportive of my research on the institute's archive of erotic photography.

This book is the result of a collaborative effort. I want to thank Carol Squiers for writing such a perceptive essay and for her wonderful sense of humor. I also want to thank Betsy Stirratt and Jeff Wolin for their participation in the selection process as contributing editors. Paring down our preliminary pool of selections and reaching a consensus was intellectually challenging and, as a result, enjoyable. Jeff Wolin also contributed to the publication of this volume by undertaking the backbreaking work of making the outstanding photographic reproductions of all of the plates for this book. Stephanie Sanders, Liana Zhou, Nancy Lethem, and Susan Straub graciously shared their insights with me while I was working on this project. I am particularly grateful to Jon Yamashiro for his unwavering support on this and all of my research. I am also indebted to James Crump, a former institute curator, for his wisdom, his warmth, and his desire to publish this book. I also want to thank Elsa Kendall and Betsey Katz for designing this beautiful book and Laura Addison and Peg Goldstein for their sharp editorial attention to this project.

The development, preservation, and, indeed, survival of the collection is owed to the commitment of Indiana University and the staff, volunteers, and other supporters of the Kinsey Institute. All of the directors of the Kinsey Institute deserve to be recognized for their many and multifarious contributions to the collections: Alfred C. Kinsey, Paul Gebhard, June Machover Reinisch, Stephanie Sanders, and John Bancroft. Without Alfred Kinsey's belief in the cultural and scientific value of visual images and his commitment to the issue of academic freedom, this collection would not exist. Homage must also be paid to the late Herman B. Wells, president of Indiana University from 1937 to 1962, for his staunch support of Kinsey's cutting-edge research, which included accumulating an archive of erotica. Paul Gebhard continued to avidly collect images and objects during the twenty-six years that he served as director. He also supervised the classification of the photography collection. As director of field research, Wardell Pomeroy did much to develop the institute's impressive archive of films. June Reinisch, the institute's first woman director, recognized the importance of the collections and made great strides in their development and preservation during her eleven-year tenure. She made works available to the public, for the first time, through exhibition. Dr. Reinisch also devoted the resources to create a curatorial position and a permanent in-house gallery. Stephanie Sanders and John Bancroft both continue to support the measures of preservation, organization, promotion, and development of the collections. In addition to the significant contributions made by all of the institute's directors, the accomplishments of the previous curators and collections staff members have been vital to improving the physical condition, organization, and intellectual understanding of the collections. Therefore, I would like to recognize and thank the past and present staff members who devoted time and attention to the photography collections: Clyde Martin, Wardell Pomeroy, Paul Gebhard, Cornelia Christenson, Blaine Johnson, Michael Cavanaugh, Scott Carroll, Joe Becherer, James Crump, Todd Smith, Paul Burk, and Amy Boles. Liana Zhou, Margaret Harter, and Ruth Beasley, current and recent collection staff members, have also done much to improve preservation and access across the collections. Much of the progress made by staff was enhanced by and, in some cases, made possible by the generous help of volunteers, interns, and students. For their invaluable contributions all of us at the institute are most appreciative.

The Kinsey Institute remains dedicated to the unprejudiced interdisciplinary study of sexuality and has begun to celebrate its spectacular collection of erotic materials through exhibition and publication. For decades, the growth of the institute's collections has depended on the generous contributions of private collectors and individual artists. I would like to take this opportunity to thank those who have donated their works to the Kinsey Institute and to thank, in advance, those who will continue to make contributions to the collection. A few recent donations have been reproduced in this volume and I thank Paul Burk, Judy Dater, Bill Paul, Leanne Schmidt, Stan Strembicki, Linda Troeller, Sam Wang, Joel-Peter Witkin, and Jon Yamashiro for their gifts and their cooperation. Also, a special note of thanks to J. B. Rund, Belier Press, Inc. The future of the institute's rich resource depends on the continuing support of those artists and collectors who understand the significance of preserving the broad spectrum of erotic expression. With a continued steady stream of generous donations, our unique and important collections will continue to thrive.

Jennifer Pearson Yamashiro, Curator, the Kinsey Institute

First edition published by Arena Editions
P.O. Box 32101
Santa Fe, New Mexico 87594-2101 USA
telephone 505-986-9132 facsimile 505-986-9138
www.arenaeditions.com

Publishing Concept: James Crump
Art Direction and Design: Elsa Kendall
Design Assistance: Betsey Katz

Printed in Italy

First Edition, 2000

ISBN 1-892041-35-9
Library of Congress Control Number: 00-132754